James A. Kirk
Dept of Religious Studies
University of Denver
Denver, Colorado 80208

PERSPECTIVES IN THE HISTORY
OF RELIGIO~

Jan de Vries

PERSPECTIVES
IN THE HISTORY
OF RELIGIONS

translated with an introduction by
Kees W. Bolle

UNIVERSITY OF CALIFORNIA PRESS
Berkeley   Los Angeles   London

ACKNOWLEDGMENT

The translator gratefully acknowledges the help given him by William W. Malandra (M.A., Brown University), Steven J. Sharbrough (M.A., University of California, Los Angeles), and Matthew L. Jaffe (M.A., University of California, Los Angeles).

University of California Press
Berkeley and Los Angeles, California

University of California Press, Ltd.
London, England

Originally published under the title
Godsdienstgeschiedenis In Vogelvlucht,
Uitgeverij Het Spectrum, N.V., Utrecht, The Netherlands.
© 1961 by Het Spectrum.

CONTENTS

INTRODUCTION

Two Approaches to Religion

There are two ways to undertake the study of religion. The first consists in asking questions about religion. It is the most common approach and seems almost to be followed universally. Just because it is so common it is hardly ever given the attention it deserves. One takes for granted that people will ask questions, superficial or profound, about religion and will proceed to form opinions on the subject. This approach is common to the scholar and the common man alike. What produces the questioning is almost irrelevant; in the one case it may be a sacrifice described in the Greek text of Homer; in the other it may be a casual interest in a neighbor who insists on a church ceremony as the only proper wedding for his daughter. In fact, the characteristic of this common approach to religion, the raising of questions and the formation of opinions, is that *it is not a matter of an exhaustive research into the data of religion.*

Some might feel tempted to call this first way the "philosophical approach," but that would be rushing things. Such a lofty designation might suggest a systematic attempt to find out what religion really is and what its claims to "truth" are worth, but the approach I have in mind is too common to be tied immediately to great philosophical and metaphysical concerns.

Rather, questions about religion are raised and opinions formed in much the same way that people observe trees, chairs, or tables. "Ultimate" questions may be related to it all but only from some distance. Whether this is good or bad for the study of religion does not concern us for the moment. If any general starting point of this first approach can be indicated, it is that some matter-of-fact thought occurs that we all already know what religion is, that we would not confuse religious matters with other things any more than we confuse trees or tables or chairs.

The second approach to the study of religion seems more "scholarly." It is concentration on the documents of a specific religion—a concerted effort to master the "stuff" of a religion. There are fewer followers of this more studious way, yet these few wherever they appear create a climate that cannot be ignored. They seem to say that in order to say anything about religion you have to know the "stuff" of religion. Of course, this principle is not wrong. The chances are that it will even gain in importance, for it harmonizes with our present craving for education, which means to an astonishing number of people that science and scholarship can be served only by knowledge of facts. Why should this not be true in the study of religion? Knowledge of facts is indispensable.

It does not require much thought to see that the two approaches are complementary; neither one can exist alone. No matter how many questions one asks about religion, it is obvious that something of religion is already known. On the other hand, even the most studious fact-finder must have some query in mind in order to locate and perceive religious facts at all. Both approaches are legitimate, and they must be related to be completed.

The distinction, then, between the common approach and the factual approach is one of emphasis. The distinction is really central to all science and scholarship. On one hand there is the problem of *method*—how to arrive at a defensible position and gain access to and define the subject matter. On the other hand there is the on-going study of the object—the facts of a religion, of a culture, of a literature, of life, or of nature. The basic distinction is simple, but as so often happens, words with a technical ring can be chosen to cover the scholarly investigator's embarrassment about his simplicity. What is at stake in the problem of method or in the concentration on this problem ("methodology") is an extension of the common search for a sensible and tenable point of view. Concentration on the *object* of a scholarly discipline is, in principle, a continuation of the other, equally common-sense realization that one must know what one judges.

As a rule, it is the simplest matters that cause friction, in scholarly methodology as anywhere else. Every astronomer will tell us that it is not so easy to say in two or three words what the subject matter of his study is. Yet we all know and have our peace with it when we loosely call his subject matter "the stars." It would be unfair to reproach the historian of religions for not being able to define his subject matter in two or three words. (The fact that with respect to religion there really do not seem to be laymen but only people with definite opinions only complicates the problems of method and object.) With religion the individual's involvement is different from what it is in any of the sciences and most other studies. If a student has some resentment against his "religious" upbringing, this is bound to influence his entry into the field of the history of religions. Similarly, a student's feeling that he has not been brought up "religiously" may result in a life-long sense of puzzlement that, brought to the subject, may be reflected in the "method." Indeed, the problem of method cannot be ignored any more than the subject matter in the student's investigation.

The distinction between the two approaches, no matter how self-evident, has often turned into conflict in the study of religion, since some students or fashions preferred one above the other. In the present book we can read about the opposition between Romantics and "scientific" evolutionists. The former had a "vision" of their subject matter and foresaw a spiritual renewal of the world they were living in; this determined their method. The latter regarded their subject matter with greater "objectivity"; they realized that much hard work must be done before the documents of religion could be interpreted with any accuracy, and even then they were not always certain that any meaning was present. The conflict between the two comes out most dramatically, and is almost caricatured, in the battle between Creuzer, the typical Romantic, and Lobeck, the great debunker. In many cases, however, we see a struggle hardly less dramatic in one and the same person. The prime example is F. Max Müller, the "father of the history of religions," indefatigable explicator of Indian religious texts and at the same time, incorrigible Romantic. We who are living so much later can afford to look at those conflicts and conflicting views in the same persons with some mildness. We can see that both sides were wrong and right and, above all, that we could have done nothing without them. We owe to the evolutionists, especially those of the late nineteenth century, a great many of the tools (dictionaries, handbooks, critical editions) with which we still work or which serve us as models. Our gratitude for those tools outweighs the realization that sometimes the predominant ideas of those scholars were incredibly shallow or even quite wrong. The fact that we still use and must use their work is a constant reminder that in the study of religion we have to give most of our man-hours to the object, not the method, of our study. The Romantics who expected a new Renaissance, impelled by the discovery of a new and fascinating idea of man outside of modern Europe and ancient Greece and Rome, were given the lie by their century. Yet history has turned the tables again by teaching us the hard lesson of "one world or none"—a lesson taught through war and gruesome technology. This is not what the Romantics could have pictured, but the slogan certainly calls for more than the mere study of man's cultural and economic conditionings; it requires a vision of man closer to some of the best Romantic writings than to any of those that only "objectified" man.

Let there be no mistake about the second approach; every endeavor to deal just with the "stuff" of a religion implies and, in fact, *is* a method. At worst it is the method of repression; while the knowledge of facts increases, the common human prerequisite for all human study—the willingness to form a new opinion—can suffer, be forgotten, and be kept to a childish proportion while the student grows. For the maturity of the history of religions as a discipline it is mandatory that both approaches be followed. This means that in the study of facts the question of the design the student makes of the facts must be asked consciously.

In the twentieth century the opposition of the two approaches has had its expression in the discussions around the "phenomenology of religion." Although earlier and other attempts have been made to present the phenomena of religion coherently,[1]

---

[1] A notable early attempt was that of the Dutchman P. D. Chantepie de la Saussaye in his *Lehrbuch der Religionsgeschichte* of 1887. And the works by W. Brede Kristensen, Norwegian by birth, professor at Leiden and older contemporary of Van der Leeuw, have an honorable place. Unfortunately the most fascinating work by Kristensen, *Het leven uit den dood,* "Life Out of Death" (Haarlem: Bohn, 1926), has not been translated into English yet.

distinct from a presentation of historical development, the phenomenology of religion is particularly the field of the Dutchman
Gerardus van der Leeuw (1890-1950). The name itself of this
branch of study raises problems in various directions: the phenomenological method in the philosophy of E. Husserl, the philosophical and psychological investigations by Jaspers and Spranger[2]
and the earlier studies by Wilhelm Dilthey on delineating a
method in the humanities. Whatever else can be said about the
phenomenology of religion, it is at the least a conscious effort to
explicate in detail what we have called the first, or common,
approach. As a group, the phenomenologists of religion—many
of lesser stature, learning, versatility, and subtlety than Van der
Leeuw—have often aroused the suspicions of the "straightforward" historians of religion. In fact, it has been the old opposition with a new vehemence. It seemed as if the students of this
phenomenology could accept nothing unless the puzzle of a
method was solved and as if the materials were dragged in only
to give substance to an argument. The most eloquent spokesman
for the historians who are considered proponents of the second
approach was the Italian Raphaele Pettazzoni. This second
group was suspected in turn by the others; its adherents seemed
to be waiting naïvely until "all the facts were in" and to think
that "facts speak for themselves." In this way they shared in the
scientific fallacies of the nineteenth century. Perhaps we are too
close to this clash to observe it with the calmness with which we
can view the earlier periods, yet we should realize that neither
of the positions can be reduced into terms of the other. Professor
Mircea Eliade no doubt spoke wisely when he described the
opposition between phenomenologists and historians of religions
as one of temperaments and viewed the conflict as a fruitful
tension.[3]

Where should we begin with an introduction to the history
of religions? One thing is certain: it would be wrong to begin
by siding with one approach against the other. It would be ideal
to bear both in mind at the same time and constantly adjust the

---

[2] For a discussion of the phenomenological method in the study of religion
and its relation to depth psychology, see especially the important study by
F. Sierksma, *Freud, Jung en de religie* (Assen: Van Gorcum, 1951). The book
contains a summary in English.

[3] M. Eliade, "The History of Religions in Retrospect: 1912-1962," *The Journal
of Bible and Religion*, 31 (April, 1963), 107.

balance to favor the individual student and his interest. It is only for practical reasons that I would choose to introduce the history of religions by giving major emphasis to the first approach, the approach of raising questions and forming opinions, rather than to the second approach, the exhaustive study of religious facts. In short, I prefer some study of "method." It should be obvious that such an introduction, chosen for practical reasons, is not a bow to some phenomenological method or other and is even less a capitulation to a Romantic bias.

What are the practical reasons for an introduction by emphasis on the first approach? For a long time our colleges have taught survey courses in man's religions. The inadequacy of most of these courses is a pedagogical scandal. In the same institutions in which the simplest course on the New Testament covers a semester, the Bhagavadgītā is dealt with in one hour of discussion at most; the other documents of man's religious heritage are treated even more briefly. The factual information thus accumulated is pitiful and the educational value nil. For many students one such course is the sum of their study of religion. They may remember the pillars of the Islam for a week after the exam, but if they have learned to ask some serious questions about man's religious expressiveness, it has happened almost accidentally. It would make much more sense to spend some time on the first, common approach, and learn to recognize and to consider such questions. Life is short and the time set aside for learning even shorter. It would be marvelous from the point of view of a historian of religions if our academic curricula devoted years to the study of religion. But as it is, the greatest educational value in introductory courses can be expected not from the amassing of yet another series of admittedly interesting facts but, instead, from a treatment of the subject of religion that relates to other spheres of the student's study—history, literature, psychology, sociology, science, philosophy. Somehow, all these and other inquiries have some bearing on the subject of religion, and the study of the history of religions has some bearing on them. The integration of the student's education is measured most truly by the manner in which he makes his approaches, aware of the interplay of the various disciplines.

Furthermore, there is sound sense in the old saw that the best place to begin is where you are. It may be somewhat frightening to speak of our first approach as method, but we have seen that this technical word is no more than an extension of what we all know and do. We begin by already knowing somehow what religion is, and it is no more than natural to begin our study by asking whether our way of "already knowing" is correct and our manner of locating things religious is defensible. Again, the second approach is equally important and necessary, but the world of religious phenomena is without limits; even if we are inclined to make the study of religious phenomena our vocation, we still cannot skip the first, common step.

I would like to put it this way; the first step must be that of method. As soon as you have made it, forget it, turn for a while to the "stuff," to an unmistakable document of religion—some Buddhist sūtra or a Purāṇa or the poetic Edda. But you should not forget for always, for by the time you want to formulate your understanding, you will do well to remember the first questions you asked or took for granted. Chances are that you will have to rectify that first orientation, but it is only in the interplay between those beginnings and those interpretations that the history of religions moves.

Working the First Approach

"Working the first approach" means increasing our awareness of what we are doing in studying religion. The crucial question is, why do we look at religion the way we do? When the first approach is shunned, it is always this question that is neglected.

Nothing is worse than a student who happens to have read a book by Marx or Freud and suddenly considers himself one who has reached the far shores of comprehension when it comes to the interpretation of religion. They are not rare. There are even adult scholars of great linguistic repute, specialists in religious texts, who insist on a mishmash of scientific, economic, political, geographical, and ecological explanations and refer the religious phenomena proper to the psychoanalyst. There is no reason to belittle any approach just because it is of a limited scientific scope or a modern fashion. But in most of these cases of modern hangers-on, old or young, the trouble is that they have not asked the natural question: why do I look at religion this way? It seems to me that this book by Jan de Vries will help them greatly in answering this question or, even better, in realizing its full significance.

Even a casual reading of the book impresses on us that human "facts," and so religious documents, never speak for themselves. Studying the history of religions must be a struggle against methodological naïveté. No doubt the study involves compilation, tabulation, classification, and explanation of religious facts, but it consists at the same time in the fostering of an attitude that is in tune with the religious facts. De Vries' book presents a panorama of scholars and thinkers dealing with religion and culture through centuries of Western learning. It is instructive and at times humiliating to see how the best of men were totally determined by the fashions of their day. The question of why we in our turn look at religion as we do is bound to occur as we read. Are we not "conditioned"? Introducing ourselves to the study of religion by answering this question in some detail is a far cry from an introduction through an easy factual survey of "man's religions." Religious and cultural facts must not be ignored and are not ignored in this book by De Vries, who was himself a notable specialist on Germanic traditions. But facts have never constituted an unchangeable body "out there"; they have come to light gradually and, above all, have stood in very different lights in different periods. Indeed, some facts appeared at all only as a result of the brightness of an illustrious investigator, as in the case of Boucher de Perthes; artifacts of prehistoric men lay in the bed of the River Somme, but only when the *idea* of prehistory was born did this great discoverer go out and find them. Conditionings can work two ways, however. They cause us to see, but they can also close our eyes to what is right before us. Until the nineteenth century, the idea had not really dawned that anything could be said about man before the days spoken of by the oldest Greek and Hebrew texts (Homer and the Old Testament); the documents of prehistoric culture did not really exist until the imagination found them.

One cannot search for the things that condition views of religion without paying attention to philosophical climates. It is true that the historian of religions is not the only student of man who has difficulties in defining his object of investigation. There are related fields of inquiry in which the subject matter is hard to define—in philology, "literature"; in psychology, the "soul"; in sociology, "society"—but more than his colleagues in other fields, the historian of religions is obliged to take note of philosophy, for two reasons. First, his subject always involves man's fundamental orientation, or the final image of the world of men. Second, if one asks why a scholar looks at religion as he does, the philosophy of his day as a rule presents the answer most articulately. Accounting for our approach to religion means broaching philosophical problems and especially tracing philosophical influences on the history of our discipline. This is one of the most effective ways of overcoming methodological naïveté.

Accounting for one's approach is not merely a matter of knowledge, not even knowledge of philosophies. Ultimately, the understanding of man and the interpretation of man's religion depend on one's own experience and intellectual integrity, and these, in spite of their constant necessity, are subject to change. I remember vividly how puzzled I was as a student by my first course in the history of philosophy. For a long time I was especially at a loss in understanding how the study of ancient philosophers could be of importance. The case of the moderns looked somewhat different. They seemed to speak a language I knew, only they spoke it much better than I did, and I think it was this realization about the great articulateness of these moderns that induced me to turn again to older philosophers. In his own way, each of the moderns—Bergson, Whitehead, Sartre, Wittgenstein, Gusdorf—had something to say about things that intrigued me and had ideas with implications for the study of religion. Somehow, my thought was influenced. Looking back, I can see that my problems in my first history of philosophy course were simply the problems of many students who have found it hard to imagine that our thought and scholarship can be so strongly determined by certain individual thinkers. Perhaps we are not always aware that we have accepted an idea. Rather, we feel we *recognize* in some philosophical author an idea *as our own*. This experience is certainly not ours alone. Seneca, in his preachy and slightly pedantic way, wrote somewhere *Quod verum est meum est* ("What is true is mine"). But the point here is that the items regarded as worthy of thought and the qualification "true" have varied considerably through the ages and in different lands and vary in the life of a single person.

A good deal of nineteenth-century scholarship was devoted to the proposal that the modern Western world was the pinnacle of human achievement. This was a philosophical idea. As long as the idea dominated, it was very hard for students of man to see greatness in other cultures. The proposal may seem flimsy and wrong to us now, but it took a long time and much exertion even to make a dent in it. For several decades in our own century it was still taken for granted by most people that an enormous distance separated the "primitives" from ourselves and primitive religion from ours. Indeed, is it so easy to substitute another and better thought for the philosophical notion of a long evolution? That notion, after all, has the great attraction that it allows us to begin our investigations with a high esteem of ourselves.

Recent anthropologists and historians of religion have agreed courageously that we can no longer believe in a gulf between primitive man and ourselves. However, when they go further they reveal our philosophical difficulties. It is entertaining to see how the "true equality" of men varies according to who describes it and how it follows unmistakably the variation in the local philosophical tradition of the investigator. The German Jensen, the Italian Lanternari, and the Frenchman Lévi-Strauss agree in opposing the idea of a separation between primitives and moderns. But in demonstrating positively what makes us the same, Jensen prefers examples of human behavior; equality seems to mean first and foremost some inclination toward an ethical system that allows men to live humanly and creatively. For Lanternari the equality is given with the fact that all people, primitive and modern, are conditioned socially and economically. Lévi-Strauss has devoted himself to an analysis of symbols and myths in various primitive traditions and convincingly shows the logical coherence of each system; in his work the unity of mankind appears to be especially the urge for such logical coherence, and hence the task of the anthropologist is the construction of some "super-logic" to which the various systems can be related. An old bias may have been overcome, but the victory is not unanimous, and the victory even shows certain ethnocentricities or, rather, "culturocentricities." We cannot say that now the universality of the idea of man has been established. No one is to be criticized for that, but it is of the utmost importance to see that the new diversity in views is due not to the subject matter itself but to the philosophical presuppositions of each scholar.

The underlying or presupposed idea of man is always the most crucial problem for every religio-historical study. This problem can hardly become clear in one's mind without philosophy. Part of the fascination of the study of religion is to see how it can affect the idea of man and how it, in turn, is affected by the prevailing idea. Yet, if anything becomes clear in the course of

the present book it is that the study of religion *per se* has affected the idea of man only rarely but was almost always determined by it.

The Art of Questions

To say that taking the first approach amounts to discovering
how conditioned we are in our views of religion is hardly inspiring. Really something more must be said. We spoke of the goal
as awareness of what we are doing in studying religion; this is
not just a necessary exercise in academic humility. It should be
above all a training in the art of questioning; it should foster
watchfulness and justice toward our subject matter.

It is true that the study of religion hardly ever influenced an
idea of man that was current in a given period, but it must be
remembered that some of the most important philosophical
ideas took many centuries to establish their influence. This is particularly true for notions and reasonings that express or bear on
some universal image of man. One early notion was the Stoic
idea that the world was a cosmopolis and the man of insight
everywhere at home. This notion seemed to disdain all customary
boundaries; it is clear that it did not greatly and certainly not
at once change the world. Cicero (d. 43 B.C.) considered the idea
too intellectualistic and incapable of moving anybody,[4] yet a long
line of thinkers was affected by these and related Stoic thoughts.
"Influence" is perhaps the wrong word to use, but there was, as
so often, a recognition of ideas among thinkers. An effect on the
activities of actual travelers—merchants and sailors—was certainly out of the question for the time being. Centuries later, the
contemporaries of Spinoza (1632-77), sailing the ocean from the
harbors of Lisbon, Amsterdam, and London, found only "hea-
thens" on the far shores. Even when national and regional
boundaries were crossed, other barriers among humankind retained all their strength. Yet, ideas like the Stoics' and Spinoza's
have "legs" too, and once voiced clearly they set things in motion, slowly but surely, even if they must await new historical
circumstances to be recognized again. The image of the world as

---

[4] *De finibus* IV 7.

a cosmopolis is one among several fertile and crucial concepts that exerted influence not because they gave a conclusive answer to a precisely formulated question but because they stimulated the art of questioning itself. It was one of the many contributing factors that encouraged people—now here and then there, philosophers and commoners—to cross the territories of the world's map and of the provincial human mind.

In the study of the general history of religions, much depends on crossing customary boundaries. It is not just a matter of conclusive theories of knowledge but a matter of living convictions. We are far from having attained a universal concept of man on which to establish the study of religions. The academic disciplines go at the problem of such an idea in very different ways. Perhaps a universal concept of man is even unattainable. This much is certain: we are in great need of honesty in the recognition of our guiding ideas. The study of religious documents cannot prosper unless the historians of religions keep their ideas of man and the universe distinct from their objects of study. There is only one way to do this, not by repressing these ideas and the ideas of their own period, but by making a continuous effort to be aware of them and thus stay alive. Religious documents always contain vital issues and burning questions. The people who study them must also know about vital issues and burning questions in order to see them elsewhere.

This is the art of questioning and of course not a magic wand. No matter what happens, Stoics, Jews, Christians, and agnostics of one sort or another will not easily agree on a priority list of vital questions, particularly not when they relate them to religious documents. But there is nothing tragic in that. The history of religions as a discipline is replete with the crucial problems of the humanities and that may well be its major claim to attention.

The Use of This Book

Every conceivable book on scholarly orientations in the study of religion is bound to be incomplete. The fact that the present book will be an excellent introduction to the history of religions and indeed serve this purpose better than any other book does not break the rule. It is true that the book is recent and hence pays attention to some of the latest important developments in the field [5] and that it also presents a total picture of approaches while only a few are covered by other works.[6] Nevertheless, the vastness of the subject itself makes selectivity inevitable, especially since the total picture is drawn by one man. The author has his preferences for certain topics in the history of our discipline. De Vries was an eminent scholar of Germanic and Celtic religion and had learned much from the study of Greek and Roman culture and, of course, Indo-European studies generally. His study of folklore—a necessary complement in Germanistics—led him naturally in the direction of the ethnological researches, with which he was well acquainted. The romance of the great excavations obviously fascinated him. Still his wide range of interests leaves many subjects untouched. Many of the great names in Indic studies or sinology are missing; at the same time, relatively obscure scholars of Nordic religion are mentioned.

These restrictions in scope have advantages. The waves of scholarly fashion and the changes in outlook stand out more clearly than they could in a complete, encyclopedic survey. Also, every student with a special interest in a specific area will be able to see his own heroes in relation to the movements depicted here. The great French sociologist Durkheim is dealt with at some length. For our discipline it is not the least of Durkheim's merits that his thought stimulated so many who in addition to their sociological knowledge have often shown a remarkable philosophical sensitivity. Some scholars attached to this school directly or indirectly are discussed; some ideas of Marcel Mauss are dealt with briefly, and one of the longer special discussions is devoted to Dumézil. However, every sinologist will think in this context also of Marcel Granet, and everyone interested in Southeast Asia's religious history will know about Paul Mus's work.

If the usefulness of an introduction to the history of religions lay in a complete nomenclature and in a balanced discussion of

---

[5] To be mentioned among the earlier works are H. Pinard de la Boullaye, *L'étude comparée des religions,* I, 3rd ed. (Paris: Beauchesne, 1929); R. Pettazzoni, *Svolgimento e carattere della storia delle religioni* (Bari: Laterza, 1924); and G. Mensching, *Geschichte der Religionswissenschaft,* (Bonn: Universitätsverlag, 1948).

[6] Still useful is R. H. Lowie, *The History of Ethnological Theory* (New York: Farrar & Rinehart, 1937).

all problems in the field, this list of important contributors and problems could be continued. Yet such a list would soon reflect the wishes, preferences, and biases of other individual historians of religions. One might note that American anthropology has not been given the attention it deserves. One might observe that some most influential philosophical systems have been shortchanged; an all-too-brief description is given of Schelling's thought about religion, while Hegel's name does not occur; also, some objection might be raised to De Vries' statements about David Hume, who appears in this work as a typical exponent of eighteenth-century rationalism. Finally, it might have been good if a special chapter were assigned to the phenomenology of religion. This did not happen, although Van der Leeuw's name occurs in sundry contexts. These last objections especially seem serious to me, but no simple remedy is available; no extra chapter could be added to meet the objection without harming the unity of the book. The only conceivable proper solution would be an additional book on the same materials, written by a student with a special knack for "systematics," or more precisely, for our first approach. The point is that De Vries was temperamentally a historian himself and not a systematician. A discussion of phenomenology, which somehow always implies an interest in methodology *per se,* may have seemed useless to him. Perhaps here the ring closes. We have a book before us most profitable for our first approach, but written by a scholar who by training and by the bulk of his own scholarship was devoted to the second approach. Let us remember that the two approaches need each other, and the very existence of this book written by this scholar is witness to that.

The frame of thought in which Jan de Vries presents the material is transparent. If this book is to be used profitably, the reader will do well to pay attention to it and raise his own questions concerning it. De Vries sees the whole period from classical antiquity to the end of the eighteenth century as inadequate in its understanding of religion, sometimes even averse to an understanding. The nineteenth century is in principle not much better, in spite of its growth in knowledge of facts. The only really worthwhile scholarly orientation was given in the brief interlude of Romanticism. Our own day is promising for the study of religion, but to make this clear De Vries points specifically to those guiding ideas of interpretation in modern scholarship that were preshadowed by the Romantics. In the end of his book, De Vries concludes his exposition of theories on myth with a eulogy of Kerényi and Walter Otto. This was not done by chance, for both Otto and Kerényi are in a way "neo-Romantics." De Vries particularly likes Kerényi's observations that compare myth to music—both provide an order, but an order irreducible to terms outside itself and demanding from the interpreter that he attune himself.

It is obvious that this manner of presenting a survey is not straight and factual. Yet it does depict the important epochs and caesuras, and the student who is informed in a certain area of religio-historical study will have no difficulty separating De Vries' inclination to overrate a Romantic bent from the actual pageant of the history of religions. It is not difficult to understand that De Vries shows some sympathy with the "archetypes" of Jung; by their nature these archetypes transcend history, and they meant to De Vries a worthwhile endeavor to view the "eternal" in religion. For Freud's analyses he has only a handful of almost scornful words. No matter that Freud, too, goes beyond history; Freud could not be taken into the Romantic chord or the eternal urge of man's "spirit." At a certain moment De Vries may surprise anyone knowledgeable in the study of religion by the uncritical ease with which his personal Romantic inclination is expressed. In discussing Carl Otfried Müller (1797-1840), a scholar in the period of Romanticism and much admired by De Vries, he observes that in some ways we can no longer follow Müller, and one of the ways he mentions is an understanding of myth as a reminiscence of historical events. Now it may be true that no one would think, now or ever, of myth in this unqualified almost blunt way, as if it were just a record of history. Yet the suggestion that a real myth cannot be related to specific happenings is open to severe doubt. Of the kingdom of Fu-nan, flourishing from about the first century A.D. to the seventh century A.D. with its center in the Mekong delta in Southeast Asia, a curious legend was recorded. According to it, the kingdom owed its origin to the marriage of an Indian, the first king of the land, and the local queen. In much later times, at the court of Angkor, a union of the same type was still commemorated.[7] It is one of the most splendid examples of a founding myth, yet there is no doubt that it expresses the historical fact of Southeast Asia's Hinduization, the alliance of Indian and local

---

[7] See G. Coedès, Les états hindouisés d'Indochine et d'Indonésie (Paris: Boccard, 1948), pp. 69 and 70, and the bibliography given there.

creativity. True myth and reminiscence of history are not mutually exclusive. A Samoyed tribal myth[8] shows this point even more emphatically. We know the history of the Russians who brought Siberia under their sway. The Samoyed myth tells about a struggle between two parties: the tribal community represented by their cultural hero Itje, and the alliance of Satan and Jesus Christ, who is called the "father of all Russians." The "evil powers" became the masters of the land. Itje left his people but promised to return to gather his tribe together and drive out the foreigners. Obviously this is a real myth, one of some primitive Messianism. But it is equally obvious how it grew up on historical fact. Finally, it must be said that De Vries' work in his own field of specialization suggests that his remarks should not be understood as a summary dismissal of the possibility of myths with historical origins.[9]

One particular point in De Vries' personal inclination stands out clearly: the strong contrast he makes between the Romantic movement and the period of Enlightenment. I have mentioned De Vries' esteem of the Romantics, and there is no reason to belittle it, but when by contrast the eighteenth century emerges over and over as the age of crude rationalism, some questions must be raised. I am not suggesting that the contrast is invalid; certainly it is possible to see such a contrast, and this gives the work a surprising unity. But I am thinking of the student who is being introduced to the study of religion. He might well make his own notes and raise his own questions at this point, using concretely what he already knows. The eighteenth century was not just the century of Diderot and not only of the cultural feat of the *Encyclopédie*—multitudes of rationalists with only here and there a lonely precursor of the Romantics—it was also the age of Vivaldi and Haydn, of the humor of Fielding, of Mozart, of Bach, and of several circles of great piety. And was there not in that century some sense of human limitation and folly and of

---

[8] I owe this example to Mr. William W. Malandra. The myth is recorded in Kai Donner, *Among the Samoyed in Siberia* (New Haven: Human Relations Area Files, 1954), pp. 84-85.

[9] I may point to the careful consideration and evaluation De Vries gives to historical events bearing on the myth about the war between two groups of Nordic gods (Aesir and Vanir). See his *Altgermanische Religionsgeschichte* (Berlin: de Gruyter, 1957), II, 208-14, and "De Godsdienst der Germanen," in G. van der Leeuw, ed. *De Godsdiensten der Wereld* (Amsterdam: Meulenhoff, 1941), II, 152.

inwardness from which a later generation could have learned, especially in the study of religion? The eighteenth-century notion of "progress" and the idea that the human race would be educated may seem shallow now—another example of a flat rationalism—but it is questionable whether one can contrast with it and raise up in glory the Romantic *oeuvre*. If the Hegelians had had some sense of relativity and some playfulness, their evolutionism (and an evolutionism it was) would have been less devastating, not in the last place in the study of religion. Could a case not be made for it, that it was precisely the Romantics who made it possible for the eighteenth-century notion of progress to turn into the nineteenth-century doctrine of evolutionism? And was not something of an ordinary human sense of self-criticism lost in the process?

Questions such as these do not concern just the biases of one author or only the thought of past centuries. Questions of this sort must arise whenever we want to go about the study of religion seriously. They lead to a critical view of our own judgments.

But let me repeat that this very introduction must not last forever; at a certain moment we must forget the problems we have learned to discern, forget the conditionings of our own questions, and deal with the stuff of religion. When we formulate in the end what we have understood, we may even have lost all sympathy for any phenomenological view of religion. It takes many different students to make up the discipline of the history of religions.

One image used by Van der Leeuw at one time in describing his method should mean something to everyone. He compared it to a cactus called "wait-a-little-bit" because of its dangerous spines that warned people not to get too close too quickly—an organic manner of not rushing our own judgments on religious facts. The history of the history of religions will be of the greatest help in training ourselves and in making our field of study sounder.

Kees W. Bolle

Part One

FROM CLASSICAL ANTIQUITY TO THE EUROPEAN ENLIGHTENMENT

Chapter One

CLASSICAL ANTIQUITY

WHEN religious beliefs are on the decline, there are always some who express their doubt outright. The history of Greek civilization shows a growing and ever more incisive criticism of everything that had been considered for centuries the inalienable heritage of the people. Even the convictions concerning the world of the gods were not exempt from this criticism. One of its results was the gross materialism in the circle of the sophists, and the historical development from Homer (8th century B.C.?) to Protagoras (5th century B.C.) leads inexorably from belief to unbelief.

Later authors often condemned Homer because of the scandalous fables he wove about the gods. It was suggested that poets like Homer and Hesiod (8th century B.C.?) be banished from the ideal state designed by Plato. Plato (*ca.* 427-348 B.C.) argued that the mythic story is a *pseudos*, a lie, although he was willing to add that a grain of truth might be concealed in it.[1] Even earlier, Xenophanes (6th century B.C.), burning with indignation, exclaimed:

> Homer and Hesiod told of the gods all that is
> Regarded as shame and as mockery:
> Theft and adultery also and mutual deceit.[2]

This criticism was leveled first against the myths. For, indeed, whoever reads the story recited by Demodocos[3] in the court of the Phaiacians, of how Aphrodite and Ares are imprisoned in the net of Hephaistos in the very act of their infamous adultery and how they are exposed to the gods' ridicule, must be shocked that the gods could be spoken of so blasphemously. Yet it is Homer who narrates this, in the eighth century B.C. That fact should make one think. We are able to observe more than once that a seemingly very disrespectful play with myths goes together with a firm belief in the gods who live in those myths. Thus one could say that we have no reason yet to doubt the seriousness of religious convictions during the period in which the epic poems were composed. And do we really know what was the proper meaning of such a myth? And is it not possible that there was more of a holy earnest in it than we, late descendants, can ever guess?

We must assume that Hesiod was a devout man. Nevertheless, even he does not hesitate to play rather independently with the mythological tradition. He does not shrink from perfecting his system with figures of his own invention in order to have a complete theogony. He is an almost classic example of the enormous influence poets have had on the composition of myths. Yet, the assumption must still be made, in the case of Hesiod, that the poet wrote with the support of an unbroken traditional certainty and with the feeling that his work unified the not always coherent narratives about the gods.

The decisive blow to popular reliance on myths and consequently on the gods came from the Ionic natural philosophers. The thought that many more gods than the Greek were venerated and that every nation had its own pantheon was bound to strike men in a city such as Miletus, where the Greek civilization had met those of Asia Minor and had received most fruitful impulses. It is true that the religious systems showed remarkable differences, yet pointed similarities could easily be found. Reflection on the nature of the gods was thus stimulated. The comparison with such very different civilizations gave the expatriate Greek mind a horizon unknown in the Greek homeland, and one that, indeed, was not to be known there for considerable time. If one reflected in a city like Miletus on the cosmos or on the essence and origin of gods and men, it was impossible to remain tied to the religious traditions in the prevailing manner of Greece proper. The natural philosophers show a striking logic in their endeavors to reduce the pluriformity of the world to a single primal principle. Thales *(ca.* 600 B.C.) considered water the primal cause of all things; Heraclitus *(ca.* 500 B.C.) thought the cause was fire. Anaximander (early 6th century B.C.) even posited a substance, which he called *apeiron*—"boundless"—as the material base of which everything is made. Let us also remember that this philosopher attributed to this "primal substance" the predicates "immortal," "imperishable," and even "unoriginated."

It is easy to see that in a spiritual realm with such eagerness for learning and such fearless theorizing the Olympic gods cut a poor figure. Believing like Xenophanes in one single god, who sets the world in motion by the power of his thought but who himself remains motionless in the same place, what is one to think of the gods of Greek polytheism, who eat and drink, make love and fight with one another? Heraclitus goes so far as to reject the idea that this *primum movens* would be some particular element, like water or fire; he calls it *logos,* which one might translate as "world-mind." We see with perfect clarity how a transcendental philosophy wiped out the whole system of solid and simple belief in the Olympic gods.

However, one point must be emphasized: the existence of the gods is by no means denied by these philosophers. Not even Heraclitus denies their existence, no matter how dissatisfied and disturbed he is about Homer and Hesiod. His dissatisfaction stems from the fear that these poets' irresponsible fiction might diminish proper respect for the gods. Aristotle (384-322 B.C.) says of Thales that that philosopher believed the world to be full of deities.[4] Let us not question here to what extent the gods of the Olympus could be meant by his "deities."

Meanwhile, the problem of how to conceive of Zeus and Apollo, of Hermes and Aphrodite, became more and more urgent. Theagenes (6th century B.C.) of Rhegium tried to solve it by regarding them as allegories for the elements of nature. If gods fight with each other, this fight signifies the enmity raging in nature among the elements. Apollo and Hephaistos are fire, one the fire of the sun, the other of the earth; Poseidon and Skamandros are deities of the water; Artemis is related to the moon and Hera to the atmosphere. Admittedly, such an explanation cannot apply to all gods. Therefore, Theagenes assumes that gods may also represent spiritual qualities. Then, of course, Athena becomes the deification of wise judgment concerning the phenomena of the world and of life; Ares becomes boundless unreason; Aphrodite desire; and Hermes the discerning intellect.[5] With this conception

Theagenes was the creator of the allegorical explanation of the gods. This explanation was to be exceedingly tenacious; it has had its proponents until the nineteenth century.

Menander (*ca.* 342-292 B.C.) reports that Parmenides (born *ca.* 514 B.C.) and Empedocles (5th century B.C.) composed hymns on physics in which they expounded the nature of the gods. This amounts to the same thing: over and over, the gods can now be explained as natural elements. According to Empedocles, Zeus is the ether and Hera the air; the earth is called Hades. Next to these, Aphrodite and Eris represent the powers of attraction and repulsion. We can only admire the sagacity with which this thinker projected a dynamic image of the cosmos into the world of the gods. According to him, the "popular gods" were the result of the connections of the four elements.

The much-traveled Herodotus (5th century B.C.) found a system of strange gods in Egypt and talked with Egyptian priests who convinced him that their religion was infinitely older than the Greek. It thus became clear to him that the Greeks, as latecomers, must have borrowed much from the Egyptians. Among other things, those priests told him that the Greek Proteus was really Pheron, who at one time resided in Memphis. In Pheron's sanctuary a "foreign" Aphrodite was also venerated, who was identified by Herodotus with Aphrodite Helena, the daughter of Tyndareus. Further, Herodotus was convinced that Poseidon was originally a Libyan and Bacchus an Egyptian god. He continually compared Greek and Egyptian deities: Zeus is Ammon; Athena is Neith; Apollo is Horus. Moreover, the father of historical scholarship surprises us with remarkable rationalistic explanations: Europa was the daughter of a king who was abducted from Tyrus by some Greeks—Cretans, in his opinion.

Reverence for the gods was critically affected by such explanations. The consequences were inevitable. If the gods do no longer rise up, as it were, from the soul of a people, but are taken as merchandise from one nation to another, what becomes of their inner validity? The opinions of the sophists, propagating their ideas in the fifth century, give us an impression of a frightening increase in unbelief among the intellectuals of Athens. Protagoras (481-411 B.C.) is reported by Eusebius[6] to have said: "I do not know anything of the gods, whether they exist or whether they do not exist, or what their nature is. There is much that stands in the way of knowing these things, especially the uncertainty and brevity of human life." It is really not astonishing that he had to leave Athens hurriedly because of a lawsuit for *asebeia* ["atheism" and "impiety" in conflict with tradition and law]. Nonetheless, we should not too quickly decry his statement as an uttering of unbelief. It is undoubtedly agnostic; yet man leaves the existence of the gods unaffected when he admits in all modesty that he is unable to "define" their nature. Thus he shows perhaps a greater respect than the great crowd of people who are of the opinion that they know exactly what the gods are worth.

However this may be, the veneration of the gods was for the Greeks a general, human custom, as it is for all polytheistic peoples. It was a duty for every member of the community, for if he did not participate, he placed himself outside the social order. The particularities of the cult were regarded as institutes by ancient legislators, who were worshipped as sages. This too is a conception that would find support until modern times. If it is not the legislators, it is the priests who give religion its final shape; soon the idea of priestly wisdom was to be replaced by the idea of priestly deceit.

Prodicus (5th century B.C.) of Ceos was also an outspoken rationalist. But with him a new idea appeared: service to the gods is a reaction of man's soul to the favor and efficaciousness of cosmos and earth with respect to human existence. The gods are benign powers, so they are entitled to worship. Thus, bread must have been envisioned as the goddess Demeter, wine as Dionysos, fire as Hephaistos.[7] This view led him further to the idea that the gods at one time were people who conferred such benefits on humanity. It is hardly possible to proceed much further in the realm of rationalistic theologies; later Euhemerus would acquire a dubious fame in this area.

With the sophist Critias (5th century B.C.) we come to the lowest point of rationalistic thought about the gods. His drama *Sisyphos* depicts human life in primordial time, when the law of the jungle prevailed and there was no punishment for injustice.

> And then, for the first time, it seems, a keen
> And cunning man invented fear of gods.
> They should strike terror in an evil heart
> Even if action, word and thought might be concealed.
> He introduced as remedy religion:
> There is a being with eternal life,

Whose spirit hears, sees and is full of wisdom,
Observing all, whose nature is divine,
He hears all words spoken by men,
No act is hidden from his eye.

This idea too turned out to be extremely fertile; in similar forms it was repeated again and again until it was worked to death. The function of the gods is to frighten evildoers. Statius (*ca*. A.D. 40-96) gives the formula that is later favored by many: *primus in orbe deos fecit timor*[8] [the first reason for the existence of the gods in the world was fear].

Socrates (469-399 B.C.) raised his voice against the sophists, as corrupters of youth. Actually, he nowhere states his religious opinion in a straightforward manner. Would he really have agreed in his heart with Protagoras? The citizens of Athens accused Socrates of *asebeia* and condemned him to drink hemlock, yet he had always emphatically declared that he venerated the gods. We may infer from his first speech before his judges that this was to him more than an empty phrase; he expressly referred to the oracle that he had been given by Apollo at Delphi and that had guided him during his entire life.[9] Still, he appeared to have too exalted an idea of divinity to assume that the gods fought with each other or spent their time making love.[10] It is probable that he regarded such images as poetical fiction, as did his pupil Plato.

Plato followed his master in rejecting the indecent fables told about the gods. He considered the poets who made up such things dangerous for a healthy society—in which, after all, the worship of gods should be an indispensable part. But it is important here to remember that Plato himself uses myth—when the flight of his thought goes far beyond logical concepts—in order to show symbolically the idea that inspired him.

Aristotle's mind was more down-to-earth. He first comes up with a psychological explanation of the causes of the belief in gods: he names as causes particular experiences of the soul, as in dreams. Next to these he mentions the observation of phenomena of the sky, which in their regular order and beautiful harmony alone would lead man to assume the existence of gods.

We can be brief in speaking of the Stoics, although Stoic teachings kept their appeal as an orientation far beyond classical antiquity and gave strength and solace to many even in the Christian Middle Ages. The Stoics favored explaining the gods' existence with the help of allegories of nature. Questionable reasonings such as the following occur in the summary of Stoic ideas in Chrysippus (*ca.* 280-204 B.C.) of Soli's work *About the Gods*: when Night arises out of Chaos, according to Hesiod, Nyx (Night) is really the haze that rises off the primordial water; this hazy air gets thinner, and ether and light evolve from it. For Chrysippus, Zeus is the supremely ruling reason and soul of the cosmos. Actually, his explanations are more than allegories of nature; they presume to explain the gods in an utterly natural way: dressed up in poetry, the gods really stand for natural proc-esses, which the ancient philosophers learned to understand al-most scientifically. Thus the belief in gods is almost a natural science, except that it makes use of primitive forms of expression.

Epicurus (341-270 B.C.) developed an idea that would not be unworthy of Freud: religion is a disease of the soul and has its origin in fear of the gods and the hereafter. It is not respect for the eternal cosmic laws, as Aristotle thought, that is at the bottom of religion. Quite the opposite. The frightening qualities of nature lead man to search for the beings behind them—that is, for beings that one could hardly imagine as benefactors. Yet man also created his gods because he was convinced that evildoers would be punished in the hereafter. In this manner man's evil conscience is posited at the root of religion!

These are only a few voices in a chorus who say the same thing with only the smallest variations. Euhemerus (*ca.* 300 B.C.), the friend of king Cassander of Macedonia, is a clear example of the triviality to which the fourth century sank in explaining the gods. He is the author of a novel entitled *Hiera Anagraphè,* or *Treatise of Sacred Matters,* in which he indulges in fancies about an island of Panchaia, which he has visited during his voyages. There was on that island a golden pillar bearing a golden engraving. He read there the biography of Zeus, who was the king of the island once upon a time. That king traveled throughout the world and estab-lished everywhere the worship of gods. He built a temple for himself and was adored in a cult as Zeus Triphylios.[11]

Euhemerus' book intended to show that the gods are nothing but mortals who were raised to the rank of gods because of their merits. However rationalistic this may seem to us, we should not be astonished that those times could engender such thoughts. In the first place, there was the cult of the heroes, and it is certainly true that Greek beliefs drew a sharp line between heroes and gods. This division is expressed in the fact that each group re-ceived very different sacrifices; those for the heroes are clearly offerings for the dead. Still, there are cases in which a hero ascended to the dignity of a god: the classic example is Heracles. Hence, Euhemerus could easily establish his thesis by generalizing somewhat. Psychologically the time seemed ripe for such things. We may think of Alexander the Great (356-323 B.C.), who was worshiped as a god even during his lifetime and never seems to have opposed that worship in earnest. The notion, even if not thoroughly acceptable to him, must have had its political advantages for a man moving about in the Eastern world.

However this may be, Euhemerus in his treatise expounded an extremely trivial conception of the world of the gods. In times when such a conception can occur, the real religious assurance must have sunk low. Therefore, it is disconcerting to realize that this conception flourished widely in late antiquity. It is easier to understand that it was accepted wholeheartedly by the church fathers and that as a result it had some sort of canonical validity in the Middle Ages (Snorri Sturluson and Boccaccio). But it did not fall at all into disfavor in the period of Humanism (Vossius and Bacon). It finds its zealous proponents, of course, in the time of the Enlightenment, and even in the nineteenth century it is set forth with conviction (Carlyle).

It will not be necessary to discuss elaborately the ideas of the late classical period. The period continues the theories that had been expounded for centuries. Polybius (202-120 B.C.), for instance, follows the teachings of Epicurus consistently: the masses, superficial and fickle, must be held back by a fear of what is unknown; therefore the ancestors wisely and deliberately introduced the gods and Hades.[12] The Greek historian Diodorus Siculus (*ca.* 40 B.C.) is at least as convinced a Euhemerist in his *Historical Library*. He shrinks from nothing: Dionysos is the same as the Egyptian king Osiris, who discovered the vine at Nysa. Journeying to Ethiopia, Dionysos took along his brother Apollo and a group of musicians, among which were nine girls —the so-called Muses. No better can be said of Strabo (*ca.* 64 B.C.—A.D. 19). Plutarch (*ca.* A.D. 46-120) likewise reels off the old explanations, fully confident of their truth. According to him, our knowledge of myths comes from three sources: poets, legislators, and philosophers. If reports do not agree, the philosophers are the preferable source. The famous adultery of Aphrodite with Ares was a warning against an effeminate temperament and against adulterous customs—an admonition that was certainly not unwarranted in Plutarch's day.

Lucretius' (*ca.* 99-55 B.C.) materialism had best be passed over in silence out of piety toward the great poet. Cicero's (106-43 B.C.) book *De Natura Deorum* raises great expectations by its title, but these expectations are not at all fulfilled. Cicero limits himself to contrasting and subsequently refuting the opinions of the Stoics, Epicurians, and Academici. Then what is the truth? Cicero did not complete the book; perhaps he intended to present his own opinion in a fourth discourse.

Summarizing these many centuries of rather sterile writings about the meaning and origin of the gods, we may first arrange the proposed explanations under these categories: natural allegory, psychology, history, and Euhemerism. These explanations are all mistaken, or at least hold only a tiny grain of truth. Some are even flatly rationalistic. At first this seems a disillusionment. We had expected more of the Greeks. Apparently, we expected too much, since we see now that the occupation of the greatest thinkers for many centuries yielded such poor results. Still, they touched and tried all sorts of possibilities of explanation with the help of the data they had at hand. This by itself is an achievement. The Greek mind—often extolled, and rightly so—proved its logical power and its universality with thinkers like Plato and Aristotle, in our area of investigation as well as in any other. Incorrect though the explanations may appear to us, scholars and thinkers were unable to provide better until far into the nineteenth century. The Greek formulas remained the highest knowledge for more than a millennium!

We shall see how the same explanations emerge time and time again. Theories concerning nature-mythologies were still presented in the middle of the nineteenth century by Adelbert Kuhn and Max Müller; the doctrine that the Greek gods were borrowings from other nations had its zealous defenders in Creuzer and Görres. And are we not convinced even today, regarding Apollo or Athena, that they are gods of foreign origin who dwelt in the Greek pantheon?

In company with the speculations of the philosophers, mention should be made of the germ of a science of religion, which one is almost inclined to call "ethnological." The Greeks were great travelers. They went everywhere and did not hesitate to touch at the coasts of barbarian nations. The colonies they established on the Black Sea and on the Ligurian—Olbia and Massilia—brought them into touch with primitive peoples. Herodotus speaks of Scythians and Libyans in the fourth book of his *History*; in his eagerness for knowledge he had not failed to inquire after their beliefs. In doing so, he found that they worshiped the sun and the moon and consequently regarded both as deities. Speaking in a general way, it can be said that barbarian nations worship as divine beings the great phenomena and powers of nature. This statement sums up what became the customary assumption in the entire ancient ethnography. We can trace it in Posidonius, Plato, and Aristotle, and until the Roman authors of the imperial era. When Caesar describes Germanic religion—which he personally has hardly seen—it is in harmony with the customary ideas of the classical ethnographers to say that the Germanic peoples reserved the term "divine" for those powers they could see in their effects: sun, fire, and moon. Of other gods nothing is known, even by hearsay. In this manner the biases of an habitual theory kept the facts from registering correctly, even where an immediate observation would not have been impossible. We should not reproach the ancients; even the nineteenth century offers plenty of the same thing. The statement—whether right or wrong—that primitive peoples worshiped the powers of nature was beautifully suited to the supporters of explanations along the lines of nature-mythology.

Chapter Two

THE CHRISTIAN APOLOGISTS

THE Church Fathers found a rich refutation of pagan religion in the writings of the pagan authors themselves. They diligently read and repeated the pagan theories, especially those about nature allegories and those from Euhemerus, that explained the offensive myths. They discovered whole compilations proving the total worthlessness of the ancient gods, whose cult the emperors sometimes forced in blood upon martyrs. The nothingness of the gods was obvious when they were compared with the one eternal God of Christianity. Let us say that we cannot expect the Apologists and Church Fathers to strive for new insights. Their work was first of all polemical; they were no exegetes of pagan convictions.

When Celsus (2nd century A.D.) wrote his *True Discourse,* in which he attempted to defend paganism philosophically against Christian attacks, he posited a supreme divinity beyond the pantheon; this divinity transcends all man's concepts and has created the other gods and the demons. Those latter powers have in their charge the history of nations and individuals. Celsus emphasizes the national character of Greek religion and sees in this national character a rebuttal of Christianity, which did not originate in the needs of the Greek people. And he adds that the

Christian God would not be more excellent than the high divinity that he construed at the summit of the pantheon.

This treatise by Celsus has not been preserved. We know it only from the retorts that the Christian Apologists leveled against it. The course of history silenced Celsus. Origen (185?-254?) is our most important source of Celsus' book, because he cites entire passages from it in his refutation. "All gods of the nations are idols," says psalm 96; this sums up Origen's judgment. Furthermore, the pagan cultic acts call forth his mockery. As more miraculous incantations are added, the cult of the gods is called more efficacious. It is clear from the cultic acts that the cult of the gods could only be a service of demons.

In spite of all this, we have reason to be grateful. If the Church Fathers had not conveyed so many particulars on so many occasions about the pagan cult, we should know even less than we do, for instance, about the Eleusinian mysteries.

The Church Fathers struck first at the allegorical reasonings by which pagan thinkers had tried to explain the myths, especially the offensive ones. These allegories turned out to be arbitrary and unfounded, for each thinker had his private theory. The ideas of Cornutus and Plutarch, Porphyrius and Julian are all different from one another. Consequently, they are useless. Euhemerism serves the Church Fathers more adequately, for did it not speak in favor of the view that the gods were really only mortals raised up? There were, first, the differences among local legends, and, also, the fact that more than one god bore the same name. Above all, these apologists liked to look at the realistic details in stories about the gods and in the temple images. Their simple explanation of the earthly variousness was that mortal people were made divine in different places and that they each had had their own historical character. But, as Pinard de la Boullaye rightly remarked, that is as far as the Church Fathers went; they argued on the same level as the pagan explicators of myth, and neither of the two made an attempt to analyze the tradition and to demonstrate the historical elements in it.[1]

Augustine (354-430) states in *De Civitate Dei* that the pagan gods are merely impure demons that make use of the souls of the dead or in the form of cosmic powers exert themselves to be regarded as gods. Abominable and full of conceit, they delight in having divine homage paid them; their doings are a crime by which they keep the soul of man from turning to the true god.

These rough words may shock us, who might be persuaded by the high dignity of an Apollo or an Athena that a spark of true holiness existed in the Greek gods. We must bear in mind that Augustine's times were times that could not tolerate anything that once was adored.

Lactantius (*ca.* 260-340) states the same opinion in his *Institutiones divinae.* Here also, Euhemerism is the order of the day. One by one, the blasphemous fables of the pagan gods are sarcastically exposed. Lactantius' teacher, Arnobius, himself a convert from paganism, explicitly names Euhemerus as the one who demonstrated the human origin of the gods. Whatever had enjoyed devout worship Arnobius regarded as a sink of iniquity. If people had believed that the behavior of the gods was a model for human life, they were shown what a pitfall this model really was.

There emerged another idea that would have a great future. No matter how the Eleusinian mysteries were ridiculed, they were nevertheless surrounded by a venerable shroud of mystery, and they promised man salvation beyond this life. Such mystery commanded respect, in spite of everything. And, even more important, one could see similarities with the sacred acts of the Christian eucharist. This fascinated both the pagans and the Christians. The pagans reproached the Christians for copying the very acts they censured. The Christians accused the pagans of plagiarism. Even worse, they accused the pagans of most condemnable sacrilege. In that case pagan religion was truly an invention of the devil.

It was not difficult to show the cause of man's fall from paradise, his abandonment of the true God and his indulgence in idolatry, when the question was raised how all this could have happened after the primordial revelation of God reported in the Old Testament. The paradise story itself fixed the blame. It was Satan, the ancient Evil One, who had played his tricks on man. Hence the Church Father Basil, who was living in the fourth century in Caesarea, regarded paganism as degenerate truth, which had been given in its pure form to the patriarchs. The devil stole our tradition, he claimed, in order to establish a cult of the demons.

This presentation met an overwhelming response. Paganism with its many gods was a degraded borrowing from the ancient Jewish tradition. The gods were in fact paganized patriarchs.

This conception made light work of so many problems that it satisfied scholars even at a much later date. It will suffice to name Gerard Vossius and Pierre Huet.

The Church Fathers employed the oddest reasonings to make the theory of degraded borrowings acceptable. So doing, they attached great importance to the explanations of names. Often these explanations did no more than attempt to pass off as proof of identity the faintest resemblance between a Hebrew and a Greek name. And, in the fourth century, the neophyte Firmicus Maternus wrote a book *De errore profanarum religionum*, in which he defended his newly acquired religion by demonstrating the worthlessness of the one he had forsworn. In this book we read the following curious passage:

> When the hot air made the crop wither in Egypt and a famine was imminent, a youth from the race of a god-fearing patriarch explained the dream of the pharaoh and foretold what was to take place. This was Joseph, Jacob's son, who had been imprisoned because of his chastity, but who entered the king's service after explaining the dream. He caused the harvest to be stored in granaries for seven years and assuaged the need of the next seven years through the prudence of his spirit, which was enlightened by God. Upon his death, Egyptians erected temples for him in accordance with their customs. The bushel, which had served him to distribute grain among the hungry, was placed on his head, so that posterity would take to heart the beneficence of a just distribution. But also the memory of his name was preserved. Since he was a great-grandson of Sarah, who by God's grace had borne a son to Abraham in his ninetieth year, he was named *Serapis* in Greek, that is *Sarras pais* [Sarah's child].[2]

After the triumph of Christianity, there was no need for polemics against Greeks or Romans who had defended their pagan persuasions. Attention was soon absorbed in dogmatic questions and the rebuttal of heretical opinions. However, an important task remained in spite of the fact that learned voices of paganism had been silenced: the work of exterminating the pagan traces still alive in the mass of the people. This effort was strenuous, especially in western and northern Europe. In Greece and Rome the gospel had been proclaimed mainly to the lower groups in society, and there it had found true adherents. The Germanic lands required a more studied approach. Preachers who convinced the king and his nobles could expect the greatest success. When these had accepted Christianity, their subjects did not hesitate to follow. We are often told of whole tribes descending to a river in the neighborhood to be baptized by the missionaries. Cases of enforced conversion and of conversion *en masse* were not exceptional. In these cases, understanding of the truths of the new faith can hardly have been profound. Paganism, just barely affected, had plenty of occasion to continue its growth. It was only then that the difficulties of real conversion began, for the population was Christian in name only.

We know various manuals from the early Middle Ages supervising the interdiction and eradication of pagan worship. Usually they tell us of sacred trees, springs, and stones. Of course, these testify to a tenacious cult, which survives until our own days, in a Christian garb. The apostle of the Suevi, Martinus of Bracara (*ca.* 515-580), found it necessary to write an elaborate refutation of pagan traditions in his diocese: *De correctione rusticorum.* He composed in this book a curious theory about the origin of polytheism: even before the Great Flood an apostasy from the original monotheism took place. This apostasy manifested itself in moral degeneration, which grew worse after the flood. Men not only forgot their creator, they began the worship of creatures, or of elements, as Lactantius called them. Once he had sunk that low, man continued falling, because for him the fallen angels assumed divine names and criminals were thus adored. Reigning at the head of those demons was Jupiter, a master at magic and incest, who married his sister and seduced his own daughters. Beneath him were Mars, the source of cruelty; Mercurius, the thief and deceiver; Saturnus, who devoured his own sons; and Venus, the demon of adultery. Temples and altars and statues were devoted to these creatures, the whole landscape—especially water and forest—was filled with evil spirits venerated as gods.

Ignoring the tendentious way in which the gods are depicted, we see here a first attempt at a developmental scheme of polytheism within the frame of Christian religious conceptions. Of course the old pet ideas, nature-allegory and Euhemerism, served well in this endeavor. Martinus appears to have had in mind an evolution that began with the original monotheism, degenerated into a worship of natural elements (sun, moon, and stars) and ended in a cult of divinized people, raised to the station of gods, this time not through their virtues but because of their vices and immoral acts.

Other authors could also be noted. An older contemporary of Martinus was the bishop of Ruspe in Africa, who was especially engaged as an opponent of Arianism. His manual, *Mythologiae,* does not contain novel ideas, but is important because it was read industriously throughout the Middle Ages and consequently kept alive the allegorical explanation of the gods.

As late as the seventh century, Isidore of Sevilla, who came to be canonized, had to struggle against paganism in his archdiocese. In spite of these exertions, he amassed an encyclopedic—though not very profound—knowledge and erudition. As a result, his *Etymologiae sive Origines* was a source of manifold knowledge throughout the Middle Ages. He broaches the subject of pagan mythology several times in his book, showing a preference for very trivial rationalistic explanations, which as a rule have their starting point in natural phenomena.

Almost all medieval clerics who were occupied with pagan mythology used to draw on the books by the Church Fathers. This explains how the hypotheses of the Greek philosophers that were adopted by the Christian Apologists continued to be popular during the thousand years of the Middle Ages.

Chapter Three

THE MIDDLE AGES

ONE might have expected the interest in the pagan gods to diminish and, finally, to die upon the complete conversion of Europe. Yet something different happened. Medieval Christianity had itself absorbed classical culture. The Greek philosophers—first Aristotle, later Plato—had a continuing influence on the theological speculations. The reverence for these thinkers, whom one might almost regard as precursors of Christian thought, did not wane at all.

There was more. Latin had become the language of the church. Every young cleric studied it, and his instruction was by no means restricted to the reading of the Church Fathers. He acquainted himself with the Latin authors in an effort to command the language. Cicero was the paradigm of an elegant Latin. It is natural that the orator was studied once again in periods when attempts were made to correct the totally corrupted Latin of the clerics, that is to say, in periods to which we now give the name "renaissance." The poets were also admired, especially Vergil and Ovid. We can see the results in the medieval imitations inspired by the *Aeneis,* adapting the materials of national sagas. The best known example is the *Waltharius* by the ninth-century monk Ekkehard of St. Gall. It followed naturally that every cleric who studied these works gained some knowledge of the classical deities and the myths that were told about them. Somehow these deities and myths had to be accounted for to avoid mental confusion. The lascivious stories especially had to be made as acceptable as possible. Again, the notion of allegory demonstrated its usefulness. Christian poets, educated in the tradition of classical literature, found an inexhaustible source of explanation and imagery. Thus it happened that the names of gods were not avoided but, quite the contrary, became an indispensable ornament of poetic diction. It is characteristic that at the occasion of the wedding of the Frankish king Sigebert with the Visigothic princess Brunichild, in 566, the poet Fortunatus wrote an Epithalamion in which Venus and Cupid blessed the marriage!

The same thing happened in the north, in the Scandinavian countries. After their Christianization, the worship of pagan gods came of course to an end; yet the gods lived on untouched, in skaldic poetry. As of old, the poets used poetic circumscriptions (the so-called "kennings") that for the most part were compounds on the names of pagan gods. This technique did not vanish. Although the poets seem to have avoided the names of gods as much as possible in the period immediately following Christianization, the tradition was not broken. The poems of pagan days were faithfully preserved and were imitated as indispensable artistic models. From the twelfth century on, Christianity seems to have been so firmly rooted in the spiritual life of the Icelanders that they felt no hesitation in employing the pagan ornamentation. The names of the gods had come to mean just as much or as little for these Christian poets as for their confreres in the south, who did not tire of setting the gods of classical antiquity upon the stage of their poems. We may assume that in connection with these kennings a good deal of pagan mythology was somehow committed to memory. It was hardly possible to use such poetical compounds without understanding what they alluded to. There is the astonishing fact that the Icelandic scholar Snorri Sturluson composed a handbook of pagan mythology almost two centuries after the triumph of Christianity, with the obvious purpose of smoothing the way for budding skalds. The book shows a surprisingly elaborate knowledge of mythology and even provides us with explanations and additions to the elaborate poetical heritage of antiquity.

But for the medieval cleric to read such texts, filled with paganism, without endangering his soul's salvation, it was necessary to make clear to him how trifling the pagan gods really were. Once more, allegory and Euhemerism were the method. When in the eleventh century Gottfried of Viterbo wrote his *Speculum Regum* for the young Staufer Frederick I, he also mentioned pagan gods and depicted them as meritorious people out of a dim past. The Franks considered themselves descendants of the Trojans; the heroes of Troy, primarily Priam, were considered ancestors of the Frankish kings. Of course, national pride played its part; since Vergil saw the Romans descending from the *pius Aeneas,* the Franks could not lag behind. They were bold enough to add that their origin in the Greek part of Asia placed their royal race far above that of the Romans. After all, the ancestor of the Trojan kings was Dardanos, the son of Zeus, and Gottfried was not afraid to place the very origin of the race of the Staufer emperors in that mythical figure. In his enthusiasm, the poet addresses the king: *"Cum Jove summo deo superi tibi regna dederunt"* ("Together with the supreme Jupiter the gods have given the kingdom to you"). This shows clearly how real the gods were to the poet and with what reverence he looked upon them.

Jerome (d. A.D. 420) provided still another brake to the dangers of pagan mythology by assuming that pagan and Christian traditions were in harmony. Isidore elaborated this, and gradually the thought was born that Israel had been the teacher of Hellas in all respects—in philosophy, in science, and in poetry. The result was that pagan mythology was assigned a place next to the Christian tradition. At the beginning of the fourteenth century, the Italian poet Albertino Mussato declared that the pagan myths proclaim the same thing as the sacred scriptures, except that the myths do it in a veiled and enigmatic way. The struggle of the Giants against Zeus is the story of the tower of Babel. Similarly, when Jupiter punishes Lycaon, one may imagine the fall of Lucifer. Later we shall see how after the time of Humanism these dubious identities grew into most curious theories—in fact they became a quasi-science, hiding the weak hypothesis under plenty of erudition.

After all, the whole line of reasoning was supported by totally unfounded explanations of names. A superficial resemblance of names or words counted for a convincing proof. This method too is old. We find it even in the thirteenth century Icelandic scholar Snorri Sturluson (1178-1241), who in these matters appears to have been a good pupil of the monks. In the preface to his mythological handbook, the *Snorra Edda,* he begins with the Christian tradition. After the Flood, wickedness reappeared among the people; they lost faith and forgot the existence of the Creator. Snorri Sturluson is of the opinion, like Martinus of Bracara, that the sight of heaven and earth led people again to believe in a creator and lord of all things in nature. But after the Babylonian confusion, the existing superstition evolved in many different ways.

At this point in his exposition he undertakes a crude Euhemeristic analysis. Also in this he is like Martinus. Obviously influenced by the Frankish tradition, however, Snorri finds his beginning in Troy. As he equates this Troy with the land of the Turks, one can see how he deals with remote resemblances in sound. A grandson of Priam, he continues, was called Trór, "whom we call Thór." Trór journeyed far and wide. Arriving in the extreme north, he found a woman soothsayer, Sibil, "whom we call Sif." One of Trór's descendants was Voden. He too decided to leave Turkey and follow his father north. He and his followers were called the Aesir because they came from Asia. The journey continued over Saxony, where Odin appointed his three sons as governors. One of them was called Beldeg (a name that Snorri must have gotten somehow from an English source), which is of course the same as Balder. Finally Odin came to Sweden where he founded the city Sigtuna, which was built "wholly according to the model of Troy." In this manner the "Asians" spread through the north, founded kingdoms, and came later to be worshiped as gods.

At the end of the Middle Ages the poet and scholar Boccaccio, who went about things in a similar way, is to be mentioned. By order of the king of Cyprus, Hugo IV of Lusignan, he wrote a handbook of mythology that appeared, shortly before his death, under the title *De genealogia deorum.* Boccaccio considered this his most important work; it was to glorify him among even distant descendants. If he meant by this no more than the next few centuries, his expectations were correct. For our part, we shall hold the poet of the *Decameron,* although he wrote in the language of the common people, infinitely dearer than the scholar of that unoriginal book. Nevertheless, the handbook was famous at one time and was considered a work of unsurpassable erudition.

Boccaccio respected the classical poets too much to think that their fables had no deep meaning. But the meaning he finds is not profound. It goes without saying for him that the pagan gods are really celestial bodies; like these, they are eternally immutable and govern the fates of men. The influence of the Hellenistic astrological speculations is clear. Of course, being a Christian author, he must add that these celestial deities can be active only as servants of the one true God.

Allegorically, everything can be made harmless. This is how Boccaccio explains the myth of Psyche: Psyche is the soul, gifted with reason; her two sisters are the vegetative and the sensitive souls. Hence they are older than Psyche, for man lives and feels before he is able to think. The soul is led up to God by Zephyrus, the holy breath of life, but God forbids the soul to desire a vision of Him. Psyche's sisters visit the soul several times, for the soul, endowed with reason, also takes part in the lower functions of life and senses. Sensuality wants to dominate reason; this is expressed symbolically in Psyche's alienation from her husband.

With Boccaccio, we close the Middle Ages. The picture we must present of the mythological "studies" in the medieval period is not encouraging. One might conclude that no more could be expected of an epoch that relied on every authority and resisted all free investigation. Yet in terms of our subject we should not castigate the thinkers and scholars of those ages often decried as "dark." When humanism ignited the light of reason, little more progress was made.

Chapter Four

THE RENAISSANCE

WITH Boccaccio we enter the confines of humanism, but his allegorical explanations still breathe the spirit of the Middle Ages. In spite of an almost exaggerated admiration for the classics, the scholars of the sixteenth and seventeenth centuries showed little comprehension of pagan polytheism. It is true that the renewed study of the Greek philosophers, of Plato in particular, had brought a greater esteem for the spirit and civilization of the Greeks, who gradually came to supersede the Romans. Scholars like Marsilio Ficino (1433-98) and Erasmus (1469-1536) had done everything to promulgate classical literature and arouse the interest it fully deserved. Before long the Renaissance was eager—especially in the realm of the fine arts—to follow the models set for all generations by Hellas and Rome. But this enthusiasm left no better understanding of the world of the pagan gods.

New ideas about the origin of those unique pagan beliefs did not appear. Protestant or Catholic, people remained bound in their considerations to a Christian faith that set the norms for all thought concerning those classical myths. This faith teaches that God revealed himself at the beginning of time as the creator of the world and mankind. The Christian point of departure could be nothing else than the belief in the One God, and the assumption of the Middle Ages was still shared that man had forgotten or failed to recognize his creator because humanity had sunk deep into sinfulness.

Of course, it was Satan and the fallen angels who tempted men and caused them to fall. This was demonstrated by Gerard Vossius in his book *De theologia gentili* with great erudition and with an overwhelming mass of unconvincing quotations. The causes of idolatry, he argued, are manifold. First is the root of all evil: the temptation by Satan to worship many demons rather than God. Then one must consider the "ignorance" of ancient humanity. With them the tradition of the revelation was long lost, and they did not comprehend the light shining in nature. They did not notice the creator in the beauty and wonder of the natural world. Each followed his limited views and thus the people's opinions about God were divided. They were blind men, leading the blind.

For Vossius, as for so many before him, the worship of natural phenomena came first, yet this worship was attached to what was created instead of to the creator. It is what Vossius calls *cultus proprius:* the worship of the sun or of Hercules. He distinguishes from this a *cultus symbolicus,* in which, instead of God himself, something that points to God is worshiped. Thus the sun was adored in the sacred fire of Vesta, as was Hercules in his statue.[1]

Still other questions arise. When the tradition inspired by God himself, and conserved in the Old Testament, is believed the basis for all development, it is logical to assume that the Greek pantheon was a degeneration of this sacred tradition. The gods of Greeks and Romans must be regarded as imitations of the patriarch in the Jewish tradition, and their names can be nothing but garbled Hebrew.

A specimen of the wild etymologies, which were offered at the time to an audience that was not demanding, is the one that Vossius presents for *Mars.* This name, he says, comes from the Hebrew word *marats,* which means "to be strong," but it can also be derived from *mechares*—"destroying, ruining." Both these designations fit the sun equally well. Thus it is "convincingly" shown why the pagans regarded Mars or the sun as a war god.[2] It is clear that this method of explanation is arbitrary. Since the sun can be considered the natural object of adoration *par excellence,* Vossius starts from a solar cult. But the sun deity was given many names, for he was called not only Zeus and Apollo, but also Mars (Ares being the same word, of which the initial letter was elided). Then, with the help of a Hebrew etymology, Vossius jumps to a conclusion about a war god.

Hugo Grotius also assumes that humanity allowed itself to be turned away from the true faith. In his *De veritate religionis christianae* he writes:

> That it was to evil men indeed that the cult of the pagans owed its origin is certain, because of significant proofs. First they did not induce people to worship the supreme God, but on the contrary, they destroyed this worship as much as they could. They wanted to equate themselves with God in all possible manners, in the cult. Secondly, they did the greatest harm to the worshippers of the one supreme God by inciting magistrates and peoples to punish them. Since the poets were allowed to sing the parricides and adulteries of the gods and the Epicurians to do away with divine Providence, there was no religion . . . however strange . . . that they did not admit, such as the Egyptian, Phrygian, Greek and Etrurian in Rome. . . .
>
> .   .   .
>
> Thirdly, a cult not becoming to a good and wholesome mind, with human blood, with naked people running in the temples, with feasts and dances full of vileness—of the sort yet observable among the peoples in America and Africa, obscured as those peoples still are by the darkest heathendom.[3]

Next to this, inevitably, Euhemerism appears again. "Worst is this, that those people whom they paid [divine] honor were clearly marked by great faults: the drunken Bacchus, the ravisher Hercules, Romulus assaulting his brother, Jupiter assaulting his father . . ."[4]

Still earlier would have come the worship of celestial bodies and the elements, such as fire, water, air, and earth. It was foolish, Grotius argues, to send prayers to all these, because they are no *naturae intelligentes*.[5]

It is not necessary to listen to the statements of the many scholars who exhibited similar opinions—Selden, Cudworth, and Bochart, among others. Only the famous scholar Pierre Daniel Huet (1630-1721) deserves to be mentioned briefly. In his *Demonstratio evangelica* he, like the others, plays with the most curious etymologies, enabling himself to identify the Greek gods with figures from Jewish history. "The objection will be raised," he writes,

> if Ashtarte is the moon, Osiris at the same time the sun, Adonis, and Bacchus, how we can identify gods and goddesses with Moses and Zipporah? But when the human race had lost the truth it wandered among many errors and piled one fable on top of the other. What pleased it most was to give to one and the same fictitious person different meanings, one physical, another historical. Thus with the name Jupiter they mean physically the planet as well as the highest atmospheric region, but historically Jupiter was a king of Crete and also Hammon, otherwise called Ham, the son of Noah. With the name Osiris they mean physically the sun and the Nile, but historically Osiris is Misram, Ham's son. Physically, Neptune is the sea, historically Japheth. Saturn is the name of the highest planet, but also of Noah.[6]

The English scholar and philosopher Francis Bacon (1561-1626) also ventured an explanation of Greek mythology. In his *Sapientia veterum* he writes that the ancient fables conceal a mystery and an allegory, although he takes into account subsequent changes as a result of insertions of historical materials or poetic additions. His explanation of Pan may serve as a specimen of his hermeneutics. Pan's tapering horns are an image of nature, ascending from the individuals to the species and from the species to the families; they touch the sky because generic concepts lead from physics to metaphysics and natural theology. Pan's hair signifies, in Bacon's opinion, the radiance of bodies that is observable with any visual perception. Bacon sees a connection between Pan's beard and the solar rays pointing downward when the sun is covered by a cloud! [7]

Although there was general concord among the theologians and philosophers of the seventeenth century that the similarity of pagan and Jewish tradition was a result of plagiarism by Greece and Egypt from the sacred scriptures, the Anglican theologian John Spencer (1630-95) proposed another explanation. In order to check superstition, God would have accepted in his liturgy a number of rites that had become venerable because of their antiquity; God would have deemed these *ineptiae* tolerable, or fit for concealing some mystery.[8] Although this explanation served the theologian to defend the rituals of the Anglican church, he nevertheless came to a much better understanding of the undeniable similarities between pagan and Judeo-Christian traditions than did his predecessors, who like the Church Fathers thought only of impious plagiary.

Chapter Five

THE EIGHTEENTH CENTURY

THE eighteenth century was the Age of Rationalism. The chief cause of this rationalism was the recent flourishing of the natural sciences. As a result, there was a tendency to look down upon faith, which was regarded as a vestige of the childhood of men. It encouraged people to criticize the Christian traditions. This criticism grew in audacity and finally shook the credibility of the traditions.

Moreover, Protestant theology led in a new direction. In trying to organize the Christian church wholly in accordance with the apostolic congregations, the Protestants came to reject as later additions the cultic forms of the Catholic church; it seemed natural to assume that these cultic forms had their origin in pagan forms of worship. Once this path had been opened, theology followed it with great consistency, then and later. The Socinians went so far as to reject the Trinity and the divine nature of Christ, since in their opinion these ideas were borrowed from neoplatonism. So the impression was now possible that Christianity, as it had evolved in the course of time, was a mixture of theological speculation and pagan superstition coming from diverse sources. Hence, it was the task of a critical study, intent on separating what was genuine from what was not genuine, to re-

move all later accretions; only then could one reach the faith
that by its simplicity would have an irresistible power of per-
suasion. Such a faith was called "natural"; it can be defined as
faith in an all-good and all-wise God, creator of world and man,
in need of no form of cult, who had withdrawn to the recesses
of heaven as some sort of *deus otiosus*. Sometimes it seems as if
this God were only the postulate of critical study: according to
Voltaire the grandiose clockwork of the universe presupposed a
clockmaker. But why continue worshiping that clockmaker, who
had completed his work in the days long past?

This spiritual attitude was wholly inadequate for a true understanding of religious phenomena. If we review the Age of Enlightenment for its appreciation of religion, we may well call it
the age of groping-in-the-dark. We may expect its speculations
about earlier, especially pagan, forms of religion to be totally
sterile. That is exactly the case, and yet there are germs of an
awareness that a new approach to the problems of religion was
called for. What contributed most of all was the finding of a
new source: primitive religions. The voyages of discovery had
opened up the world, and there was now plenty of opportunity
to become acquainted with primitive tribes all over the earth.
We have already observed that Hugo Grotius compared Greek
cultic acts with feasts and dances that still occurred among tribes
of America and Africa in the obscurity of darkest heathendom.
This manner of comparison could only be to the disadvantage
of the Greeks. The initial contacts with primitive religions were
superficial and the conclusions disappointing. Nevertheless, the
contact with those savages was never again lost and thereafter increased continually. Gradually, Europeans acquired a more solid
knowledge of those barbarous peoples, and their understanding
of strange beliefs profited by it.

This growth of knowledge was owed primarily to the Catholic
missionaries, particularly the Jesuits, who tried to bring Christianity to all parts of the world. They made serious efforts to penetrate into strange and forbidding worlds of thought, and it must
be said that they were keen observers. In China, the missionaries
did their work among a people of a millennial high civilization;
they found religious ideas that were in no way, either in subtlety
or purity, inferior to Christianity. There seemed to be reason to
ask oneself in all humility whether the Christian faith alone had
a high and pure awareness of God.

From India at the same time came the first reports of a spiritual and religious life dating back more than 3,000 years. In 1730, the Jesuit Jean Calmette announced that he had discovered the first two Vedas, and two years later he had learned about all four of them. The truth of this information may be open to doubt, but undeniably this priest must have spoken with Brahmans and must have listened with the deepest respect to their profound and refined metaphysical speculations.

Of eminent importance were the discoveries made among the North American Indian tribes. The missionaries had plenty of opportunity to propagate Christianity in Canada, which had fallen to France. They made their way to the tribes in the interior and began their salutary work. A trace of the significance of their work is, perhaps, that later investigations of tribal mythologies brought to light elements that apparently had been accepted from the missionaries. The beliefs of the Indians were carefully examined and reported in conscientious publications, of which the *Relations de la Nouvelle France* were the most important. There is no better proof of the accuracy of these communications than the fact that present-day ethnology still utilizes them as sources for our knowledge of the Indian religions of the past.

The ideas about religion that were thus collected did not go unnoticed. Scholars and philosophers found much use for them. Traces of these ideas are found in two French authors who speculated on the origin of religion. Bernhard le Bovier Fontenelle (1657-1757) began his book *Discours sur l'origine des fables* with the assumption that the truth revealed to the Jews either had not become known to the other nations or had been allowed to perish because of mental dullness. To make this point, he draws attention to some astonishing similarities between the Greek and the American "fables"—for that is what he calls the myths. It is a childish philosophy of both peoples that, according to him, explains the similarities. This childish philosophy thinks of the unknown in terms of what is known and is inclined to accept what is probable as true. He arrives at the conclusion that all peoples have the same spiritual predisposition—a conclusion that twentieth-century scholarly research seems to have forgotten completely and one that could have saved it from errors and even embarrassment. Another conclusion by Fontenelle is that the red Indians could have reached the high level of Greek culture if they had had the chance for development without external hindrance.

Charles de Brosses (1709-77) showed greater originality. He focused his attention on West African fetishism and became convinced that it provided the key to an explanation of Greek paganism. In 1760, he published anonymously *Du culte des dieux fétiches*. In this work he rejected the allegorical as well as the Euhemeristic explanation of the Greek myths. But he too begins with the thought that the original revelation had perished among the pagan nations. Further, he considers ignorance and fear the principal motivations for religion. Fetishism is for him a primordial form of religion. He assumes that it existed among all peoples, including the Greeks, and tries to collect proofs for this thesis. We may deplore the fact that he did not give a sharper definition of fetishism; for him, it was simply the cult of animals and objects. It is not difficult to locate that primitive cult in the Greek myths in which animals are significant. It goes without saying that his argument is insufficient, but this is secondary. Of greater importance is that for the first time a scholar tried to approach Greek religion not from Christian presuppositions but on the basis of primitive forms. In the final analysis, this method means that Greek religion must be considered as the result of a development with roots in a much simpler and earlier religion, which can still be found alive among the later "savages" and can still be studied there.

The two authors mentioned were *rarae aves* in their time. How exceptional they were becomes obvious when we turn to another scholar of the period, Abbé Banier (1673-1741). For him Euhemerism had lost none of its old prestige. His book *La mythologie et les fables expliquées par l'histoire* ("Mythology and Fables Explained by History") indicates by its very title which way the author turned for explanations. The unoriginal thesis is again that paganism appeared after the degeneration of early humanity and particularly in the race of Ham. Like many before him, Banier looked to Egypt, for that country had always had the reputation of being the oldest culture in the world. There was an Egyptian solar cult, and it seemed likely that adoration of the sun was the first form of worship. From Egypt, the sun cult would have spread to all parts of the world. However, Banier sees that this does not suffice to explain the whole store of myths. Hence he gives most significance to the divine veneration of people who were raised to the state of gods because of their deeds. Their names served also as names for celestial bodies. But the diligent abbé fails to show the historical foundation of mythology in all cases; he then comforts himself with the thought that it is not a real and thorough history preserved in the myths but a history that he has had to deduce from these myths. It will not be necessary to demonstrate that this totally imaginary history is just as mythical as the myth it was meant to explain.

Curious ideas were presented also by Nicolas Sylvestre Bergier (1718-90). In his *L'origine des dieux du paganisme* ("The Origin of the Gods of Paganism") he assumes the task of drawing the developmental scheme of Greek religion. This is how he sees it: the most ancient times knew only a cult for a single god, Uranos. After this came the rule of Chronos and the Titans, during which the worship of nature unfolded. Then the real polytheism of the Olympians followed, and in the end the veneration of people as gods. It is obvious that Bergier followed Hesiod step by step; his scheme presents the traditional sequence of the various dynasties of gods. Bergier's merit lies elsewhere. It is that he formulated the idea of some sort of *animism*; in his opinion, the cult of the Negro peoples presupposes a belief in spirits that are present through the whole world. This belief, he continues, also forms the foundation of fetishism and even of Greek polytheism. Thus we see in Bergier's work the first hesitant steps toward an evolutionistic theory of religion that would not become dominant until a century later.

Actually, in the eighteenth century the influence of the philosophers on the problem of religion was of much more importance than that of the theologians and other scholars. The philosophers were quite unhampered by the biases of the official creeds. Sometimes they arrived at almost frighteningly radical conclusions. This can even be said of David Hume (1711-76).* In his opinion, the contemplation of the cosmos teaches us that this cosmos is a huge machine, divided into smaller machines. Thus, even by the eighteenth century, a mechanical image of the world was drawn. The machines function in harmony. This can be explained only by assuming that they are designed by an intellect

---

* What follows in this paragraph is principally a summary of Cleanthes' argument in the *Dialogues Concerning Natural Religion,* and it is doubtful whether it represents Hume's position *in toto.* It does not do justice to the soundness of Hume's skepticism—his profound awareness of the limitations of the human mind. However, De Vries makes the point that will strike the historian of religions first and foremost: Hume seems to miss any organ for an appreciation of concrete religious phenomena and in this respect is a child of his time.—TRANS.

infinitely greater than man's, yet in essence not different from it. In this manner Hume demonstrates in his *Dialogues Concerning Natural Religion* that the existence of a deity is a necessary postulate of a contemplation of nature and also that this deity must be of the same nature as the human spirit.[1] It follows that natural religion must be the worship of a creating Supreme Being.

However, Hume also believes that the development of religions is of a very different character. At the beginning of history Hume sees polytheism, which must in no way be regarded as a contemplation of nature. Why should there be a polytheism? Hume finds the answer in psychological processes. Human experiences evoke fear or hope. This leads to questions about the causes of events, and here the anthropomorphic manner of thinking plays its part: men find it impossible to conceive of beings other than those with a man-like nature as a cause of events.

As the century grew older, the tongues of the philosophers, who became more and more like philosophizing journalists, became sharper. The arch-mocker Voltaire, pseudonym of François-Marie Arouet (1694-1778), commences with a deism devoid of sense and finds the origin of polytheism in priestly ruses and craving for power, for it was priests who introduced idolatry and superstition to establish their own authority.

In the *Encyclopédie,* Denis Diderot (1713-84) exhibits similar opinions. According to him, there are three forms of religion:

1. of the philosophers who attempt to approach the essence of God and nature;
2. of the pagans—a form that is taught by the priests and protected by the kings for selfish purposes;
3. of the superstitious populace that becomes the victim of every appearance.

Concerning the beliefs preserved by the priests, Diderot says that the dogmas are demonstrably untrue and yet not so absurd as they seem at first. For it is possible to interpret the gods and their cult sometimes mystically and always allegorically. Moreover, for Diderot, too, Euhemerism is a way out. The earliest pagans venerated their great benefactors as gods—Jupiter, Apollo, Ceres, or Bacchus.[2] An unimaginative, flat rationalism always seems to be in need of Euhemeristic support.

The Italian Giambattista Vico (1668-1744) has a special place

in the eighteenth century. His principal work, the *Scienza nuova,*
went almost unnoticed in his own time; it was to exert its great
influence only much later. This "new science" is what we would
call cultural history; we can well understand that Herder was at
one point fascinated by it. Vico assigns a great role to imagination
in the creation of religious ideas, for it is the imagination that
provides the shapes for religious and mythological imagery. He
also attributes to man an intuitive knowledge of God. In addition, fear created by certain natural phenomena is for him a factor of great significance. Presenting an outline of the development of Greek religion, he distinguishes four stages:

1. divinization of nature: heaven with its thunder becomes
   Zeus, the sea Poseidon;
2. gods that can appear only after man has succeeded in ruling
   over the powers of nature: Hephaistos, the god of fire;
   Demeter, the goddess of grain;
3. still later gods, who embody civil institutions and parties:
   Juno is the institution of marriage; Diana was born as a
   result of hygienic measures taken by the police;
4. the total humanization of the gods, as found in Homer.

Much in Vico's book is not fully developed, but how else could
it be in his century? It is to his credit that he had an open eye
for the similarities of different peoples and the underlying one-
ness of human nature. These insights are quite surprising in the
eighteenth century; how far ahead of their time they were is
clear only to us today. Indeed, for a true understanding of the
development of religion, the unity of human nature must be the
point of departure; all comparison of Greek or Roman religion
with the mythology of the primitives rests on this postulate.

Part Two

THE INTERLUDE
OF
ROMANTICISM

Chapter Six

THE ROMANTIC PERIOD: INTRODUCTION

WITH the Romantic period came a spiritual climate much more favorable to an understanding of religion and mythology than the rationalism of the eighteenth century. While reason ruled for a century, the spiritual emaciation was alarming. The clearest examples were in literature. The supreme sway of reason had to be dislodged to clear the way for new life. This was no easy task, for the intellect had been set firmly on a throne, and the illusion was strong that the intellect was the chief, if not the only, element of the human spirit. All other elements had to submit to it. Man—it was thought—acting rationally could not fail to reach the height of perfection.

But what of emotion, of will, and of imagination? Perhaps they could be suppressed for a long time, but they would never cease to exist. They lived in almost wilfully forgotten regions of the soul, ready to return in full force at the favorable moment when the aura of the intellect had diminished.

If we recall the trivial manner in which the great philosophers of the Enlightenment used to speak of religion, it is no surprise that the really faithful were disgusted. There was no necessity to refute intellectualism with arguments. Emotionally it was evident that intellectualism was wrong. As soon as one was aware of this and realized that emotion was entitled to a part in the discussion, the spell of intellectualism was broken. The intellect lost its position of superiority and was placed side by side with the other activities of the soul. (As a matter of fact, at first the place of the intellect went far below the others.)

Emotion and imagination become the catchwords of the new movement. It is characteristic that the change occurred most forcefully in Germany. It was no longer the French scholars who took the lead, as in the eighteenth century, but German philologists and philosophers who devoted themselves to the study of religious problems.

The reaction against the Enlightenment began with the *Sturm und Drang* period and was tempestuous. French classicism, which had been admired and meticulously imitated, was finished; now it was Shakespeare who set the tone in art. Subservience to the compulsory artistic norms became despised; one celebrated freedom and spontaneity. Theories of art were not in demand. Originality was called for more than anything else; the notion of genius came into vogue. Reason had been overprized in former days, and the new fashion was a conscious inclination toward irrationalism. Despite all the exaggerations that went with the transition, it must be recognized that this reaction was necessary and sound. For those who desired some insight into the essence of religion and the history of its forms, a good dose of irrationality was perhaps more useful than a complacent, positivistic intellect.

The *Sturm und Drang* was powerfully influenced by Jean Jacques Rousseau (1712-78). He propagated a profound feeling for nature and led the search for a more intimate contact with nature. God was immanent in creation; he was not thought of as being outside or *versus* his creation. These thoughts led naturally to a pantheism, which Goethe remained faithful to all his life. Christianity seems to evaporate to some extent; it has no hold on those glowingly enthused by nature. Pietistic circles are alight with a devout faith, yet this faith is not fixed by the traditional dogmas and, again, has its main support in a feeling of harmony with God.

When this tempestuous period had run its course, Romanticism proper began. Many distinguished figures felt attracted by a positive form of Christianity. Clear examples of this mood were certain conversions to Catholicism that caused quite a stir at the time (Friedrich Schlegel, Joseph von Görres).

It was a fortunate coincidence for the more thorough study of religion that in this period a number of Egyptian and Indian sources could be presented to the European public. By the end of the eighteenth century, English scholars had access to religious scriptures that until then had been scrupulously guarded by the Brahmans. As early as 1784, William Jones (1746-94) had been able to point to curious similarities among various myths of Indians, Greeks, and Romans. (He also included the Biblical tradition in his comparison.) The Frenchman A. de Polier, who was born in Lausanne and who later had entered the British-Indian military service, had been able to acquire various Sanskrit texts and had sent some manuscripts with Vedic texts to London, where the possibilities for scholarly research were best. After his death, his niece M. E. de Polier, utilizing manuscripts that he had kept, published a book, *Mythologie des Hindous* ("Mythology of the Hindus"), in which she emphasized the relation to the Biblical tradition. It is clear from her work, published in 1809, that she made use mainly of epic and philosophical texts and that the Vedas were hardly known to her. This one-sided book gave an inadequate view of Indian religion but for the time being it provided European scholars with their only knowledge of the subject. That its influence was harmful is quite obvious in the work of Friedrich Creuzer, for whom M. E. de Polier's book was really a foundation. Fortunately, soon after, Henry Thomas Colebrooke was able to know the important sources more thoroughly, but his beneficial knowledge made its influence felt only after the Romantic Period.

However this may be, the little that became known in Europe of the Indian religions and philosophies was quite important. It aroused an interest bordering on passion. We see this in the book *La langue et la sagesse des Indiens,* published in 1808 by Friedrich Schlegel: he predicted a spiritual rebirth in Europe not unlike that of Humanism.

At that time no distinctions were made among Vedic periods, Brahmanism, Buddhism, or Hinduism. This fact is one of many typical of the confusion rampant in the discussion of Indian religions. Relatively recent speculations in texts and commentaries were thought to report the ancient religion of India, and the Upanishads were put on the same level with the Vedic hymns; the possibility of an accurate history was confounded.

General Bonaparte's expedition to Egypt (1798-99) was accompanied by a staff of scholars who were to study the buildings and inscriptions of Pharaonic times. This conscientious enterprise was crowned with a success that could never have been imagined, when in 1799 the stone of Rosetta was found, which bore an inscription in hieroglyphs, demotic, and Greek. In 1822, Jean François Champollion (1790-1832) deciphered the Egyptian script. The very next year he ventured an outline of the Egyptian religious beliefs in his book *Panthéon égyptien* ("The Egyptian Pantheon").

For the time being, the rapid succession of startling discoveries whetted rather than satisfied the appetite for knowledge. It was to take many years of painstaking research to gain some true insight into the religions of India and Egypt. But it should be said that these discoveries gave a strong impetus to the religio-historical studies of the Romantics and thus gave rise to ideas far superior to those of the preceding centuries, which were totally wanting in such stimulating materials. Now for the first time classical antiquity could be illuminated by much more ancient civilizations. True, insufficient facts and enthusiasm over the first discoveries led to quick conclusions and irresponsible generalizations. But one thing had been achieved: the endless and sterile argumentation confined within the classical tradition had been broken.

Chapter Seven

THE ROMANTIC PERIOD: PHILOSOPHICAL THEORIES

IN BEGINNING with Gotthold Ephraim Lessing (1729-81), we look back for a moment to the eighteenth century. Yet as the precursor of a new age he should be mentioned here, for the turn of the tide is manifest in him; he is not typical any more of eighteenth-century rationalism. In his treatise *Die Erziehung des Menschengeschlechts* (1780, "The Education of the Human Race") he discusses among other things the development of religion. Providence reveals its activity in history. This revelation given to mankind conveys nothing that mankind will not find for itself, while the form of revelation is always in harmony with any given epoch. Thus, every religion is such a form of revelation and at the same time a phase in a perennial development. The spirit of his time makes Lessing emphasize the moral character of religion; dogmas, rituals, and priests are of secondary importance for him. The development he speaks of is to find completion in a rational religion that will no longer be in need of revelation.

The most important figure in the period of transition to Romanticism is Johann Gottfried Herder (1744-1803). During his study in Königsberg he was greatly stimulated by Johann Georg Hamann, the "magus of the North." During a voyage to Nantes in 1769, a storm in the Baltic Sea moved Herder so profoundly that the experience marked the beginning of his original thinking. He writes in his diary: "There are a thousand new and natural explanations for mythology when one reads Orpheus, Homer or Pindar . . . aboard ship." Oriental poetry also had its influence on Herder; it gave him a deeper view into the essence of mythology, which was for him at the same time the essence of poetry. Compared with Oriental poetry, which seems to show him a primordial mythology, the Greek pantheon is for Herder not quite original, although he grants that it was suffused with a unique beauty by the poets.

Herder's passion for synthesis combined mythology, poetry, and language into a grand unity. With its help he wanted to penetrate to the sources of human nature. Herder's logic is not keen; he is rather intuitive. His thoughts are often lofty but not always well defined. However, this quality fitted the spirit of his time perfectly. At any rate, he had insights that were novel at the time and turned out to be extremely thought provoking. In his enthusiasm, he saw the mythology of the nations expressed in their very languages. What else could the primordial language have been but the imitation in sounds and images of nature, moving and revealing itself to man—pure personification, a living mythology! If one compares to this the ideas Max Müller would develop a century later about the role of language in the origin of myths, it becomes clear how successful Herder really was in disclosing the essence of mythology and language at the same time. In this respect, he was far ahead of his day. One could even say that ideas comparable to Herder's reoccur only in Walter F. Otto. For it was the latter who said:

> Language and myth cannot be separated from each other.
> I have tried to show not only that myth must be understood
> as language, but, much more significantly, that language
> must be understood as myth.[1]

Herder arrived at the conviction that whoever would understand a mythology like that of the Greeks must come to it without the feelings and concepts of modern man. If religion is the awareness of God's activity in creating order, we must try to place ourselves within the soul of those in whom that awareness is born. For Herder, the Greek gods are living personalities who cannot be grasped by a general concept. Concepts are too small for the totality of their being; concepts, after all, are fundamentally no more than *ex post facto* abstractions.

In his *Älteste Urkunde des Menschengeschlechts* ("The Earliest Document of the Human Race") he observes that all of nature, just like its creator and his replica, the human soul, is spiritual and symbolic. For that very reason nature can be understood by us. In the same spirit he states that the whole creation is nothing but a symbol, a hieroglyph of God, through which he wants to educate man; the earliest doctrine is the dawn of day, light, the symbol of beauty and perfection.

Herder is one of the founders of the later scholarly discipline of mythology. From his time on, thanks to his influence, myths were no longer regarded as a collection of allegories; he often emphasized the religious elements in myth and art. Of equally great significance is the idea that the course of human history shows a development—an idea he accepted from Lessing.

The nature of Herder's thought shows in his reproach against Kant. Kant's philosophy, he claims, would dry up the soul. And it is true that the Königsberg philosopher tries to solve the problems of man and world purely rationally. In trying to establish faith on a firm foundation, he shows that speculative reason cannot know the essence of things but that it is the practical reason that discloses to man the certainty of freedom, of the existence of a supreme legislator and of the immortality of the soul. In Kant's opinion, ethics do not rest on religion, but the other way round—religion rests on ethics.

Kant's influence on his time was great. According to him, faith is the province not of reason but of emotion. Thus knowledge and faith are separated, for they belong to different spiritual faculties. It will become the task of the post-Kantian philosophers Fichte and Schelling to resolve this dualism again; this happens in their "idealistic philosophy."

Let us confine ourselves to some remarks on Friedrich W. J. Schelling (1775-1854). Starting in 1828, Schelling lectured on a *Philosophie der Mythologie (Philosophy of Mythology)*.[2] In his view, myths must not be considered as fancies and fabrications. Myths have a reality—one of a peculiar nature. It is true that initially mythology appears an incoherent mass of fables, but it is the task of philosophy to discover reason in that incoherence and sense in that apparent senselessness. One should not take refuge in the method already followed too long—of calling crucial in the myths only what the investigator can accept as crucial and calling the rest poetic foliage or later bunglings with the text. What is at stake is not any fixed contents of the ideas but the significance that myth holds for man. The spiritual power of myth over the human soul is precisely what makes it impossible to see in myth something invented or thought up by poets or philosophers.

The speculative nature of Schelling's construction is clear from the scheme he draws for the development of mythology.*

A. MOMENT I — The unconquered and unconquerable central character of the first principle.

B. MOMENT II — Process by which the first principle becomes peripheral and, consequently, may be conquered = Urania.

C. MOMENT III — The real struggle between the resistant principle and God who sets free. To be distinguished are:
  a. the struggle for victory goes on, yet he who is really God frustrates the final victory = moment of Chronos, negation of true victory.
  b. transition to true victory in which the true God shows himself ready for a real victory.
  c. the Egyptian, Indian, and Greek mythologies.[3]

---

* This can hardly convey much to one not acquainted with Schelling's philosophy. For the history of scholarly attitudes to religion it is interesting to notice that the religions of the world and the Christian religion find their place here in one and the same scheme: the development of the *idea* has precedence over historical divisions as well as over theological biases. It is a purely *philosophical* scheme, whose seriousness is particularly striking. As I said in my introduction, the Romantic idea of unfolding became so very serious in comparison with the eighteenth century.—TRANS.

Chapter Eight

THE ROMANTIC PERIOD:
THE SYMBOLISTS

E. CASSIRER says of the Romantic philosophers and poets what could also be said of some mythologists of this period:

> [They] were the first who had drunk from the magic cup
> of myth. They felt refreshed and rejuvenated. From now
> on they saw all things in a new and transformed shape.[1]

Among these men, whom we call the Symbolists and who had their center in Heidelberg, were Joseph von Görres and Friedrich Creuzer. Each came to the fore in 1810 with a book, and their thoughts were so similar that one can see evidence of their simultaneous activity in the University of Heidelberg in 1806. Of the two scholars, Görres (1776-1848) was rather more a politician and journalist. He began as a zealous adherent of the French Revolution, then became an opponent of Napoleon, and then one of the most influential authors of the German independence movement. After his appointment as professor of history in Munich in 1827 he became a leading figure in the Catholic movement.

In contrast, Friedrich Creuzer (1771-1858) was professor of classical philology and ancient history at Heidelberg for nearly

45 years with the exception of a short time spent at the University of Leiden.

In 1810 Görres published his *Mythengeschichte der asiatischen Welt* ("History of Myths in Asia") in two volumes and Creuzer the first part of his *Symbolik und Mythologie der alten Völker, besonders der Griechen* ("Symbolism and Mythology of the Ancient Peoples, Especially the Greeks"). The very title of Görres' work shows that he wanted to draw into his investigation the Oriental religions, which had become known recently and quite insufficiently. On what little was known he built the boldest hypotheses. He begins with a primordial state in which the peoples of the earth are still undivided; he considers this a true natural state, the same as a priestly state or a theocracy. He describes that time as the golden age remembered in the traditions of every people. All things in it are characterized by simplicity: no temples and no images. Görres, who likes to speak in a glittering, sometimes rather oracular style, continues his extravagant enthusiasm for that primordial humanity on the banks of the Ganges and Indus in the following manner:

> They looked from the earth upward. There in heaven was the real realm of fire. There was the sun burning continually. There the stars, the planets and the fixed stars both, pierced through the darkness like flames. There the fires which only shine sparsely on earth were burning for ever unconquerable. Then the cult of fire became a cult of stars and the religion became pantheism. . . . And because all the nations were together in this great primordial state, these worldviews . . . form the inheritance which they bore with them on their long, later journeys. . . .[2]

The motif of the paradise story is recurrent in Görres' rhapsodic expositions. Indeed, it was not difficult to point to an original state of bliss in other religions than that of Israel. Yet Görres' imagination in presenting it is somewhat too vivid. He moves his primordial paradise to India, for he considers that the cradle of humanity. This figment of the imagination goes to show how strongly the new-found Indian writings enthused the intelligentsia at the time. But it is noteworthy that Görres in his exaltation seemed to have a vision of a truth that only later scholarship could demonstrate as reality: long before Franz Bopp showed the coherence of Sanskrit with Greek, Latin and Germanic and drew the conclusion that these languages must have one mother language, Görres conceived of an Indo-European unity originating—as would be commonly thought until long after him —in India.

Friedrich Creuzer drew a slightly different picture of primordial days. This is so because he looked at the development of Greece. He began with the Pelasgians, of whom Herodotus said on the basis of what he heard in Dodona[3] that they used to offer to the gods everything that could be offered. But they did not call the gods by their names for they learned these later from the Egyptians. Noteworthy in Herodotus' account is the notion of an ignorant primordial people that has yet to receive everything cultural from a more intellectual nation. Creuzer accepts this notion from Herodotus and then faces the problem of how, from such primitive ignorance of divine matters, the rich mythology, blooming as early as Homer and Hesiod, could have come into being. According to Herodotus these poets were the first to speak of the names of the gods, their cult, and their functions; it is the poets who gave the gods their shape.[4] In Creuzer's opinion there was a transition—in which the Pelasgians learned a higher idea of the gods—between the first speechless veneration of nameless presences and the later religion with its wealth of fables. Therefore, he assumes a period of activity by certain priests. These priests, coming out of the Orient, would have brought a message of a higher faith—an explanation that no doubt occurred because Creuzer thought of later missionary activity by prophets and founders of religions in the East. The nature of the wisdom brought by these priests is easy to guess when we recall that he deduced it especially from the later philosophical writings of the Indians, convinced as he was in all naïveté that those writings contained the earliest beliefs of the Vedas.

Creuzer elaborates his argument. The highly talented priests faced a great difficulty. Their exalted conception of divinities was to be communicated to a people who were very "poor in language." A straightforward communication was quite impossible. However, even Pausanias says that "the best of the sages among the Greeks expressed their thoughts not clearly, but enigmatically." [5] Similarly, in Creuzer's opinion, the form in which the Oriental priests conveyed their teachings to the Pelasgians must have been no more than a matter of hinting and (mysterious) revelation, because discursive thought was as yet nonexistent. The instruments of this communication were symbols.[6]

Creuzer's statements about symbolism are among the best ever made. The Greek *symbolon,* as described by Plato,[7] was something composed of two parts. It confirmed all relationships by a visible sign, like the little stone or die broken in two that signified an established right of hospitality. A symbol has a double face: it reveals something that cannot be expressed conceptually, but at the same time it conceals that thing because it can never be its adequate expression.

Then Creuzer continues:

> The idea of "the original" in symbolism evolved at an early time from the belief in the animation of the whole material world and the signs people attach to it. The fundamental powers, personified as deities, ruled over these signs and it is they who as inventors of divination were also the first diviners. Hence the relation of such signs to what is signified by them is original and divine. Just as the whole cult continues that help which the gods themselves first gave to the people, all symbolism through which the priests know how to reflect the higher reality rests not on names arbitrarily designated by people, but on that original relation itself.[8]

It cannot be denied that this is a subtle understanding of symbolism. It is justifiable to recall Goethe's poem:

> Youthful from heaven she comes. Uncovered to him who is
> both
> Priest and sage the goddess appears. In silence he casts
> down his eyes
> Then, raising the censer, in humble devotion enshrouds her
> With a transparent veil, that we may suffer to see her.

> *Jugendlich kommt sie vom Himmel, tritt vor den Priester
> und Weisen,*
> *Unbekleidet, die Göttin; still blickt sein Auge zur Erde,*
> *Dann ergreift er das Rauchfasz und hüllt demütig verehrend*
> *Sie in durchsichtigen Schleier, dasz wir zu schauen ertragen.*

A symbol enables us to intuit what is unknowable, what would strike our mortal eye blind. Only, for Creuzer it is not priests and sages who placed symbols between the godhead and man but the gods themselves who revealed themselves in symbols. This is how Goethe later expressed himself in his *Aneignung:* here the goddess weaves a hazy veil and with it drapes herself, and Goethe has her say: "The veil of poetry from the hand of truth" (*"Der Dichtung Schleier aus der Hand der Wahrheit"*). Poet and scholar thus meet in an awed approach to symbolism.

Creuzer stated that the earliest people thought of the powers of nature as animated. We must not confuse this with animism in the earlier sense of De Brosses and even less with the later sense of Tylor's theory. What Creuzer means is a pantheism that is still very primitive and anthropomorphic; it is far from the doctrine of the world soul formulated by Neoplatonism. But it is a seed slow to germinate in the human soul. What finally attracts Creuzer is the thought of Schelling, on whom he depends: everything in nature is alive, and man is within nature in a mystical unity.

In the period between the primitive Pelasgians and the polytheism of Homerus Creuzer saw all sorts of influences at work—Egyptian and Phoenician and Indian. They must have reached the Greek Pelasgians via those priesthoods that came from the Orient to the ignorant primordial nation. Traces of those Oriental teachings could be expected in later Greek mythology. This is what Creuzer tries to prove. He compares the Indian myths and cults with those of the Greeks. His attempts show an unmistakable genius, but of course a conclusive argument was out of the question, because of the insufficient knowledge of Indian religion. The knowledge Creuzer thought he could rely on came from the work by M. E. de Polier, which we mentioned before and which led him astray with its wild and baseless symbolic explanations. The extreme antiquity attributed to the newly discovered texts by William Jones could only strengthen Creuzer's opinion that this philosophy reached back to the most ancient times. Finding comparable teachings in Orphic and Neoplatonic writings, it was Creuzer's manner to assign such an early date to these teachings—at least to their essential contents—that it became possible to link them to the primordial Indian doctrines.

Creuzer sensed the danger of attributing a highly developed philosophy to primitive people and resisted this danger. Those early people must have lived in a state of innocence. This would be apparent in the nature of their rituals. Even when the rites were obscene, they embodied lofty ideas. If we moderns feel repelled, we reveal our own degeneration.

Obviously, Creuzer's whole argument is defective. He chose the wrong points of departure because he had no access to the real sources. The missionary priests from the Orient are pure fancy;

they never existed and could not exist because polytheistic religions show not the slightest inclination to force themselves on other nations. He attempted a great synthesis when the time was not ripe for it. And yet, it is true that he gave with his work a stimulus that was perhaps unequalled, not in the last place because of the opposition he evoked but especially because of his enthusiasm for Indian antiquity, which would turn out to be immensely fruitful for the future study of Greek and Roman and also Germanic religion.

How much more profound Creuzer was than most of his contemporaries we learn from a comparison with one older contemporary, the scholar Christian G. Heyne (1729-1812). Heyne regarded myths as philosophical expositions on the cosmos; they came from philosophers who were not yet able to express their thought in a conceptual language. Primitive man, facing the great phenomena of nature, was deeply moved. So he recreated with his imagination what he had perceived objectively and expressed it in a language of images that derived from sense perceptions. In this manner the *sermo symbolicus et mythicus* was born. An example given by Heyne is the concept "to cause." This concept, he reasons, is much too abstract for the primitive mind, which can express the idea only more graphically with the word "to beget." This mythical language had incalculable consequences in the course of time, for as soon as a conceptual language had developed, it was inevitable that a word like "to beget" was heard no longer in its symbolic but in its real sense. This theory of the *sermo symbolicus* is most unsatisfactory, for it means that if a myth mentions the sons and daughters of Zeus, it does so only in a symbolic expression no longer understood. Myths then are the results of misunderstandings. Ideas of this sort anticipate the even cruder theory of the "disease of language" as the origin of myths, which was to be put forth by Max Müller some seventy-five years later.

However, one should not attribute to Heyne an idea that the move from a symbolic to a "real" conception of begetting could give rise to the personification of natural powers. He understood too much of the essence of mythology to suppose that the gods owed themselves to a change of meaning, let alone to a misunderstanding. On the contrary, Heyne believes that the idea of God is innate in man. Because of this, man—no matter how educated and advanced—feels compelled to veneration. Even the ancient Pelasgians, after all, venerated with sacrifices the divine powers, although the names of the gods were not yet known to them! Thus in Heyne's work the notion of an original monotheism crops up again—a notion the seventeenth- and eighteenth-century scholars derived from the biblical tradition and one that in the nineteenth century would even become a doctrine of very scientific ethnologists. Polytheism is a later phenomenon or, if one will, a form of decay. Man receives benefits from nature, while from nature he also suffers inconvenience and damage. Thus, at every moment he meets the play of a divine power, and the power manifests itself in various ways. He gets the sensation that his life is determined by various powers. Here he moves toward personification. Gradually he creates a series of gods who are always experienced as acting persons. Hence what he wants to tell about his experience takes a dramatic form. This is how Heyne explains the origin of myths.[9]

Heyne's power lies elsewhere, in the importance he gives to the fact that we do not know the myths in their original form. Therefore, he warns against too sophisticated an interpretation. It would have been good if Görres and Creuzer had taken to heart this well-considered thought, for those two understood the simple philosophemes of the barbarian Greeks in terms of the Upanishads. Heyne points out that the subtlety of our modern thought does not at all blend with the habits of thought in primordial days. There are at most similarities, and they are hard to delineate. This is the more urgent because myth does not unfold according to the laws of logic but is often influenced by tangent associations of thought. In later times, Heyne continues, the role played by the poets makes our researches even more difficult. The poets transformed the myths with their skilful imaginations. These thoughts of Heyne bespeak a clear approach, which is also apparent in many other places in his writings. He insists on the importance of archaeology, which he wanted to see in its rightful place beside the literary tradition. Further, he pointed out that it was necessary to arrange and investigate religio-historical traditions topographically—a task that only the nineteenth century would undertake in earnest.

In many of his researches Heyne was a typical eighteenth-century man, but his work does point to the future. When at the end of his days the first reports were heard of the Indian traditions, he was delighted by the broadening horizon and the new possibilities there. But indubitably he would have taken a critical view of Creuzer's wild associations.

Chapter Nine

THE ROMANTIC PERIOD:
THE HISTORICAL SCHOOL

MORE than enough criticism was leveled against Creuzer. In passing we may mention the poet Johann Heinrich Vosz, who found Creuzer a "Jesuit agent in disguise" and wrote a vehement *Antisymbolik* ("Antisymbolism") that cruelly mocked Creuzer's profound explanations. For Vosz the gods of the myths are no more than personifications of nature; it is wasteful to search for an esoteric meaning.

More powerful and more effective was C. A. Lobeck's opposition. In his *Aglaophamus sive de theologiae mysticae Graecorum causis* (1829. "Aglaophamus, or about the causes of the Greeks' Mystical Theology") he razed Creuzer's whole construction; yet what he put up in its place was an incoherent series of drolleries, some of them obscene. Lobeck lacked all religious sensitivity; hence his judgment was that of a blind man judging colors. The Greek mysteries, which had seemed sufficiently important to the Church Fathers to inspire serious refutations, are for Lobeck "juggling-tricks," like the tricks of the Freemasons' lodges. Discussing Lobeck's rebuttal of Creuzer, Walter Otto notes:

> It is true that the weakness of Creuzer's method was now exposed, that the mysterious doctrines he thought he had

deciphered in the ancient myths were held up to ridicule
and that all who wanted to follow the same way were given
an object lesson. But what did the serious critic have to
offer himself? What place could there be for pride now that
a holy earnest had been put to silence because of errors it
had made? In fact it was the flattest Rationalism! It was
easy for this type of mind to expose inspiration as fanciful-
ness because for this type of mind everything was so simple
and unproblematic that every child could understand. Actually there was absolutely nothing behind the venerable
cults and myths that deserved serious thought.

The struggle unchained by Creuzer's *Symbolism* gave the
death-blow to the true study of myth, which would not come
back to life until our days.[1]

Of greater significance was the criticism brought against Creuzer by Gottfried Hermann (1772-1848). According to Hermann,
myth is the figurative expression of an idea. This is of course in
harmony with what Creuzer could have said. Hermann agreed
even further with Creuzer and assumed that priests were important in the formation of the myths. And, again like Creuzer,
he thought that these priests, who arrived at their higher wisdom
through a right observation of nature, could not convey wisdom
to the people directly. They chose a tongue of images. But the
people never grasped those images for what they were and understood them in their ordinary sense; this understanding was
the basis of the popular belief.

Hermann also assumes that the myths came for the most part
from the Orient. We see, he claims,

how the knowledge of divine and human things came to
Europe from Asia via Lycia; we see how the poets then
freed the alien lore from the monstrous exuberance of the
East and recreated it in its Greek form. Further we see how
these wise teachings, distorted by the confusion of the religions, corrupted by the ignorance of the interpreters and
clouded by wanton pleasure-seekers, gradually receded as
the secrets of the Mystery religions.[2]

At this point the ways of Hermann and Creuzer separate. For
although the myths embody a great deal of lore, they are not
necessarily very profound. And unfortunately, the wisdom that
Hermann has in mind is particularly simple-minded. He explains the myth of Io as follows: Io is a running water loved by

the skygod, who fills the stream with rain water. Argus is a dam made of porous and brilliant pumice stone. But the water breaks through this dam and runs along as a river with a horn-like whiteness!

The most important scholar of the period we are considering is Carl Otfried Müller (1797-1840). The basic theses of Romantic mythology were the coherence with Indian religion and the idea that the myths concealed a profound philosophical wisdom and hence were the work of priests. These theses were rejected by Müller. In later times rejection would not be so complete, but we should remember that what was known of the Eastern religions in Müller's day was too slight to bear any theory of relationships. According to Müller, Zeus had absolutely no counterpart in India; this is a striking expostulation, because for us it is this very Greek deity whose Indo-European origin is beyond doubt.

Nevertheless, Müller's sound judgment is clear from his observation that myths are no store of wisdom or priestly invention but a product of "the people." We may trace the influence here of a specific conception of the authentic character and value of popular tradition—a conception that grew continuously from Herder to the Brothers Grimm. Müller considers myths an endeavor to express experiences of cosmos and nature according to popular emotion and understanding. This could only lead to the idea that at a certain stage of cultural development myth was the only and the necessary way to contact the principles of cosmic and human life.

We could make a remark on the basis of an idea that was given attention only in later times, the idea that the romantic notions of "the people" and of popular tradition contain a peculiar overestimation. "The people as a whole" (das Volk) does not create myths any more than it writes poetry. It always is gifted individuals who give form to what is alive in a people; the form does not just correspond to the popular ideas but raises them to a new level. There is no need to exclude the possibility that the making of myths owed a great deal to the ones in charge of cultic affairs—the priests.

At any rate, Müller regards myths as a certain type of expression of reality. The myths as we know them were not as they were in older days. They have changed considerably in the course of many centuries, and Müller was the first one to see that clearly.

First of all Müller points to the oral tradition, which always transforms materials; ancient motifs got lost and were replaced or were confused with others. Culture gradually altered in form and content; the myths had to be adapted to these changes. Of course he also refers to the influence by poets; they transformed myths according to their own taste or the fashions of their time.

With these insights he vehemently rebuts Creuzer. One must not expect, he says, that the basic idea of a myth can be "envisioned" by an inspired intuition. What is needed is patient and painstaking research. Hence Müller emphasizes that a historical product like myth must be approached with the tools of historical research. This means above all a historical analysis of the tradition. Thus, he reformulates the requirement already set before him by Heyne, his predecessor at Göttingen: it is necessary to observe the local differences in cult and mythical tradition. Further, with respect to etymology, which he considers an indispensable tool, he cautions the student of myth.

Yet in many ways Müller is a typical Romantic. He too feels one should really draw close to myth in the same manner as one draws close to a work of art. A certain talent is needed for it, a special gift of imagination, perhaps of identification.

> This much is clear, that combinations and syllogisms alone, even if they are very subtle, cannot lead to the final goal, although they approach it, and the final act of proper, inner understanding requires a moment of inspiration, uncommon tension, and extraordinary cooperation of spiritual powers which surpasses all calculating efforts by far.[3]

These thoughts about myth as a work of art are extraordinary. A scholar of our own days, Karl Kerényi, has noted time and again that our relation to myth is like our relation to music: both myth and music are autonomous realms of the spirit and are not accessible to everyone.

When Müller attempts to reveal the origin of myths, he makes two cases. Often he sees in a myth a reminiscence of ancient colonies, like Byzantium, Syracuse, and Corcyra, or, even further back in time, a reminiscence of the ancient wanderings of nations. For it is certain, he argues, that the ancients could not experience such important events except as divine interventions. If all this were true, it would be possible to assign a date to the myths. They originated in the "mythical time," which must have been the time before the return of the Heraclids.* In the second place, now, when the historical period proper has begun, and a sense for history and philosophy begins to grow; the time of mythological creativity is over. Myths originating now, as far as they relate to physical and astronomical phenomena, may be considered the first beginnings of science. Finally, Müller points to the apocryphal character of myths that have their origin in false etymologies or serve to explain rites and symbols that were no longer understood; these myths show no trace of religion.

Although we can agree with Müller's sound critique of the exaggerations of the Symbolist school and should recognize the secure foundations of his method of investigation, still it seems to us that his view is in many respects too rationalistic. The idea of myth as the remembrance of history or as primitive science can only seem antiquated. Yet because of this feature in his scholarly thought Müller shows a curious similarity to the nineteenth century; therefore, he certainly is a precursor of the modern study of mythology.

---

* For a brief account and source references concerning this event in Greek legendary history, see Robert Graves, *The Greek Myths* (Baltimore: Penguin, 1955), Vol. II, sec. 117h and 146.—TRANS.

Part Three

THE NINETEENTH
AND
TWENTIETH CENTURIES

Chapter Ten

THE NINETEENTH AND TWENTIETH CENTURIES

BY THE end of his life, Creuzer himself could not help noticing that the spiritual climate was changing drastically. Taking a bird's-eye view of history, the period of Romanticism is only a short interruption of a movement that remained dominant from the seventeenth century until the beginning of the twentieth. In the eighteenth century we spoke of Rationalism, in the nineteenth century we speak of Positivism, but both times we have to do with the dominion of the *ratio* over emotion and imagination. The nineteenth century is characterized by two further movements that are closely allied to this dominion of reason: historicism, which arose in the humanities, and evolutionism, which had its great day in the science of biology. It goes without saying that they are in principle most closely linked. The doctrine of evolution was tremendously stimulated by Charles R. Darwin's book *On the Origin of Species by Means of Natural Selection*, published in 1859, which depicted the conditions that could explain the alterations of plants and animals in the course of time. What particularly fascinated Darwin's contemporaries was his opinion that all plants and animals in the final analysis derived from only a few original species, perhaps even from a single one. If the name of Goethe occurs to us here—since he too spoke of

an "original plant" (*"Urpflanze"*)—then the great difference between his thought and the thought of the nineteenth century
stands out: what for Goethe was an "idea," an entelechy that
unfolded itself separately in the various separate species, became
for Darwin a more or less causal sequence of changing plant and
animal forms, directly following one from another. Finally, the
idea that man was the end result, after a long procession of
earlier and simpler forms of life—ultimately even a unicellular
primal form—greatly furthered reflexions on cultural phenomena.
And it is true, it does seem to us as if modern culture is much
more complex than, for example, the culture of the Middle
Ages; yet the Middle Ages show a greater complexity than primitive forms of culture. In the field of technical achievements this is
particularly clear. The idea of evolution was transferred to the
study of the spirit and culture, with the conclusion that art, religion, and morality had "evolved" in the course of time. Various
theories that we shall discuss about the "evolution" of religious
ideas began with this assumption and sought basis in the beliefs
that reputedly prevailed in primitive tribes.

More important for religio-historical study was Positivism. The
great thinker of this philosophical system was Auguste Comte
(1798-1857). In his *Cours de philosophie positive* (1830-42) he
composed a theory that man had passed through three stages:
the theological, the metaphysical, and the positivistic. This sociological law (*loi des trois états*) has had great influence on
further investigations. In the theological state man explains the
phenomena of nature as the interventions of supernatural beings.
In the second state abstractions replace these beings. Finally, in
the third state, man restricts himself to a search for causes and
purposes and is no longer concerned with "the absolute." Human life is directed toward what is real, certain, useful, and
relative—in a word, what is positive. Comte believes that the
same development occurs in the individual. If this is so, there are
far-reaching consequences, for humankind, like an individual,
must leave behind each preceding phase in order to ascend at
last to the highest. In the positive state the remnants of theology
and philosophy can only be considered mementos that have to
be discarded in the end. To be unconcerned with the absolute
means in fact the same thing as killing it. The task of the positive
examination of material phenomena is to establish laws that
govern them. But then, establishment of laws must be the goal of

all investigations, also in the areas of social, moral, and psychological phenomena. If, here too, objective laws can be shown to rule, the person loses his significance, as Comte himself states it; the person is fundamentally a pure abstraction; only humanity is real, particularly in the realm of the intellect and of morality.

This Positivism treats religion as a dated point of view, a primitive structure in the evolution of man. The Positivist, the man of the nineteenth century, is able to and should lead his life without religion. While in eighteenth-century Deism the idea of God was already a vague abstraction and the cult was at most an expression of gratitude toward the "Supreme Being," the nineteenth century took the inevitable next step to atheism. A stark example is Ludwig Feuerbach (1804-72), who proclaimed an unmistakable materialism. God and all religious concepts are no more than projections of human ideals and wishes. In his *Vorlesungen über das Wesen der Religion* (1848-49. "Lectures About the Essence of Religion") he says:

> Religion is born only in the darkness of ignorance, dire need, indigence, in conditions in which human imagination is bound to dominate all other faculties, and at a time when man lives in the worst mental tensions and the most exalted stimuli for his emotions.[1]

Since the object of the science of religion is a wraith, it hardly pays to make it an object of serious research!

The English thinker Herbert Spencer (1820-1903) was less extreme. He agreed with Comte that science presides over the realm of what can be known, but Spencer left a space for the unknowable. The unknowable domain is given to religion, which is thus assigned its place next to science. In this arrangement Spencer clearly expressed the antagonism of science and religion that dominated nineteenth-century thought. And to the extent that science would gather the unknown into the fold of knowledge, religion would lose its domain. The kingdoms are adjacent—on the same level, as it were. It does not occur to Spencer that religion is found somewhere else altogether. It must be said, though, that for Spencer the absolute, which is beyond human comprehension, is nonetheless something indubitably real.

Spencer hails the doctrine of evolution proclaimed by Lamarck, which enables science to coordinate the data of experience. Spencer assumes a similar evolution of religions. Monotheism is a final form; it is preceded by polytheism and, before that, even more primitive religious levels. Spencer's notion of primitive man is clear in the following exposition:

> When, however, we cease to figure his mental processes in terms of our own, the confusion disappears. When, verifying *a priori* inference by *a posteriori* proof, we recognize the fact that the primitive man does not distinguish natural from unnatural, possible from impossible; knows nothing of physical law, order, cause, etc.; and that while he shows neither rational surprise nor the curiosity which prompts examination, he lacks fit words for carrying on inquiry, as well as the requisite power of continued thinking; we see that instead of being a speculator and maker of explanations, he is at first an almost passive recipient of conclusions forced on him. Further, we find that he is inevitably betrayed into an initial error; and that this originates an erroneous system of thought which elaborates as he advances.[2]

Inevitably this man, intellectually so ill-equipped, speculating on the transcendent—if ever he found the strength to do so— would arrive at the most absurd ideas. How it is that this primitive man managed to stay alive, inventing all sorts of tools, building houses and ships, practicing agriculture—that Spencer does not disclose to us.

For the simple reason that each cultural phenomenon occurs in its own time and place, it is justified. This is also true for religious forms. All religions deserve the place they have; wherever they are, they are good, in a relative sense.

It is not necessary to assume that the primitive religious forms we see today, which are repugnant in their crudeness and cruelty, must be original; Spencer regards them rather as secondary deteriorated forms. And he is inclined to assume in general that the lowest forms of culture, observed among primitives and contrasting with our own, are to be considered phenomena of decay. Many ethnologists still pay homage to this idea. In Spencer's case there may be a trace of Rousseau's dream of the "good savage."

However one assumes religion evolved from primary forms, the conclusion will come that there must have been a time when religion did not exist. When ethnologists think they have established the fact that some tribes lack an idea of god, Spencer is not surprised: it fits his system. Religion can originate only when man develops some conceptual sense for the supernatural power present in phenomena. This conceptual sense is not given with creation; it can come to pass only through the experience of many generations. It grows clearer and more subtle in the course of time, in accordance with man's evolution in general.

The nineteenth century was marked by a growing agnosticism. It could hardly have been otherwise. Certainly the positivistic turn of mind was not conducive to the study of religious phenomena. Accurate descriptions were attempted of the facts observed in primitive and more advanced religions, and the positivistic mind tried to uncover "laws" of the evolution of religious forms. Yet that mind had no access to anything central in religion, for even the most specialized knowledge of external facts (cultic gestures, priestly organizations, myths) is insufficient. Kerényi speaks of a "mythological form of thought";[3] there are other modes beside it. They belong to the essence of man; they did not appear in the course of his history in order to wither in the bright light of reason. On the contrary, the mythological form of thought is a structure in the human soul.

What is true of the mythological form of thought is certainly true of man's religious disposition. This disposition is not a form that once had to be put on. It is the most profound secret of the human soul. It is wrong to suggest that the observation of facts in the world outside or in himself compelled man toward a religious sentiment. Rather, the religious disposition toward the world is in man from the beginning, beside and together with his reason, his imagination, his sense of beauty, and his will.

Chapter Eleven

NEW MATERIALS FOR THE HISTORY OF RELIGIONS

DURING the nineteenth century, materials for the study of the history of religions accumulated fabulously. This happened in three ways. First the work of editing and explaining Oriental religious texts, especially those of the Indo-Iranian peoples, was undertaken. Soon after, numerous other texts followed that had come to light in archaeological excavations. They came from Babylonia-Assyria and Egypt, as well as from Asia Minor and Syria. But archaeology did more than discover texts and deserves to be treated separately. Third, the intensified colonization that took the place of economic exploitation resulted in an increasing concern for the fate of the dominated nations and gave rise to an elaborate and more responsible missionary activity. The result was a greater knowledge of the religious ideas of the primitives.

The Literary Texts

When Creuzer attempted to explain the Greek religion from an outgrowth of Indian and Egyptian traditions, there was a dearth of material. In his time, knowledge was insufficient to distinguish the great religious movements of India: Brahmanism, Buddhism, and Hinduism. This changed with nineteenth-century scholarship. The edition of numerous Buddhist writings from India—and from Tibet, Nepal, Ceylon, and Mongolia—and the edition of Chinese and Japanese translations made it clear that in Buddhism itself there were various movements whose relation could be assessed more accurately.

A task even more significant was the edition of the writings of Brahmanism. The scholarly world had of course awaited particularly eagerly the publication of the Vedas. Still, the work proceeded slowly. The first complete translation of the most influential Vedic texts came about under the care of Max Müller, who saw to its publication between 1849 and 1874 in the series *Sacred Books of the East,* which he had established and to which he devoted himself completely from 1876 on. This series finally comprised fifty volumes, which made available for scholarly research texts in good translations of the Indian and Iranian religions. Naturally, the interest in the Rigveda was paramount. Nevertheless there was a good wait before a complete text edition was published. It appeared (1861-77) eminently edited by Aufrecht. A series of new translations by Graszmann, Geldner and Renou penetrated further and further into the text and also enabled nonspecialists to study the Rigveda. Often the archaic language made the meaning of the text uncertain, and these uncertainties produced a series of exegetical treatises. Gradually, the nature of these poetic collections gradually became clear. Scholars at first entertained ideas about some sort of popular poetry. In particular, its original descriptions of nature created the notion that the Rigveda was a primitive and spontaneous poetry. It was, rather, the opposite that turned out to be true.

The Rigveda is a highly artificial poetry of hymns composed by schools of priests and poets, but this conclusion could be drawn only after scholars had learned to recognize the use of fixed liturgical formulae and the sophisticated rhetorical style. Although the text is ancient—the origin is thought to date to a period of which 1200 b.c. is the earlier limit—it presupposes a long priestly tradition, far removed from any immediate expression of the ancient beliefs of the Indians. None of this diminishes the religio-historical value of the text. Although the priestly tradition may have grown more literary and subtle, it does not seem to have altered the central beliefs: the ideas to be found about the gods and their myths have validity also for non-Brahmanic circles. Of course, this cannot be said of the interpretations of more recent commentaries, for these present truly Indian philosophical speculations and thus differ from the early texts. For the study of Indo-European religion and mythology the Veda remains a crucial source.

The Avesta presents a different case. Editions and translations of this Iranian text begin to appear in 1850. The manuscripts are of Parsi origin and date back no further than the thirteenth century, so they are quite recent. No wonder the text consists of very ancient and relatively recent parts. Most ancient and important are the *gāthās,* strophic songs ascribed to Zoroaster himself; there are many passages obscure in language, full of archaisms. The Avesta contains the teachings of the religious reformer Zoroaster, whose very existence was doubted by scholars like Tiele (1830-1902) and Kern (1833-1917) and whose date is still far from certain. His teachings show a sharp reaction against the ancient Iranian pantheon; we learn about it from Zoroaster's polemics, although the pantheon was not contained in his system itself. After Zoroaster's death the ancient popular religion appears to have renewed its power. Hence in the later writings, composed in Pehlevi, ancient religious and mythical features emerge clearly.

New sources were discovered for other Indo-European nations. As to the religions of Greece and Rome, one could hardly expect that the texts would greatly increase. However, the ancient inscriptions, found and published in ever greater numbers, were of special significance. Their publication was scattered throughout numerous journals, and scholars felt a need to compile them. The result was the appearance of the *Corpus Inscriptionum Graecorum* (1828-77), the *Corpus Inscriptionum Atticarum* (1873-82), and, finally, the *Corpus Inscriptionum Latinarum* (1863-85), to which supplements added new discoveries. These collections soon proved to be an inexhaustible source for knowledge of the common beliefs and thus were a welcome addition to the literary texts. Examples of a meaningful addition to our knowledge of Italic religion—which used to be based exclusively on Ovid, Varro, and Servius—are the tabulae found at Iguvium (written in Umbrian) and the ritual of the Fratres Arvales.

Then there came a swell of editions of Germanic and Celtic texts, slowly improving our understanding of the images and ideas of these peoples. The two Eddas—the poetic, with its number of mythological poems, and the prosaic, in which the Icelandic scholar Snorri Sturluson surveyed the Scandinavian pantheon—laid the basis for a more profound understanding of ancient Germanic religion.

The greatest surprises, however, came from the diggings in the East. The archaeological investigation of the palaces of Assurbanipal (668–627 B.C.) and other excavations uncovered documents from the libraries of kings. There were thousands of clay tablets of cuneiform script and thousands of documents, varying in content. There were religious texts, such as prayers and charms. Among the most important discoveries were the fragments of the Gilgamesh Epic, which entranced the world of scholarship with its parallel to the biblical story of the Flood. In addition to these overwhelming finds the Babylonian and Sumerian texts were discovered.

In Egypt, too, an abundance of new material was found. The walls of pyramids and temples—uncovered with cautious care—bore hieroglyphic texts, sometimes very elaborate ones. On the coffins scholars read fragments of the *Book of the Dead,* a collection of sayings given to the dead in their graves; these formulae proved to be of great significance in the religion of Osiris. There was much more. Thousands of papyrus scrolls and fragments came to light, partly from the refuse heaps of cities in the Faiyum, partly from the graves of mummies. Since 1896 the so-called Oxyrhyncus texts have become known; they are written in Greek, Coptic, and Arabic, and among them are important gospel texts.

The excavations, which were vigorously continued in all regions of the Near East, unearthed more and more texts. It is impossible to enumerate them here. But one surprising discovery should be mentioned—the royal archives of Boghazkoy in Turkey found by Hugo Winckler in 1896. The civilization of the Hittites was revealed. The Hittites belonged to the Indo-European language group, and, consequently, this discovery was an unexpected enrichment of our knowledge of Indo-European religion. Of eminent importance was a writing of the fourteenth century B.C. in which the king of the Mitanni made a treaty with the Hittite king, Subbiluliuma, who had restored him to his throne. On this occasion the king of the Mitanni, Mativaza, called as witnesses the gods Mitra, Varuna, Indra, and the two Nasatyas. This document, several centuries before the text of the Rigveda, shows us the great gods of the Indians together and in the same order in which we know them in the Indian texts.

Finally, let us mention that Syria and Palestine also began to yield their buried treasures. The result was an elaborate collection of Semitic inscriptions. Next to these the finds of Ras Shamra Ugarit are worthy of mention; the texts here were written in a totally unknown script, which in a few months' time was deciphered by two scholars, A. B. C. Baver and E. Dhorme, who were not aware of one another's researches. Among these Canaanite texts the history of Baal drew much attention.

The editing and explication of this constant stream of materials occupied many scholars; the twentieth century sees a continuing increase of materials, and there is no telling what discoveries the future will bring. Our growing knowledge of religious life in the Near East has reversed many long-established opinions. Naturally, the findings led often to hurried conclusions, which were corrected by new findings. The Babylonian-Assyrian materials, which shed such an unexpected light on the Old Testament, suggested that the Jewish traditions derived for the most part from Babylon. Some scholars went so far as to suggest that all the myths in all the world stemmed from Babylon. (This is known as Pan-Babylonism.) In a period of secularization, these and similar suggestions supported the conviction that the Old Testament—which for so long had been the revealed Word of God— was just a collection of stories, borrowed in part from other nations, and must be treated like any other "literature." What remained of all this was the sober view that the Jewish people, like all peoples, had been influenced and had borrowed from surrounding civilizations. This did in no way detract from the originality of the Jewish faith.

The Excavations

We have seen how thoroughly the excavations increased our knowledge of the ancient religions. However, texts were not our only benefits from the diggings. Other documents have also had great significance.

The beginning of the nineteenth century brought the first glimpses into the prehistory of man. Even in the preceding century human artifacts had been found in holes beside the remains of animal fossils, but at that time they aroused little attention. But when Boucher de Perthes, beginning in 1841, found in the old sediments of the Somme flints processed by men, it began to be clear that human life must stretch back far before the word of history. In his book, *Mémoire sur l'industrie primitive et les arts à leur origine* ("Primitive Industries and Arts since their Beginnings") Boucher claimed that the origins went to the Pleistocene. Initially, few were inclined to believe him, but in the long run the strength of his evidences, which increased in number, could no longer be disputed. Thus the idea of a Stone Age—which in western and northern Europe must have preceded the historical civilizations—was born. Before long the idea grew that primitives who still exist on earth could be compared to the "primordial man" of Diluvial days, the ancestor of the present inhabitants of Europe.

Around 1863 a beginning was made with the investigation of caves in the Dordogne, followed shortly by investigations in the Pyrenees. Here were the remains of still more ancient periods. Soon various phases came to be distinguished in the Stone Age: a Paleolithic and a Neolithic period. Later a separate Mesolithic period was inserted between the two. This was not the end. The growing number of finds and an ever subtler method of examination caused the Old Stone Age to be subdivided into periods named for the excavation places: Moustérien, Aurignacien, Solutréen, and Magdalénien.

There were astonishing finds that proved that a plastic art existed and an art of unexpected beauty. The earliest examples are figurines of women, like the famous "Venus of Willendorf" (Lower Austria) and those of Laussel and Lespugue in France. They are marked by heavy bodily forms (particularly steatopygia) and a strong emphasis on sexual characteristics (breasts and genitals). Are they images of deities? And may we conclude that there was a fertility cult as early as the Stone Age?

Even greater surprises were in store. In 1880, Don Marcelino de Sautuola announced that he had discovered a number of rock paintings in the cave of Altamira in the province of Santander. Other sites were searched and comparable paintings found in France in the caves of Combarelles in Font-de-Gaume, close to Les Eyzies (Dordogne), of Marsoulas (Haute Garonne), and elsewhere. They show animals—reindeer, bison, mammoth—pictured true to nature and in natural positions. Sometimes an arrow is drawn in the body, which suggested to some that these paintings played a part in hunting magic—an explanation that Leo Frobenius could confirm later because of hunting customs he had learned in Africa. The animal figures stand out sharply against the walls and are so truly drawn that at first a fraud was suspected, but later finds showed that they are genuine. Moreover, strikingly similar drawings were discovered among the Bushmen.

Human figures are more scarce, but when they occur, they are even more interesting from the standpoint of religion. In the *Grotte des trois frères* (Dordogne) a human figure was found in dancing posture; he has a pair of stag antlers on his head and a stallion's tail and genitals. It can hardly be doubted that this represents a cultic activity. Masked men occur elsewhere too: in La Mola Remigia (eastern Spain) five masked warriors are depicted armed with bow and arrow.

Drawings that are naturalistic and sometimes resemble impressionism are typical of the Paleolithic period. In the later Stone Age they do not occur. At that time there was a preference for schematic drawings, which no doubt had a symbolic meaning. Although such drawings are not totally absent in the Early Stone Age, they may be assumed to express new religious ideas. Further, the opinion seems warranted that in the later Stone Age the Paleolithic hunting magic was replaced by fertility rites.

These and other finds acquainted us with human life in prehistoric Europe. We have noted that parallels could be pointed out among present-day primitives. Thus it became possible to connect archaeology and ethnology. This was very significant, for it stimulated a new scientific task, viz., to outline on the basis of parallels the evolution of religious notions. Such a scheme of evolution was meant to apply universally. These endeavors were quite appealing, if only because Darwin had characterized biological life as an evolution.

Archaeology did not restrict itself to the most ancient periods of civilization. Its great value lay especially in the study of historical civilizations previously known only from written sources. The sensational discoveries by Schliemann—who from 1870 to 1880 excavated the ruins of Troy, and then of Mycenae, Orchomenos, and Tiryns—stimulated others to continue these examinations with even greater zeal. Schliemann's successor was the architect W. Dörpfeld, who greatly improved Schliemann's rather primitive method. Schliemann had embarked on his expedition with the intention of finding the Troy of the *Ilias,* and he really thought he had found it, even including what he called the treasure of Priam. Dörpfeld was not so ambitious to find something in particular; he wanted only to observe and investigate. The archaeologists had to turn from treasure-seekers into methodical scholars. Finally, no detail escaped the attention of the archaeologists; they have learned to study even apparently insignificant finds.

As early as Schliemann's digging, other excavators were at work as well. They hunted the remains of ancient temple sites. This work began in 1862 with Newton's excavations in Halicarnassus and Cnidus and was followed by Wood's excavations in Ephesus (1877). Still earlier was the work done by Lenormant at Eleusis (1860). Later came the painstaking excavations at Delphi, Olympia, Delos, and Samothrace. These yielded many indications of the structure of temples in the classical period but also of much more ancient constructions, which belonged to prehistorical times.

Crete gave up its secrets to Sir Arthur Evans, who in 1900 discovered King Minos' famed "labyrinth" in Knossos. Excavations, continuing for years all over Crete, brought to the surface a civilization that had formed the foundation of the Mycenaean culture; the background of the later classical civilization was revealed.

Similarly, researches in Egypt were not limited to the pyramids and temples (no matter how much understanding they gave of pharaonic social and religious life, with their rich inventory of objects, images, and inscriptions). Traces of much earlier civilizations were found, reaching back even to the earlier Stone Age. They were discovered by Flinders Petrie in the Nile delta, in the Faiyum, and near Thebes. Afterwards it fell to A. J. de Morgan to find between Abydus and Thinis the graves of Menes and of the first dynasty, which until then had been considered fictitious.

The expedition of Jacques de Morgan to Persia in 1897 sought to examine Susa, the ancient capital of Elam. There de Morgan distinguished seven layers of dwellings. At a depth of fifteen meters there were clay tablets covered with hieroglyphs. Their date of origin is estimated at three to four thousand B.C. These inscriptions were successfully deciphered, and because of them a number of ancient Elamite deities became known. Fragmentary annals of Babylon and Nineveh were also unearthed, but most curious of all was that it was here that the code of Hammurabi was found.

As the excavations increased in the Near East, they yielded surprise upon surprise. We can mention only a few, which are of special interest for the beginnings of history. First, there are the excavations of Boghazkoy by Hugo Winckler. Here a hitherto unknown and mighty empire lay in ruins—the kingdom of the Hittites. Winckler discovered the remnants of the city of Khattushash, capital of the Hittite empire, which flourished in the fourteenth and thirteenth centuries B.C. It appeared from the inscriptions, deciphered by the Czech scholar Hrozny, that the language spoken there was an Indo-European dialect, mixed with the language of a substratum.

The significance of ancient Phoenicia became more evident through the discoveries in the ancient harbor city Ugarit (present-day Ras Shamra). In 1929 a French expedition guided by F. A. Schaeffer and C. Virolleaud arrived there and discovered remains of almost all the ancient cultures that had imposed their influences on this maritime center. In addition, the investigators gathered a number of cuneiform tablets from the fourteenth century B.C. and written in the Phoenician language, which was akin to Hebrew. We have already referred to the epic of Baal-Alein, which shows some similarity to the myths of Adonis and Tammuz; it appears to deal with a myth of natural powers, which either conquer or are conquered during the change of seasons.

Finally, we mention the discoveries made in 1920-22 in the valley of the Indus. First, at Harappa (Punjab), a number of seals covered with animal figures and pictography were found. Then, an ancient settlement was uncovered at Mohenjo-Daro, where a number of cities had been built in succession, one on top of the one before. The seals brought to light here allow a dating to the third millennium B.C. This precedes the invasion by Indo-European tribes in the Indus Valley by a thousand years. Yet this prehistoric civilization was far from primitive. To the contrary, it was characterized by great technical achievements. The city plan (with a sewer system) and the structure of the houses (including bathrooms and windows) bespeak an amazingly high cultural level, superior in many respects to the other civilizations of the ancient Orient. The absence of temple ruins is conspicuous at Mohenjo-Daro; is it possible that the gods were worshiped in the open air?

Lacking data, we can say nothing about the nature of religion in this civilization. If their peculiar script is ever deciphered so that we can read what the seals say, we may become informed. But in spite of the fragmentary nature of our knowledge, even now we can assert that we must think of the Indo-European invasion of India in new terms. The opinion was held—and the epic narratives lent support—that the conquering Indians met a most primitive populace. The facts are quite different. We might look for a comparison in the invasion of the Mycenaean civilization of the Peloponnese by the primitive Dorians. In that case we can expect that the urban natives exerted great influences on the semi-nomadic peoples who attacked them. It is quite possible that this holds for the Indians and their religion, and it can be expected that continued research will be able to point to certain features in the Vedas that have an Austronesian derivation. Here we have an example of the importance of archaeological discoveries: they can change our perspective considerably and correct previous views. Views of specific problems often originate in existing conceptions that scholarship rather unconsciously accepts and applies.

Our image of the ancient world around the Eastern Mediterranean basin changed completely because of the archaeological researches. Not only was our historical perspective amplified—sometimes by millennia—but there came to light various totally unknown civilizations that had played a great role in the cultural development of Mesopotamia and Egypt and that had to be considered from now on. With respect to Greek religion, these changes in our orientation should be particularly clear. In the past—actually since Herodotus—it was taken for granted that the religious ideas of Hellas were shaped under the influence of Phoenicia and Egypt. The findings on Crete discredited these beliefs. Scholars like M. P. Nilsson presented a Greek religion built on a Mycenaean substratum (hence, non-Indo-European). Furthermore, the deciphering of the so-called linear-B script on tablets found in Pylos caused a revision in the chronology of Greek polytheism. The discovery that Dionysus—reputedly originating in Thrace—occurs perhaps as early as 1400-1200 B.C. on the documents of Pylos is so startling that it is like a revolution in our thought.

Archaeological researches in the dwelling places of the Celtic and Germanic nations have taught us more about the material civilization than about the religion. Concerning the religion, mention should be made of ideas on death and the hereafter, which became somewhat clearer from the shapes of graves. Also, archaeologists succeeded in uncovering ancient pagan temples. As to the Scandinavian world, reference may be made to some excavations in Iceland and especially to that of the ancient pagan temple at Uppsala. As to the Celts, the excavation of a Gallic temple structure in the Altbach valley near Trier has been important;

it gave us some insight into the development of this type of architecture. Certain images of deities demonstrate strikingly primitive cultic forms customary among the common people. Finds of the grave of Kivik, or the Gundestrup kettle, raise more questions than they can answer. It is unlikely that much more can be discovered. Nations that build almost exclusively in wood leave only scanty cultural remains in the ground.

The Ethnological Data

Even in the eighteenth century some scholars had grasped the similarities between the religious ideas of the classical peoples and those of the primitives. The French Jesuit J. F. Lafitau (1670-1740), who had been a missionary among the North American Indians, wrote *Moeurs des sauvages américains comparés aux moeurs des premiers temps* (1724. "The Customs of the American Savages Compared with those of the Ancient Times"), a study of the Canadian tribes, and noted several points of similarity between them and the peoples of classical antiquity. He concluded that the religious ideas of the whole world are of the same nature and found the explanation in a primordial gift of revelation to the first people, Adam and Eve.

In 1757 C. de Brosses presented the Académie des Inscriptions with a treatise that the learned society did not have the courage to publish. The treatise appeared anonymously in 1760 under the title *Du culte des dieux fétiches ou Parallèle de l'ancienne religion de l'Egypte avec la religion actuelle de Nigritie* ("The Cult of the Fetish Deities, or the Resemblance of the Ancient Egyptian Religion with the Religion of the Sudan at Present"). The author proposed that fetishism can be demonstrated among all peoples. Of course, we could not subscribe to such a thesis, but that does not at all detract from the book's extraordinary significance. After all, de Brosses was the first to attempt a developmental sketch of classical polytheism with the help of the religion of primitive tribes.

It is easy to understand that after the triumph of evolutionism, developmental schemes were constructed on the basis of the increasing ethnological data; in these schemes all forms of religion would find their place. We shall deal with these theories later more extensively. What should be noted at present is that in order to refute or confirm these theories, still greater documentation of the primitives was required. This need was more than answered. The more intensive colonization became among the primitives, the more necessary it was to be acquainted with tribal cultures. Explorers who gradually filled in the map of the world collected every kind of information; on the whole, they gathered data rather incidentally. Moreover, since there were usually translators, the work done by these explorers was not trustworthy in all respects.

Civil servants, posted at one place for a long period, sometimes seized the occasion to penetrate into the spiritual world of the people among whom they did their work, but it was especially the missionaries who tried to account more accurately for the religious ideas of the tribes. They did not stop at similarities to Christianity. They had to be familiar with the religion they wished to replace. Misunderstandings, arising from lack of knowledge on the part of the missionaries, could be very harmful. Furthermore, the missionaries could acquit themselves well only if they presented their message in the native language. They had to understand the nuances of the pagans' religious vocabulary; and since it was of the utmost importance to translate the Bible into the language of the primitives, a painstaking comparison of religious terms was called for. Only then could an assessment be made and indigenous words assigned to Christian conceptions. Here the very same questions arose that a thousand years earlier had occupied missionaries among the Germanic or Celtic peoples.

Excellent work was done by these Protestant and Catholic missionaries. Nevertheless, the trained ethnologist must often have felt that their communications should be consulted with some caution. It was inevitable that their examinations of the primitives should sometimes, ingenuously, force a result. Many a native's reply is affected by the tone of the question he is asked. A question originating in the thought-world of Europe and Christianity can easily bypass the train of thought in a primitive man. It is also well known that a native who is wary yet eager to please is likely to answer yes when questions are posed in a somewhat positive way. A certain laziness of thought can easily lead him to make short work of troublesome questionings. Finally, it may be said that not all men think in clearly delineated concepts and that it is always difficult to present religious imageries in words.

There is also another objection to some communications by

Christian preachers. When they take their task seriously they will often inform themselves of the pronouncements of scholarship on the nature of the primitive religions. Then it is almost inevitable that they become more or less influenced by fashionable ideas. We can observe that at the moment when animism was fashionable ethnological theory, missionary reports frequently abounded with evidences of animism. It is interesting that in some cases ethnographers, visiting the same tribe at a later date, established very different and much more important religious facts, which had escaped the missionary, who was absorbed with what he was expected to find.

As the primitive peoples were influenced more and more in the civilization of the West, and primitive traditions began to fall apart, an urgent necessity was felt to fill at the last minute the lacunae of earlier research. Trained ethnologists, equipped with a method of objective investigation, tried to register accurately what was alive among the primitives. The exactness of those investigations is often admirable, the knowledge that was acquired surprising. Wholly novel views were gained. In the first place, more attention was given to the sociological structures that codetermine the form of a religion. Second, scientific psychology made itself felt: it was not necessary to restrict oneself to what primitive man said. All sorts of indications, sometimes indirect, made it possible to gain insight into his soul. Quite naturally, this gave scholars a closer contact with the primitive spirit; the man who so quickly felt defensive when questioned by missionaries was more relaxed vis-à-vis the ethnologist.

Expeditions often went out to search for particular religious ideas or to put hypotheses and theories to the test. "Schools" were established, such as the school of Frobenius (d. 1938) in Frankfurt, of Schmidt and Koppers in Vienna, of Boas (d. 1942) in North America. Although there was a danger that the investigations of such schools could yield biased observations, they also had a great advantage. The study of primitive man could be undertaken in the light of precisely formulated problems, and phenomena might be revealed that had been hidden from earlier investigators.

The scientific researcher can come into much more intimate contact with the population he studies. The representative of Christianity has an aura that may make it impossible for the native to open his mind to him. The modern ethnologist has no such problems. A brilliant example is the American investigator

Margaret Mead, who lived on New Guinea as a member of a village community. Bronislaw Malinowski expresses humorously what the change in attitude means:

> The anthropologist must relinquish his comfortable position in the long chair on the veranda of the missionary compound, Government station, or planter's bungalow, where, armed with pencil and notebook and at times with a whisky and soda, he has been accustomed to collect statements from informants, write down stories, and fill out sheets of paper with savage texts. He must go out into the villages, and see the natives at work in gardens, on the beach, in the jungle; he must sail with them to distant sandbanks and to foreign tribes, and observe them in fishing, trading, and ceremonial overseas expeditions. Information must come to him full-flavored from his own observations of native life, and not be squeezed out of reluctant informants as a trickle of talk.[1]

The result of this development of anthropology was that in the second half of the nineteenth century most guesses about the evolution of religious thought were made with the help of ethnographic data. The significance here for the scholarly views of polytheism, as exemplified among the Indo-European peoples, does not need to be discussed. If questions were raised about the basis of specific religious forms, it was possible to find support in facts assembled from all parts of the world. This method had its dangers, however: it was too easy to assume that religious thought was uniform, and thus the conviction could grow that certain religious and social phenomena, such as totemism or matriarchy, had been transitional phases everywhere in the world. But then, where these opinions were held, the ever more intensive ethnological study could provide the necessary corrections.

Chapter Twelve

THEORIES CONCERNING "NATURE MYTHS"

AT THE start of the nineteenth century, religio-historical investigations were mainly confined to the Indo-European peoples. The study and growing knowledge of the ancient language of India and of the texts made a path far deeper into the past than the Greek or Germanic sources had allowed. And the overestimation of Sanskrit was not a disadvantage but a strong stimulus. Initially, it was felt that this sacred language of the Brahmans was virtually identical with the root tongue of all Indo-European languages. It took many years of painstaking comparative study to find that in many ways Sanskrit had deviated from that original language as much as had Greek and Latin. Sanskrit was merely among sister languages. At any rate, the result of the exaggerated attention paid to Sanskrit was that the ideas crystallized in the Vedas were treated as more ancient and original than those of classical antiquity.

The one-sided orientation toward the Vedas held a further pitfall. The Rigvedic hymns give mythical allusions and descriptions with an imagery inspired principally by nature. A figure like Ushas, the goddess of dawn—comparable to Eos in Greece—inspired the poet to sing of daybreak and the triumph of light. The great myth of Indra's struggle with the Vritra, which the

Veda says released the heavenly cows, seemed to be a story about thunder, which caused the long-awaited, long prayed-for rains to pour down. An idea developed that the Indian gods were powers of nature and that the myths were fanciful enactments of natural phenomena.

If one phenomenon seemed to be preferred, it was taken as the center of the mythological system. Thus, theories of thunder and storm were born and thus the theories about the sun and its manifestations.

The thunder mythology had its main proponents in Adalbert Kuhn and his brother-in-law Wilhelm Schwartz. Kuhn had begun his research into Indo-European culture on the basis of linguistics and became the founder of the Indo-European archaeology. Then, following the example of Jacob Grimm, he turned to the collection and study of popular traditions, and this brought him to mythology. His principal work, in 1859, *Die Herabkunft des Feuers und des Göttertranks* ("The Descent of Fire and of the Divine Drink"), is a book of high caliber, when seen in the light of his time, and still receives deserved attention. In his mythological expositions he begins with atmospheric phenomena, the passage of day and night, summer and winter, but especially with thunder and storm. By their nature the myths of Indra and the Maruts give an apt documentation. He also tries to support the coherence of the various Indo-European mythologies with linguistic data; this attempt was very important in a time when the coherence of the languages had just been discovered. It seemed obvious to compare Varuna with Uranos or Surya (Sanskrit: sun) and Helios (Greek: sun). Kuhn also saw a resemblance between the Indian Gandharvas and the Greek Centaurs. He related Saraṇyū, the mother of the Aśvins, to the Greek Erinys, which was more risky, as was his comparison of Hermeias with the Sanskrit Sarameya, the name of a dog. Kuhn's method did not bear up to criticism as the phonetic laws that determine the relation of languages gradually became better known and a scientific etymology became possible. The modern science of linguistics made quick work of the beautiful parallels he had established between Indian and Greek mythical figures. As a result, scholars hesitated for a long time to attempt the comparative study of Indian and other Indo-European names of gods. This was certainly at scholarship's expense, for in spite of everything, later research concluded that it is precisely in the area of religion that names and words can deviate from the "phonetic rule." Exceptional forms of this order could occur in the sacred sphere, where the usage of language was unlike profane speech. Taboo phenomena may have played a role in the peculiar conservation of religious words. Finally, a growing sophistication in the study of phonetics could make some comparisons of divine names acceptable, though the efforts looked unsure at first.

One cannot deny in the "nature mythologists" an intimate, romantic feel for the phenomena of nature. We read in Schwartz:

> The thunderbolt—the most universal and original magical fetish among almost all peoples—seemed to trace in the sky the source of rain, or, slightly differently, the thunder "opening up," or mythically expressed, "the unfolding flower of thunderclouds," brings on the stormy night with its shadows, or seems to disclose, as lightning tears the clouds, the mountains of the clouds with their radiant treasure.[1]

No nature mythologist lacked imagination, and this helped them in locating all sorts of physical phenomena in the ancient myths. Above all else, Schwartz expounds, Wodan (the chief Norse god) is the storm, and the comparison to the Indian Vayu immediately offers itself. The Indian deity, veiled in clouds, has his sphere of action in heaven. In the case of Wodan thunder and lightning are rather secondary accompaniments. They are central in the case of Donar or Zeus. Donar was believed to be a gigantic, demonic being, moving through the clouds, urging his thunderous steed around the sky in the wild commotion of the storm. The flash of lightning that shot underneath the clouds was believed to be the flash of his eye, which was shaded by the clouds as by a hat. But the flash of lightning could, at the same time, be a spear hurled from the heights, or a gleaming sword. These motifs could, in turn, be interpreted as the trappings of a hunting or a warrior god.[2]

In the same context Schwartz observes that in the "lower mythology" of the Germanic tribes, Wodan absorbed a great many elements that occur more faintly in Greek and Roman mythology and yet are analogous to the Indo-European popular beliefs. "Lower mythology" and "popular belief" were the new concepts coined by Schwartz. Since Jacob Grimm, popular traditions had been collected and examined with increasing intensity. Grimm saw them as precious survivals of a distant pagan past; the ancient myths, he thought, lived on in the fairy tales, and in the sagas he found the last traces of the pagan gods, who after Christianization had been brought to the state of trolls and giants.

Schwartz developed a different view. What is still alive among the folk, he thought, is not at all the echo of an ancient pantheon but the ground on which polytheism sprang up. Popular belief, or "the religion of the people," is precisely that belief in all those supernaturals, dwarves, giants, elves, and nixes that have had their home in the mind of the people since time immemorial. Moreover, this elvish populace is much more ancient and original than the great gods of the Greeks and Indians. Therefore Schwartz believed that the figures of the gods were born in the course of millennia by virtue of more highly refined ideas. To understand this higher religiosity we should find out what "the people" (*das Volk*) at one time believed and thought and what it still believes and thinks.

There is some sense in Schwartz's train of thought. Nineteenth-century research always began by assuming that all elements of civilization, and consequently also of religion, passed through an evolution; the schematic series of fetishism / polytheism / monotheism was familiar even to the eighteenth century. Its validity went unquestioned. And it is not impossible that in present popular religion much of the ancient lower mythology really does survive with the gods long since toppled by Christianity and transformed to demonic beings. It would be wrong to assume that the superstition leading a veiled existence among the people represents the primordial Indo-European beliefs, yet its testimony cannot be ignored. As long as one assumes—like Schwartz —a pantheon that was common to the Indo-European nations and must have preceded their division, the danger of overestimating the primitive beliefs in demons is not too great. It seems quite obvious that the anthropomorphic pantheon of an intelligentsia (as we know in the Vedic liturgies)—the work of sophisticated schools of priests—cannot have the same sway over the lower strata of the population. With the latter we certainly may assume there was a much simpler and more naïve religiosity, in which spirits and demons figured significantly, and where, from day to day, the great gods of the pantheon hardly played a part.

Nevertheless, Schwartz's conception of a lower mythology became fatal for scholarly investigation. Before long, the collapse of the ideas that Adalbert Kuhn had proclaimed—that Indo-European gods could be inferred from similarities in names—also hurt the notion of a pan-Indo-European pantheon. An incisive linguistic critique did not leave intact much of the identifications that once were so striking. The one god who was unaffected by this scholarly turmoil and who really could have been worshiped by the Indo-Europeans was the ancient skygod, for the identification of the names Dyaus pitar (Sanskrit), Zeus pater (Greek), and Jupiter (Latin) could hardly be denied.

The net conclusion of the discussion was that, next to the worship of the skygod, nothing must have existed but that popular religion or so-called lower mythology. Gradually, in the course of centuries, the variegated pantheon we know from the sources must have come into being. Supposedly this happened after the Indo-Europeans had left their "homeland." Each nation had its own names for the "secondary" gods and thus proved to have discovered (or appropriated) them independently. This reasoning fitted miraculously well into the frame of nineteenth-century historicism, which we shall discuss more elaborately later. It became a most appealing task to demonstrate how that pagan pantheon had been slowly structured. This process was not so much the result of a need for new gods because of growing cultural complexity but rather of an interplay with alien civilizations, from which whole sets of imageries and customs were borrowed. This hypothesis was already dogma in the study of Greek mythology: Zeus-Ammon came from Egypt, Dionysus from Thrace, Apollo from Libia; all those derivations that were held by the ancients themselves were still immutable among scholars of the Greek pantheon. A foreign origin seemed probable for other deities as well. The Romans were considered a nation that accepted almost completely a world of gods; did they not appropriate the whole Greek pantheon? The Germanic people and their deities were treated similarly. Since the cultural superiority of the Celts was beyond dispute it was presumed that the Germanic tribes who met Belgians and Gauls along the lower Rhine received gods like Donar and Wodan from them. Even in the twentieth century Gustav Neckel defended the thesis that the Germanic god Balder had come to Scandinavia from the Near East through Thrace.

But let us return to the Nature Mythologists and the problems related to Schwartz's lower mythology. It was Wilhelm Mannhardt (1831-80) who became the nineteenth century's most successful student of this lower mythology. At the beginning of his work he was still an adherent of nature-mythological explanation after the manner of Adalbert Kuhn. But later the great significance of popular tradition for religio-historical study became clear to him. At the sacrifice of his own money and time he decided, independently, to collect accurate data by means of questionnaires, and his research went far beyond the borders of Germany. He concentrated on harvest customs. His results were published in 1865 in the book *Roggenwolf und Roggenhund,* followed by *Die Korndämonen* in 1868. In these works he explains that in popular religion certain beings—personal beings—were supposed to be present in the cornfield as "fertility spirits"; these spirits could be caught at the harvest time. Some curious customs involving the last sheaf of grain revealed this tradition to Mannhardt. In his main work, *Wald- und Feldkulte* (1875-77, "Cults of the Forests and the Fields"), Mannhardt assembled much material showing how closely the popular ideas of Greeks and Teutons corresponded and how the mysteries of Eleusis were rooted in similar ideas. "The same psychic process," he writes,

> which explains so many elements in tree worship, is also the germ of the Demeter myth. What I have in mind is the comparison of plant-life with human life. Not only that the growth, flourishing and withering of trees have been compared at an early date with the conditions and development of animals and man; but still more clearly perhaps in the language and customs of the peoples, a similar association of cereals and man comes to the fore.[3]

With Mannhardt the "folkloric" mythology begins its triumphal procession. It has had its day, and left a number of important insights. But like so many branches of study it became marred by onesidedness and exaggeration and provoked sharp criticism. The great importance of Mannhardt's ideas is shown most decisively by his influence on the English anthropologist Sir James Frazer (1854-1941). Frazer's books, *Spirits of the Corn and of the Wild* and *Adonis, Attis, Osiris,* give witness to this influence.

In a letter of May 7, 1876, to Karl Müllenhoff, Mannhardt writes:

> I am far from considering all myths psychic responses to natural phenomena—like Kuhn, Schwartz and M. Müller with their whole school—and even farther from considering them exclusively sky phenomena (solar or meteoric); I have learned to value poetic and literary production as essential

7787777777777

factors in the formation of mythology and to draw the necessary conclusions. On the other hand, I am convinced that a part of the earliest myths owed their origin to a poetry of nature which is not immediately comprehensible to us any more but needs to be explained by analogies [to contemporary primitives]. That we can make these analogies does not imply a complete historical identity, but takes advantage of a similar conceptualization and a similar predisposition on a similar developmental stage.[4]

This is an idea that in 1881, a year after Mannhardt's death, was to be formulated by A. Bastian in his treatise *Der Völkergedanke im Aufbau einer Wissenschaft vom Menschen* ("The Function of 'Collective' or 'Ethnic' Ideas for the Science of Man"). Bastian discusses here the *"Elementargedanken"* ("elementary ideas"), which seem to be inherent in the human psyche and for that reason can become manifest everywhere and in any age. It is a stimulating thought and has much weight in some of its forms; it can restore the balance in the case when similar beliefs in separate places are taken as emanating from a single place of origin. Thus Mannhardt, who always evinced a touching modesty, is one of the pioneers of modern scholarship in the areas both of folklore and of the history of religions.

Later investigations showed, however, that the agrarian customs and ideas existed far outside the Indo-European areas. We should not attribute the popular beliefs as reconstructed by Mannhardt to an earlier stage of Indo-European culture but instead to much more ancient, prehistoric substrata.

In his letter quoted above, Mannhardt mentions the name of Max Müller (1823-1900), who was no doubt the most important nature mythologist. He was not only a student of the history of religions but also a great linguist. An eminent student of Sanskrit, he had immediate access to the Indian sources—which was only partly true for Adalbert Kuhn. Max Müller was also the first to edit Vedic texts and gained fame by interpreting those archaic and often obscure hymns. Indeed, he had everything needed for an intimate knowledge of Indian mythology.

But the spirit of one's time usually fixes one's interpretation. In Max Müller's day the opinion was generally held that polytheistic religion was a nature cult. This idea came from the Romantics, who were strongly inclined toward nature-pantheism and panentheism. As we have already noted, the Brahmanic metaphorical language readily allowed such views.

For Max Müller, the central point for the formation of the Aryan pantheon is not the terrifying thunder but the lovelier phenomenon of daybreak. He placed this phenomenon at the origin of the struggle of winter and summer and the return of spring. With a rather modern feeling for nature he delights in the dawn of day. "There is no sight in nature," he says,

> more elevating than the dawn even to us, whom philosophy would wish to teach that *nil admirari* is the highest wisdom. Yet in ancient times the power of admiring was the greatest blessing bestowed on mankind; and when could man have admired more intensely, when could his heart have been more gladdened and overpowered with joy, than at the approach of
>> 'the Lord of light,
>> Of life, of love, and gladness!' [5]

This must be regarded as merely the poetic rapture of a modern and very romantic person. Extravaganzas of this type were rebuked by Malinowski, who knew about primitive thoughts and feelings:

> From my own study of living myths among savages, I should say that primitive man has to a very limited extent the purely artistic or scientific interest in nature; there is but little room for symbolism in his ideas and tales; and myth, in fact, is not an idle rhapsody, not an aimless outpouring of vain imaginings, but a hard-working, extremely important cultural force.[6]

To illustrate the type of explanation presented by Max Müller, I want to mention the Indian goddess *Saraṇyū*. With Kuhn, he attaches importance to the similar sound of the Greek *Erinys*. Still he does not consider her the personification of the thundercloud but, again, the dawn of day. Therefore, he compares her to Ushas, and particularly so because both are the mothers of twins (Saraṇyū is especially known as mother of the Aśvins, celebrated twin deities in the Vedic pantheon). However, Athena is also a mother of twins. Hence Athena is another goddess of morning twilight; proof is the myth of her birth from Zeus's head, as the morning twilight is born from the eastern sky. (After all, the east in India is called "mūrdhā divaḥ" or forehead of heaven!) Now Athena's wisdom is explained, if only one thinks of the Sanskrit verb *"budh,"* which means both "to awaken" and "to know," for the goddess who awakens men also leads them to knowledge.[7] It is not necessary any more now to waste words on such fanciful reasoning.

One point in the nature-mythological explanations needs to be clarified. How could the admiration for a phenomenon of nature ever give rise to a personal deity? How could the thrill—or with thunder, the fear or terror—develop into the mythology we know? This was the problem that haunted Max Müller. He did not rest until he found a solution—one that formed the keystone of his system. Being a linguist, he found his clue in the form in which primitive man expressed his feelings.

In the philologist Christian G. Heyne we met the idea that "primordial man," charged with emotion, recreated what he perceived in terms of imagination. This image occurs in a language of sense impressions because the primitive cannot form abstract thoughts. The abstract "causation," for instance, appears in the immediacy of "begetting." Max Müller developed a similar train of thought. He, too, believed that the primal language is not abstract but visual. Even in an expression such as "the day breaks," is there a pure concept of time or is there not rather an agent who can be expected to do something like "breaking"?

As long as the mind was sensual and filled with words, Max Müller argues, it was impossible to speak of evening and morning, of winter and spring without attributing to these something individual, active, sexually determined, and so, at last, a personal character. Either these phenomena were nothing—as in our own withered thought—or they were something, and in that case they could be conceived not merely as powers but as beings endowed with power.[8]

The sensual, visual nature of language appears also in the verbs. They have their full, primitive significance and have not yet faded into abstractions. The verb "to follow," for instance, presupposes someone going after someone else and must not be understood as "to appear later in time." Therefore, when it is said that the sun follows the dawn of day, we conceive a being loving another being and attempting to embrace it. For primitive man, sunrise was also that moment when the night gave life to a beautiful child.

If we assume such an imaginative language, we should expect shifts in meaning with the course of civilization and abstraction. However, Max Müller invokes another linguistic phenomenon: polyonymy and synonymy. Since most objects have more than

one attribute, in the course of time each was given various names
—polyonymy. Because one quality can be attributed to more than
one object, it became possible to understand the word for this
quality in different senses—that is, for one adjective to invoke
various different objects—synonymy.

What this implies for the evolution of mythological ideas can
be shown in the Indian tradition, according to Max Müller's
reasoning. Śiva's or Mahadeva's myths, or Vishnu's and Krishna's
myths, which were the starting-point of Creuzer's studies, are
worthless; they originated late, as a wild and fantastic plant from
the Indian soil. The Veda is the true theogony of the Aryan
tribes; Hesiod gave no more than its caricature.[9] The human
spirit, which always and by nature knows divinity, was compelled
in a peculiar direction by the irresistible power of language, by
the quirk in images of the supernatural. If we want to know
this direction, we find it in the Veda. The gods in the text are
masks without players, made by man and not his makers; they
are *nomina* ("mere names"), not *numina* ("divine powers"):
names *sans* reality, not ineffable real beings.

This development Max Müller called a "disease of language."
The polyonymy and synonymy, which were once meaningful,
confused imageries that were initially separate. A mythological
phraseology appeared, because within a collection of predicates
a single one was pushed to the fore and became the acknowl-
edged proper name of a god.

The term "disease of language" is unfortunate and reveals the
weakness of Max Müller's whole construction. After all, how
could an unnatural linguistic process of confusion and mixture
be responsible for a mythology that had been meaningful and
trustworthy for generations? *Nomina,* not *numina!* How could
one say such a thing about the gods of pagan polytheism, who
move us time and again exactly because of their strong personal
character? Indeed, were Zeus and Wodan, Indra and Donar no
more than empty names? They were true gods—one could almost
say of flesh and blood—so human were they in their imagery, so
persuasive in their doings. They demanded veneration because
of their powerful intervention in life; awe and confidence, fear
and love were felt for them in accordance with their power and
character. Mythology is not a disease of language; it is a reality
immediately apparent to man; it has its being in all that is limit-
less and enigmatic in nature or in himself.

Max Müller's theory demonstrates once more the gap that lay

between nineteenth-century man and the sundry faiths he knew existed. To the extent that modern man's soul detached itself from Christianity, to the extent that Christianity was allowed to deteriorate into a mere moral lore as the core was taken out of its dogma and the sense for its mystery got lost, to that extent also man's understanding for other religions disappeared. It seemed to him that these religions were so naïve that they could not have any connection with deep human experience. Max Müller's theory makes abundantly clear that he never fathomed belief.

He was a man of his time. For many years he had enthusiastic supporters. In England, G. W. Cox was his faithful disciple.[10] In France M. Bréal, who was at the same time a linguist and a historian of religion, as was Max Müller, propagated his theories.[11] A scholar of stature like A. Réville argued as late as 1881 that the mythical explanations of natural phenomena are poetic flights empty of every really religious element. Hence the cult is the imitation of a process of nature; Réville analyzes the elements he regards as separate symbols that nevertheless relate to a central idea and can unite in a complex cultic act.[12]

Analysis alone, no matter how subtle, is insufficient. So are constructions of thought, no matter how cleverly thought through. Only an accurate observation of primitive religious life will lead to worthwhile insights. (See Chapter Fifteen.)

Chapter Thirteen

THE HISTORICAL SCHOOL

BEFORE we turn to the contribution of Ethnology to the revival of the study of the history of religions, we should review some studies of religion done from historical documents. Here, classical mythology has the place of honor.

We already noted how C. Otfried Müller advised historical study of the mythological traditions. The myths cannot have been constructed in a college of priests (as Creuzer believed) and consequently cannot have had from the beginning the coherence and profundity they show at a later stage. Creuzer's thesis was impossible because it never explained how for centuries people lived among and revered the myths. The myths could not have been imposed on them but must have been a product of the people's souls. The myths must have interpreted what everyone knew. If, in the forms we know, they seem too complex to warrant this conclusion, the answer is that they have not always been so involved. Their intricacy was the result of a long evolution, partly unconscious in the course of oral tradition, partly conscious in the minds of poets and thinkers. Consequently, the task of the modern scholar is to unweave the myths, to track their development through centuries, to separate more recent strands, and thus to arrive at the germinal form from which the whole variegated mythology evolved.

The scholarly predisposition of the nineteenth century is a clear-cut historicism. This new attitude was stimulated by the expansion of the spiritual horizon in archaeology and in the ever increasing knowledge of primitive cultures. Moreover, the growing convictions about evolution drew attention to the course of history as a process of becoming. Everything that exists has become. Each branch of the humanities was affected and inspired by this new vision. We owe it a wealth of historical knowledge. Certain oversimplifications were inevitable in its wake, and tangled phenomena were reduced to simpler forms. With occasional interruptions, the movement of culture was believed to be a constant ascent. We shall see the influence of these ideas on the history of religions. It cannot be denied that the idea of a historical development—justified in itself—was often overstretched. This had to produce a reaction. In the realm of language and of social structures, original elements turned out to be far from the simplest.

This period had no eye for transhistorical values, which have the utmost importance precisely in the area of religion. The movements of history appear rather more at the surface. Beneath lies an unchanging mode of being, capable at all times of yielding similar reactions to cosmic and psychic experiences.

The flood of documents on all sides made new outlooks possible. A growing number of Greek and Roman inscriptions discovered revealed beliefs of the ordinary citizen. They disclosed a more genuine, perhaps a more primitive religion than that of the poets and philosophers. Mythology began to seem no more than the beguiling fringes of the cult, so the cult became the center of scholarly investigation. Here too archaeological research showed the value of the evolution hypothesis. The temples arose in the course of time and became ever larger in dimension and ever more beautiful in structure. Local cults gradually became great festivals celebrated throughout Greece.

The study of classical religions was intensively cultivated. Scholars such as Theodor Mommsen (1817-1903) and Georg Wissowa (1859-1931) tried to establish the stages of Roman religious development. Franz Cumont (1868-1947) studied oriental religions that penetrated Rome in late antiquity. Jules Toutain (1865-1921) demonstrated through inscriptions and plastic art how the

Romans had affected the religious evolution of Gaul. With the archaeological discoveries on Crete and in Pelopponesus a wholly different and earlier world was disclosed behind the image of pagan tradition presented by the Greek literary sources. Martin Persson Nilsson (1874-) wrote a new chapter on the Mycenaean people and the numerous traces of them in later religious forms and thus altered the traditional exposition of Greek polytheism. More accurate knowledge was also gained of the religious development of ancient Rome. It had long been known that the Roman pantheon was virtually a copy of the Greek, but now it became possible to mark various moves in this appropriation. In the earliest days of Rome, Greek deities were accepted beside the Etruscan: Liber, Ceres, and Vulcanus. The Greek deities did not come straight from Greece but were imported via Kyme and probably southern Etruria.

Here again historical investigation suggested that very little of the Greek or Roman religion really went back to the early beginnings. Now it seemed there had been no broad basis from which the pantheon of the Indo-European nations could have developed. Indeed, the one thing that seemed to be ubiquitous was a primitive and barbaric religiosity. That was all, when the Indo-European tribes—including the Celts, Teutons, Romans, and Greeks—began their independent existence. The "folkloric" school had already created the view that the real gods had "evolved" rather recently; in the beginning there was only the simplest belief in demons. This view was made prominent in a particularly crude and one-sided fashion by Sophus Bugge (1833-1907). In his Studier over de nordiske gude-og heltesagn ("Studies of Nordic Sagas of Gods and Heroes"), published 1881-89, he concludes that many Scandinavian sagas are adaptations of stories and teachings that pagan or semi-pagan Norsemen had heard in the Viking day from Christians on the British Isles, especially from monks or from men educated in monastic schools. The influence of monks occurs to Bugge because he assumes there are traces in the Nordic tradition of classical mythical narratives that could have been found in English monastic libraries.

It fell to a real folklorist, however, to push this theory of borrowings to the extreme. The Finnish scholar Kaarle Krohn (1863-1933 wrote in 1922 a Skandinavisk Mytologi (Scandinavian Mythology). In his naïveté he dedicated it to the archbishop Nathan Söderblom, a well-known historian of religion and a great name in the ecumenical movement, and went on to try to show that a number of old Nordic myths were no more than adaptations of Christian legends.

Such provoking historicism and diffusionism had to be objected to. Yet real criticism came only later in the twentieth century, although the Swedish poet and scholar Viktor Rydberg (1828-95), to whom we shall return, may be mentioned as a precursor.

Even the prominent scholar Otto Gruppe (1815-1919), who had sharply criticized the nature-mythological hypotheses, fell victim to the extreme historicist fashion. He was unable to see in comparable cultic forms and myths a common heritage but explained them as borrowings. Unlike Creuzer, he did not turn to India but looked to the Near East, which during his time began to yield the secrets of its soil. He remained a realist in the sense that he assumed that such borrowings could take place only among peoples in close and continuous contact. He saw many things correctly—for those much earlier civilizations of Asia Minor really did influence Greece considerably via the Ionian colonies—but he also exaggerated a great deal. He ignored the fact that religious convictions are usually not "imports." They are that only in the latest phase of historical development, when the revealed, monotheistic religions feel called upon to bring their doctrine of salvation to all the nations of the earth. That is what we find with the universal religions, Buddhism, Christianity and Islam. By nature, these religions are super-national and are called to bring the other nations to the true faith through missions. But the ancient polytheistic religions felt no urge of that nature. The inner coherence of these religions with the whole social structure of the people made the belief system a form *sui generis* functioning only in its own landscape. Of course, every living nation is ready to accept cultural riches from foreigners, but as long as it is alive it does not allow itself to be touched at its inner core. And that core is first and foremost the ancestral religion.

Chapter Fourteen

PANBABYLONISM

PANBABYLONISM can be called a specific set of applications of general historicistic and diffusionistic views, and therefore deserves to be reviewed now before we move to anthropological theories concerning the history of religions. A review of the topic entails ideas that were actually expressed only later but, nevertheless, are linked to the earlier period by their nature-mythological character.

The exaggerations by Adalbert Kuhn and Max Müller might lead one to deny to the experience of nature all significance in the birth of religious feelings. That would be wrong. We pointed out several times that the phenomena of nature played an important role in the Indo-European myths. Their presence, in the Indian Vedic hymns in particular, motivated the construction of the thunder and daybreak mythologies. The veneration of natural phenomena is universal; on the most primitive cultural level, the sun, the moon, and the other celestial bodies have an important place in the cult.

This explains why it is precisely the ethnologists who have often underlined such nature cults. The very title of his book, *Das Zeitalter des Sonnengottes* ("The Age of the Sun God"), implies that the great Africanist Leo Frobenius (1849-1917) wanted to explain the majority of myths by celestial movements of the sun, at least at the beginning of his scholarly career. In 1910, six years after this work of the young Frobenius, Paul Ehrenreich (1855-1914), who had concentrated on South American ethnology, published a mature product of his studies, *Die allgemeine Mythologie und ihre ethnologischen Grundlagen* ("General Mythology and its Ethnological Foundation"). He decided that lunar phenomena are most frequently at the sources of myths. The moon and the phases of the moon were bound to appeal to the imagination; its hold on nature and its supposed connection with vegetation and the menstruation of women account for the age-old importance of the moon.

A remarkable theory, in the form of Panbabylonism, emerged by the end of the nineteenth century. The Assyriologist Hugo Winckler (1863-1913) had seen the significance of ancient Babylonian astrology and astronomy. The Babylonians acquired an extraordinary knowledge of stars and planets. This was not the result of scientific curiosity but of the belief that the stars influenced men's lives and even the course of nations. The routes of the stars, determined by strict laws, seemed to make predictions possible. This compelled a continuous observation of the sky and, in time, a mass of accurately recorded data. Astronomy is thus the daughter of astrology.

The stars, and especially the sun and moon, together with the planets, were believed to be manifestations of divinity. The influence of these ideas in Europe in late antiquity is well known. The days of the week were named after the planetary deities. Even in Gaul we find them, depicted on the so-called Jupiter-giant pillars,* whose enigma has not been solved. Astrology still has its votaries.

Hugo Winckler thought he could demonstrate the influence of these Babylonian ideas over a much wider area. He caused a stir with his assertion that this influence can be established even in the Old Testament: granted that Saul, David, and Solomon were historical persons, their portrayal in the Jewish tradition is in the image of a mythical scheme derived from Babylonian astrology.[1] It is possible, no doubt, that the Jews were in contact with those teachings, but that they were directly influenced by

---

* About 150 in number, erected by the Gauls between A.D. 170 and 240, principally in the Rhine, Mosel, and Saône regions.

them—despite their strict monotheism and the scrupulous care with which its purity was guarded—seems most improbable.

This was not the end. Winckler found disciples who went much further. Eduard Stucken (1865-1936) believed that he could show the astral myths in all parts of the world; it would follow that the mythical ideas were diffused from Babylon to all the nations, including even the primitive tribes. For Stucken the constellation of the Pleiades is the key to the diffusion. Stucken even believed in a precise date when the influence diffused from Babylon. The date was an equinox when the sun was in the sign of Taurus, to which the Pleiades belong, in about the year 3000 B.C.; the calendar reform connected with the equinox was established by Stucken at 2800 B.C. on the basis of cuneiform documents. So we may thank the Pleiades and the accuracy of Babylonian astronomers, which inform us of the starting point of a worldwide mythological development! [2]

However, it should surprise us if the astral myths spread at such a late date. More has been learned since Stucken did his work, and we would now allow much longer spans of time to the births and reappearance of myths if they diffused from one geographical center. The fact that other peoples, perhaps less scientifically, traced the courses of the stars and that they too might be credited with some imagination does not have the least role in Stucken's theory.

For a short while this Panbabylonian hypothesis enjoyed great popularity. This was in the wake of the deciphering of cuneiform texts, when Babylon was revealed as a leading civilization in antiquity. Her astronomy, her age-long observation of the heavens, was most impressive. Her influence on the nations of the Near East proved to be greater than had been conjectured. But just as the Romantics overestimated the Indian texts, these scholars exaggerated the significance of Babylon.

The spell of Panbabylonism could not last. Today we can only be fascinated that it dragged along with it so many eminent minds. As soon as specialists in other areas—Egyptologists or ethnologists—tested the assertions, they were reduced to almost nothing. Besides, the Panbabylonian theory contained no reason why other peoples could not arrive themselves at astral myths. The sky and the night were over all nations.

There was a further objection along this line. The adherents of the theory were absorbed in the civilization of Babylon; Stucken himself was absorbed in one year, 2800 B.C.; he was not interested in what happened before. But the history of mythology does not begin when Babylon has accumulated plenty of information about the stars. There were immeasurable spaces of time before, in which religious and mythical ideas were in play all over the world. It is curious that Panbabylonism occurred at a time when ethnology had already made many attempts to clarify this most ancient period of religious history. The ethnological contribution is our next topic.

Chapter Fifteen

ETHNOLOGICAL THEORIES

John Lubbock

Only in the nineteenth century did it become possible to extend religio-historical and mythological study beyond the Indo-European traditions. Immediate access was gained to primitive life and beliefs. "The proper study of mankind is Man," an eighteenth-century remark, is really the adage of the nineteenth century, which saw the birth of the new science of anthropology.

John Lubbock (1834-1913) was one of the first to study prehistoric man closely. That meant man in the archaeological eras but particularly man of the living primitive peoples. In 1870 Lubbock wrote his principal work, *The Origin of Civilisation and the Primitive Condition of Man.* He tried to sketch the evolution from the lowest stage of civilization, which prevails in some primitive tribes, to the peaks reached by the Greeks and by the western Europe of his day. He examined various aspects of culture—marriage and kinship relations, morality, language, juridical institutions—and devoted careful attention to religion. Here he marked off stages of development.

The first level is characterized by a total lack of religious ideas. He believed he could deduce this atheism, which various investigators doubted, from data collected among extremely primitive peoples. His findings are no longer persuasive, since we know how very difficult it is to penetrate the religious symbols of a primitive people. It seems quite naïve of Lubbock to list among his authorities sailors and merchants. These informants—like so many scholarly investigators even at a later date—had the barest knowledge, if any, of native languages. How could they pass on religious ideas, using words they had misunderstood, from languages whose structure and spirit they were unaware of?

Atheism is followed by fetishism, says Lubbock. He describes fetishism as an illusion that man can compel some divine power to carry out his designs. It can be called a phase of magic. Lubbock does not make clear how divine powers suddenly can be spoken of. How they suggested themselves, and what was their actual nature, is not really explained. He does mention some sort of belief in spirits that would originate in sleep and especially in the presence of death.

The third stage is nature worship or totemism, veneration of the elements of nature: trees, rivers, stones, and animals. Lubbock's identification of nature worship with totemism shows how inaccurately that concept was understood at the time. One year before the appearance of Lubbock's book, MacLennan had made an attempt to present totemism as the source of all worship of animals and plants.

Shamanism is the next stage. Man has advanced far enough to regard the divine powers as fundamentally different and greater by far in power. These powers are also supposed to exist at a great distance from the world of man, and the shaman alone is able to reach them.

The fifth stage in Lubbock's account is idolatry or anthropomorphism. The gods have assumed a human shape; they can be approached reasonably and persuaded. Although they are within nature, they are creators. Now, too, their essence is pronounced through images.

The next stage reveres one deity as creator of the world, and here originates the idea of a godhead absolutely transcending man.

Finally, Lubbock concludes that he is able to point to the stage at which religion is connected with morality.

Lubbock's scheme is most unsatisfactory. It proves how superficial the knowledge of primitive religious forms still was in his day. It is true he knew of fetishism, totemism, and shamanism, but he did not perceive their real significance. This ignorance enabled him to assemble them in a fashionable evolutionistic design. It is also totally arbitrary to posit an initial atheism and arbitrary to provide an evolutionary circle that returns to atheism by way of various foolish religious forms. It is also astounding that he saw a link between religion and ethics only at a late stage. Even in the most primitive state of culture, the establishment of order in human society—and hence moral ideas—is inseparable from religion.

Animism

One year after Lubbock's work appeared, a book was published that was to have a profound influence on religio-historical study. It was *Primitive Culture* (1871) by Edward Burnett Tylor (1832-1917). Inevitably, Tylor was a typical evolutionist. In the beginning, he says, was a very primitive religion. It was not the atheism of Lubbock; Tylor was convinced that man has always been religious. Whoever considers him otherwise has failed to notice some religious form, for the simple reason that the Christian in himself has too high a concept of what it means to believe.

Tylor created the theory of animism. For him, animism is the basis of all religion and continues in modern spiritualism. He looks at the phenomena that are common to humankind: sleep, ecstasy, sickness, and death, as well as dreams and hallucinations. In dreams man has experiences that are impossible when he is awake. He finds himself in a place other than the one in which he went to sleep, visits with relatives and friends who are far away, sees regions where he has never been. And the other way round, people approach him who he knows are long gone, whose death he can recall. How can these meetings be explained? While his body lay in the hut—a certainty, his housemates assure him—he was somewhere else. In a sense, he must be two. Besides a physical body, he must have a double who is immaterial and invisible.

Death too was a riddle for primitive man. A second ago a man was alive; he breathed, moved, and spoke. Suddenly, life departed. It is as if something made an exit from the mortal body. Moreover, it is as if whatever detached itself from the body has begun an independent existence, because it manifests itself, as noticed, in other people's dreams.

Tylor's theory is that these experiences suggest to man that he is threefold. First, there is his body; next is some principle of life, which vanishes at the moment of death; finally, there is a spiritual being, which can remove itself from the body during the lifetime and continues to live after death. Before long, man merges this spiritual phantom with the principle of life to form a single concept. This is the "soul," something immaterial, like a vapor, with the power to cause movements and thoughts.

Tylor tries to explain several phenomena by means of this concept of a "soul." But it is especially important to note how he derives from the doctrine of "soul" a doctrine of spirits that becomes a systematic "philosophy of natural religion." This is what he says:

> Conformably with that early childlike philosophy in which human life seems the direct key to the understanding of nature at large, the savage theory of the universe refers its phenomena in general to the wilful action of pervading personal spirits. It was no spontaneous fancy, but the reasonable inference that effects are due to causes, which led the rude men of old days to people with such ethereal phantoms their own homes and haunts, and the vast earth and sky beyond. Spirits are simply personified causes. As men's ordinary life and actions were held to be caused by souls, so the happy or disastrous events which affect mankind, as well as the manifold physical operations of the outer-world, were accounted for as caused by soul-like beings, spirits whose essential similarity of origin is evident through all their wondrous variety of power and function.[1]

"Ghosts," the souls of the dead, can become troublesome demons, but they can also develop into benevolent deities who take care of their relatives and those who honor them. This is the origin of ancestor cults. And with these spirits the savage explains diseases, oracles, and the horrifying phenomena of madness.

When men located these spirits in specific objects, fetishism was born, and the veneration of trees and stones. When a stone or a pole was no longer considered the house of a spirit, but a symbol of the divine, men had created idols.

We have been climbing to the higher forms of religion. Step by step the world has been populated with a multitude of spirits, elves, and gnomes, all at work in nature. Finally, the gods of polytheism arrive. The moment man became the model of divine beings, his society became the model of the life of the gods. The great gods among the lower spirits were like kings among their subjects. Although they were different from the common spirits, it was only a difference in estate and by no means essential. They were personal spirits reigning over personal spirits. In principle, the great gods of polytheism were already present among less advanced peoples. The poet and priest, theologian and philosopher made these gods ever more noble and more real.

The skygod is the most special in the pantheon of polytheism. Sometimes he is the sun god or the ancestor of the tribe. The lesser gods fade away and the religions of mankind reach the stage where one God is adored. The Father of Heaven, once supreme among a nation of gods, becomes the Father in Heaven, and there is no space for other deities at his side.

A similar exposition of the course of religious development is given by the English philosopher Herbert Spencer (1820-1903) in his *Principles of Sociology* (1876-96), with the important difference that he places ancestor worship in the foreground. Like so many others, he thought that fear was the basis of all religion. The object of dread is the spirit of Tylor's theory, the phantom of a dead man who appears in dreams. The primitive was led inevitably to worship the dead, and from this all the forms of religion arose.

In its immediacy and power, the dream image arranges around itself the vague concepts of animism. It may have been very early that man became aware of a certain duality in himself. But this more or less spiritual *Doppelgänger,* which he had noticed in his dreams, became a ghost or a shadow upon his death. This ghost is the central point of primitive belief, according to Spencer. It gives the primitive a beginning in explaining all enigmatic and supernatural experiences. Then Spencer enumerates the same phenomena we met in Tylor: shadow and echo, epilepsy, and, above all, death. When fear and awe arise for this complex of phenomena, which revolve about the spirits of the dead, ancestor worship is the immediate result.

With great virtuosity, Spencer demonstrates how all further forms develop from this cult. The first evolution is the cult of plants and animals, and nature worship in general. The personality of divine powers is not problematic, since from the beginning the "ghost" was personal. But personality heightens in significance. Veneration of the dead is ancestor worship, hence, already "personal" in principle; together the ancestors become concrete in a tribal hero or a tribal god. Thus, the "personal" element grows.

It is interesting that Spencer takes refuge in a confusion of names to explain the occurrence of personifications. He notes that in Homer, "Aides" begins as the name of a personal being but later becomes the name of his home, the netherworld. Therefore, nature cult is derived from the worship of souls. Spencer also believes that taking metaphors literally can lead to the worship of heavenly bodies. Or, if the Pharaoh was called "Horus, courageous bull," it must mean that originally Pharaoh was simply compared to a bull. These metaphors could only confuse the man and the animal and result in animal worship.

A pinch of Euhemerism is added to Spencer's account. He asserts that in their normal and their abnormal forms all gods come into being through apotheosis, for the god is first a living, superior man, whose power seems superhuman.

Obviously, this reduction of animism to "manism" is not convincing. It is arbitrary to posit the ancestor cult at the root of all beliefs. Tylor was more cautious: he abstained from offering any opinion as to a more primitive form that might have preceded animism or as to the nature of such a form. He only believed he had established an early stage that made the way to all later forms discernible. Spencer, by training an engineer, tried to finish off his construction. For precisely that reason, it remains an experiment of thought; it may be admirably ingenious, but it does not mirror life.

What is striking in both systems is the unconcealed evolutionistic thoughts. Descending step by step through civilizations, we arrive at a lowest point where man emerges from the animal stage. In this hypothetical primal situation one cannot speak of religion. Man must first live as man with the outside world and with his own psyche to become aware of the supernatural. Animism is the first fruit of such experiences. From this starting point in the theory, logical deduction can derive one stage from another and ascend in the end to monotheism, which itself will give way to a pure philosophical deism. Beside this there is an evolution of morals, from a savage horde existing in total amorality to the Christian community, in which the high moral standard reflects lofty concepts of God.

The exposition is completely a priori. Some bestiality is posited at the beginning, and a man is conceived who is lower than Neanderthal. The method of this evolutionistic hypothesis is to compare what is unknown or little known to what is known. One looks for constant factors, which acquire the significance of general phenomena. Further thought is given to the function of these phenomena in religion. The most simple of these constant factors are assigned their place in the realm of child psychology. Indeed, no hesitation is felt in descending into the psychic life of animals, who already show the signs of fear and awe.

The comparative method separates the complex from the simple. More involved material must be dated to a later stage. Thus, one can establish what are the later products of a stronger intellect and more developed culture. A residue remains that is universally human and part of the primitive stage, for whatever is common to men must have the deepest roots in his being and must have been with him since his appearance on earth.

Then, by comparing religious phenomena, the evolutionary scheme acquires the aspect of unshakable reality. Humanity must have passed through the listed phases in the indicated sequence; there is no space for spontaneous growth or for any singular predispositions among different races. If at a certain level the religious forms of a people are not what the scheme suggests, one is entitled to remedy the deficiency. If a step in the development cannot be established, it must have disappeared through an unnatural atrophy or because of outside pressure.

The nineteenth century could think only along these lines. Cultural development, too, must have had its fixed course. The spirit was an aspect of biology; it was subject to the same laws. Theories such as Tylor's and Spencer's are pure intellectualizing. They attribute the idea of a soul to an attempt to explain some phenomena of the world. Indeed, according to Tylor, primitive man was a pure logical causalist when he concluded that the person of a dream-experience or the agent of life in a body must be explained as what is called soul.

If religions take form according to the laws that reason can establish, what then is faith? It becomes a by-product produced at a certain moment when inexplicable and powerful emotions suddenly rise up in man. Moreover, it is suggested that religion really has its origin in dreams and hallucinations—wholly unreal phenomena that have no value for modern man. It is no surprise that such a view was ammunition for all those who belittled religion as "imaginary."

The evolutionistic view must be a mistake. Next to *homo faber* or *homo oeconomicus* there is certainly reason to speak of *homo religiosus*. Emotion and imagination, as well as the intellect, have been human qualities from the beginning and so has a receptivity for the transcendent. This is man's heritage. When a primitive sees spirits in animals, in things, or in nature, he sees by virtue of his religious sense and not after a process of thought arrived at through certain psychic experiences.

The animism theory cannot be the definitive answer to the problem of religion. The problem is more subtle. Yet, few hypotheses in the science of religion have been as successful. Particularly in ethnological circles, this theory has been dominant for a long time. Many historians of religion and philosophers of culture accepted it, perhaps in a somewhat modified form. For the theory was modified in the course of time. Most of the rigorous scheme had to be dropped. What remained was the conviction that some evolution must have occurred and that the ascent to higher forms must have come with political and social changes—especially with the development of the intellect as disclosed in science and philosophy.

Preanimism

In 1900 R. R. Marett published an essay entitled "Preanimistic Religion" in the journal *Folk-Lore*.[2] It immediately raised great interest, which was to be expected during a time that was eager to trace the line of evolution as far back as possible. Marett notes that Tylor's animism is vague: it manifests itself in feelings that are barely related to any idea. Therefore, he asks himself whether the belief in spirits might not have been preceded by something yet more original.

Marett finds this more ancient belief in what is usually called by the Melanesian word "mana." He defines mana: it is an element spirits and gods have in common; it is present in what is magical and mystical, in what is beyond and below the world, in what is unknown in us and what is unknown outside us. It is the supernatural and supernormal. Or to reword it: it is the "awful" and everything in which it shows itself is an awe-inspiring power —or in short, a "power."[3] When phenomena of nature reveal this "power," we can speak of "animatism"; we cannot say animism, as the notion of "spirit" or "ghost" is still lacking. In a phenomenon like the storm, primitive man discerns some sort of personality or will but no more. Real animism comes only from the fear and respect ("awe") for animals that make an uncanny impression, like the serpent.

In his preface to the collection *The Threshold of Religion* (1909) Marett disclaims Wundt's interpretation of his own thinking. Wundt had credited Marett with the preanimistic hypothesis, and he used it to design a theory of the origin of religion that conflicted with Tylor's animism. Wundt's thinking was partly hazy, for Marett accepts animism unconditionally as a primitive form of religion, while he also wants to assume an earlier, still simpler stage of religion. One should not, however, infer from these two things that he has in mind an evolution from something abstract to something concrete. What he has in mind is a vague notion that comes into focus and becomes differentiated.[4]

In a later article, "The Conception of Mana," published in the same collection, Marett clarifies his ideas. He begins by quoting Bishop Codrington on the Melanesian "mana." Marett compares it with similar concepts among the North-American Indians; Siouan "wakan," Iroquois "orenda," Algonquin "manitu." Although mana can be present in a setting of animism, it is nonetheless distinct from it. Mana is the minimum religious definition: "supernatural power."[5] According to Marett, this preanimism should be understood not historically but in a purely phenomenological sense; it is an endeavor to classify facts. As Marett himself notes, the time for writing a complete history of religion has not arrived.[6]

Because preanimism sounds older than animism (in spite of clarifications to the contrary), the more neutral term "dynamism" developed. Dynamism refers to power alone. The theory of dynamism shortly became an elementary part of the ethnologist's study of primitive religions. Before long it was also believed that in higher religions traces of this belief in power could be demonstrated, as in the "brahman" of the Indians or the "numen" of the Romans.

It is obvious that religious objects are charged with power. The question is whether man has ever conceived of power without an agent. Since it is always Codrington's book that is quoted on mana, we shall pay close attention to what Codrington actually said. Bishop Codrington, who made scrupulous observations of the Melanesians, defines mana as:

> . . . what works to effect everything which is beyond the ordinary power of men and outside the common process of nature; it is present in the atmosphere of life, attaches itself to persons and to things, and shows itself in results which are unmistakably its own.[7]

At first glance this is like Marett's definition. Codrington says that mana "attaches itself to persons and to things"; one could deduce that it also exists by itself, even though it becomes apparent through agents. But if we read on we are told:

> But this power, though impersonal itself, is *always connected* with someone who directs it; all spirits have it, ghosts generally, and some men.[8]

Further he says:

> A man may have so close a connection with a spirit or ghost that he has mana in himself too, and can so direct it as to effect what he desires . . . If a man has been successful in fighting . . . he has certainly the mana of a spirit or of some deceased warrior to empower him.

And further:

> The Melanesians believe in the existence of beings personal, intelligent, full of *mana,* with a certain bodily form which is visible but not fleshly like the bodies of men. These they think to be more or less actively concerned in the affairs of men, and they invoke and otherwise approach them. These may be called spirits; but it is important to distinguish between spirits who are beings of an order higher than mankind, and the disembodied spirits of men, which have become in the vulgar sense of the word ghosts.[9]

Thus, in fact, the religion of the Melanesians is a form of animism. They have known an impersonal power, which supposedly appeared very early in their religion, but who can separate what is in living practice inseparably connected? What is noteworthy in the beliefs of these Melanesians is that the efficaciousness of the spirits is clearly distinguished from them and given its own name. But this is not so curious. Let us take the classical example by Codrington: someone finds a peculiarly shaped stone and leaves it at the foot of a fruit tree or buries it in his garden. A good harvest follows: the stone has mana.

What else would one expect a man to say? A relic is brought to an invalid, and he gets well: the relic has mana. Someone who suffers from scrofula touches the cloak of a French or English king, for the cloak has a therapeutic power: the cloak has mana. This much is observed; what causes the power is not so obvious. Of the relic we know that its miracles must be the work of a saint. Of the royal cloak we know that its power derives from the person of the king, consecrated at his coronation in Christian times, or, in pagan days, descended from the gods.

The Melanesian observes that his stone gives him a good crop and decides that the stone has power, or in Marett's words, a "supernatural power." The source of this power is hidden from him. Yet it would be naïve of us to assume that the cause of the power lay simply in the stone's peculiar shape. The shape is just an indication of the stone's peculiar potential; stones can be tested only by experience. If the test is successful, the stone has mana.

Consequently, I think we should agree with Codrington that the efficacious power of mana is always the influence of a spirit, although other ethnologists, such as Graebner, find this doubt-ful.[10] With this picture of mana, we have approached ideas of magic. Those scholars who consider magic more ancient than religion—a problem we shall come back to—are of course inclined to extend their theory here and take mana into the sphere of magic. Then the idea of mana becomes religious only when it becomes related to personal beings.

It is clear that in his relations with power, man cannot always locate its source. The example of the stone proves that. One must call the thing miraculous. Tregear's *Maori-Polynesian Comparative Dictionary* circumscribes mana as "supernatural power, divine authority, having qualities which normal persons or objects do not have." Just this dictionary listing shows convincingly how complex the concept of mana is. Let us note that our word "sacred" is not less complex.

Considering Codrington's evidence, it seems to me that we have no right to separate the Melanesian concept from its animistic context. Power must always be related to an agent, even if we have to leave the agent undefined for the present. For an elementary definition of religion, it is dangerous to use the circumscription "impersonal power." Yet it is in that sense that Marett formulates it: a certain coherent, concrete state of reflection, in which ideas and states of emotion together directly evoke an activity. Marett's reasoning is imperfect: it veers dangerously close to that school in the history of religions that sees the origin of religion not in a veneration of gods but in a stage at which no god at all existed.

Finally, it should be pointed out that the concept of mana is lacking precisely among the most primitive tribes but occurs in societies on the cultural level of the patriarchal kinship system, mainly nomadic cattle breeders. These are predominantly totemistic peoples, with a strictly organized social structure and powerful chiefs or kings. They are very far from representing a "primal" civilization. The real representatives of a primal civilization are the Australian tribes and the African Pygmies; among them we will not find mana unmixed with animistic strains but something entirely different.

Beliefs in a Creator-God

Andrew Lang (1844-1912) was an avowed opponent of the philological school (as that of Kuhn and Max Müller) and chose Tylor's idea of animism as the earliest form of religion.[11] Then he chanced on a report of the Benedictine missions in West Australia that established the fact that the tribes in the area, who were most primitive in all other respects, held a kind of belief that seemed far from primitive. This problem intrigued Lang. Naturally, he began by doubting the accuracy of the report. He extended his own research to other peoples on a low cultural level: the Andaman Islanders of Southern Asia, the Zulus, Middle African tribes, and North American Indians. But everywhere he confirmed the report of the Benedictines, and he abandoned his skepticism.

Among the Australians, who were living at the most primitive cultural stage of hunting and food gathering and who did not even know the art of baking pots, there proved to be a belief in a highest being, named differently among different tribes. Anthropologists usually represent this type of high god by Baiame, the god who is venerated by the Wiradjuri and Kamilaroi tribes in southeast Australia. Baiame is foremost a creator-god, who made people out of animals or clay and gave them laws. He watches over the execution of his commandments; after death, everyone must appear before him. Three things are unforgivable to him: murder, deceiving the eldest of the tribe, and taking another man's wife. An especially emphatic commandment of Baiame is to be good to the old and weak. The women pray to Baiame for rain; sorcerers pray for a long life and at burials pray that the dead be accepted into his realm. The tribe of the Euahlaji, who worship Baiame, call him "All-father" in their secret ceremonies and say that all tribes are obedient to his laws.

Naturally this creator-god shows small variations in other parts of the world. The Bushmen on the Kalahari Desert call the god Kage, and tell of him that he created everything. When they pray, they say: "O Kage, Kage, are we not your children? Do you not see our hunger? Feed us!" It is interesting that this god is said to have been very good in the beginning but grew ever more disposed to evil because he has had to endure so much. Perhaps this Kage is connected with the grasshopper "Kaggen" who created the moon.

This deity is also known to the Bantus. He is always good to them. But he has become a *deus otiosus*: he lives in heaven and has withdrawn from humankind. And he is not really worshiped any longer. On the other hand, some tribes consider him the dispenser of rain and sunshine. This lesser significance of the deity may be because of the court of gods beside him, whom he has created and who execute his will. The people address their offers and prayers to these intermediaries. Moreover, the Bantu tribes have a highly developed ancestor cult.

If we try to define these beliefs, which occur only in very primitive tribes, we might speak of some sort of monotheism. This is very surprising. Furthermore, these tribes prove to have high ethical norms. One report concerning the Australians on the north coast—dated as early as 1668!—mentions that a major trait of the population is beneficence. The native shares his food and even his possessions. Whether much or little, everyone receives his portion, youngsters and weak old men who cannot gather food as well as the strong.

All this information was a complete departure. Primal man was supposed to be a semi-animal, an atheist and an immoralist. In sexual matters he was imagined as completely promiscuous. But the least developed peoples, as a rule, have a monogamous marriage form. In fact, in each specific, the exact contrary of the customary opinion proved to be true. Had Rousseau been right with his romantic words about the good savage? It was hard to believe. Lang was accurate when he wrote that, like other martyrs of science, he expected to be regarded as inopportune and troublesome, as a man fixed on one single idea, and a wrong one at that.

Opposition was indeed on the way. Lang's findings were in flagrant contradiction with long-standing ideas. Tylor, who must have felt particularly affected, took up the gauntlet. He tried to explain that bothersome faith in a creator by suggesting that the missionaries had been its inspiration.[12] The creator-god is then an imitation of the Christian god, somehow conveyed to the natives and somehow accepted. This hypothesis would be supported by the vagueness of the god's character. He would be a supreme deity superimposed on indigenous beliefs. Hence, the natives would not really know what to do with him. This all too easy rebuttal by Tylor was itself negated by the fact that a similar monotheism was recorded among the North American Indians before the activity of Christian missionaries. Moreover, there was sound evidence that the Australian tribes believed in a father-like creator-god long before any missionary's arrival.

Other scholars found other solutions to the puzzle. Lang had emphasized that this high god could not be a mythical portrayal of a powerful chief, for the simple reason that these Australian tribes did not have such chiefs. Nevertheless, Howitt tried to suggest that the god was analogous to the tribal chief on earth. He even thought that the god's name, "Father," could be explained in this manner. It is true that Lang overshot the mark, for among the Australian tribes such tribal chiefdoms do occur. All the same, Howitt's solution is too far-fetched. How could the All-father, sitting alone on his heavenly chair, be an imitation of a tribal chief surrounded by a council of elders?

Another ardent opponent of Lang's thesis was Sidney Hartland. His a priori point of view is striking in itself; it is improbable, he argues, that naked savages without any organized government—primal horde!—unable even to count to seven, would have developed such a lofty philosophical concept. Hartland's criticism seems more serious when he denies the attributes of eternity, omnipotence, omniscience, and creativity to the deity discovered by Andrew Lang.[13] Nonetheless, this argument is erroneous. There are many among the missionaries and ethnographers who emphatically attribute these qualities to divine beings like Baiame. Hartland was carried away by his antipathy to Lang's "troublesome" hypothesis and denied without qualification the remarkable moral concepts of the Australians.

Arnold van Gennep, who made a special study of the religious concepts of the Australians,[14] tried to eliminate this type of god as a cultural hero or mythical ancestor divinized only in later times. But these heroes occur rarely among the Australian tribes and, besides, how could they explain the creator-god? R. R. Marett was even wilder when he suggested in "Preanimistic Religion" (mentioned above),

> I have to confess to the opinion with regard to Daramulun, Mungan-ngaua, Tundun and Baiame, those divinities whom the Kurnai, Murrings, Kamilaroi and other Australian groups address severally as "Our Father," recognizing in them the supernatural headmen and lawgivers of their respective tribes, that their prototype is nothing more or less than that well-known material and inanimate object, the bull-roarer.[15]

Indeed, the roaring sound of this wooden slat, swung round the head on a string, must have aroused deep awe, and of course life and power were attributed to it. However, it should be noted immediately that women and children, who are outside the mysteries of initiation, are frightened by the sound of the "bull-roarer" coming from the forest; the male initiate knows exactly what it is. And among these tribes it is not the women who create myths. Marett, without winking an eye, goes on in his arbitrary construction: after the fear of the bull-roarers come all sorts of stories about them; these stories in turn are enforced by a symbolic ritual. Thus, Marett suggests a cult that is based on fabricated stories. Such a sequence is probably very rare, if it exists at all. We can only establish the fact that the aversion to sudden, new, and disagreeable thoughts is a poor counsellor in scholarly matters. Marett's construction lacks all probability.

The debate over the existence of "primordial monotheism" ("Urmonotheismus") at the lowest level of civilization had begun. But the very idea seemed out of place among the fashionable evolutionistic opinions. Despite the inadequacy of counterarguments and the low validity of explanations offered for the phenomenon, it appeared that Lang's theory would be passed over and gradually disappear.

A change occurred when Father Wilhelm Schmidt (1868-1954) decided to enter the argument. Naturally he began with Andrew

Lang's work. But he thought it desirable to assemble more material. A special investigation was essential to study the high gods in greater detail and to discover how other and more recent religious ideas might have been affected by them. It was essential to examine tribes on the lowest culture stage for notions of a creator-god. At Schmidt's instigation, ethnologically trained missionaries were sent out to find tribes that had not previously been studied. They found the same or similar ideas among other very primitive tribes. Father Gusinde and Father Koppers went to the Fuegians, Father Schebesta went to the Negrillos of Ruanda. It has been insinuated—and this is unfair—that these expeditions went out explicitly to establish a primordial monotheism in various parts of the world. Rather, we should say that we usually find what we are looking for. Who will take offense—and this is as true with respect to spiritual life as in the natural sciences—if an investigator collects material in order to confirm some hypothesis he has already conceived? After all, when the theory of animism was in full swing, evidence on its behalf was sought continually among the primitives, and time and again it was maintained that convincing proofs had been established.

No matter how ethnologists resisted, there is no reasonable doubt that the most primitive peoples do not have an extraordinarily crude culture. There are conspicuously high moral concepts among these people, and they believe in one single creator-god, who is just and good. The problem becomes: how should primordial monotheism be explained?

Lang, a sober-minded nineteenth century man, tries to solve it in the realm of the *ratio*. According to him,

> As soon as man had the idea of "making" things, he might conjecture as to a Maker of things which he himself had not made, and could not make. He would regard this unknown Maker as a "magnified non-natural man." These speculations appear to me to need less reflection than the long and complicated processes of thought by which Mr. Tylor believes, and probably believes with justice, the theory of "spirits" to have been evolved. (See chapter 3 [of Lang].) This conception of a magnified non-natural man, who is a Maker, being given; his Power would be recognised, and fancy would clothe one who had made such useful things with certain other moral attributes, as of Fatherhood, goodness, and regard for the ethics of his children; these ethics having been developed naturally in the evolution of social

life. In all this there is nothing "mystical," nor anything, as far as I can see, beyond the limited mental powers of any beings that deserve to be called human.[16]

Hence he can define religion elsewhere[17] as the speculative belief in a superhuman power, as the moral belief that this power, transcending law, sanctions a certain manner of life, and finally as the affective belief that this power loves its children.

This view could just as well have been presented in the eighteenth century. The deistic concept of god is curiously close to the monotheism of the most primitive tribes, but it hardly seems fitting to arrive at this conception by a formal argument. Admittedly that "maker" fashioned useful things as well as many that were extremely dangerous to man. Lightning, tornados, carnivorous animals, and poisonous plants were also his work. Why did the primitives look upon this powerful maker as a loving father? Why was love suddenly the mover *par excellence,* instead of the fear that had been posited so often? Could one really imagine that such a god was born through an argument?

Understandably, a Catholic scholar such as Father Schmidt could not imagine it. Nevertheless, he emphatically recognized,[18] in accordance with Catholic theology, that faith in God must be preceded by the natural knowledge of God through reason. The question is: from where did this knowledge of God come? Here Father Schmidt allows the possibility that in primordial days at a certain moment God revealed himself to man. This idea of a "primordial revelation" is a matter of faith; it relates particularly to Christian theology. I am not refuting its validity, but I want to point out, for the sake of clarity, that in the purely scientific problem of the origin of religion a concept of a totally different order is thus inserted. Whether or not the fundamental problems of faith and religion can be solved exclusively with the ratio will be a question forever: we are here at the dividing line between faith and knowledge.

In the meantime, even if we do not pursue the origin of primordial monotheism, our difficulties with that phenomenon are not over. Even the title "monotheism" has been debated. The word means faith in one single god. Is it certain that in the case of the Australian aborigines we may speak of faith?

Nathan Söderblom (1866-1931) doubted this. It is true, he admits, that the trust of the most primitive tribes in a primordial father is well established, and we may even assume it is an essential element of religious evolution. But he will not call the type "divine." Instead of "god," he wants to use a more cautious term—"*Urheber,*" a power that brings things forth. That there is no real god he infers from the fact that this power has no cult and receives no offerings.[19] Then Söderblom makes his own hypothesis on the origin of faith, distinguishing three beginnings: animism, preanimism, and the belief in supreme beings (the last would not be present in every tradition). The odd thing is that he does not want to grant a real religious meaning to any of these three forms: they lead into religion only in the course of time; in the primal day religion was missing.

An idea similar to Söderblom's about an *Urheber* occurs in Gerardus van der Leeuw (1890-1950).[20] According to him, men must have felt the need for a very high authority, perhaps in the background, from which all other powers could be derived, including man's own, and which gave authority to the religious rite, but for the rest was not too troubled about man and would not disturb him in his human capacities. However, the institutions of this highest being must be obeyed: rites, commandments, and interdictions. He observes men in this respect and to do so even better he retires to the sky (which was not always his home). Thus, the deity is rather a preserver than a creator. Although sometimes the world's whole existence is derived from him, often he has created only a few particular things. This deity no longer acts, although once he caused a beginning and everything further is unthinkable without this first act.

Consequently, this supreme being is close to the cultural heroes and saviours or to the tribal ancestors. As *Urheber* of the rites he is, as it were, the primordial medicine man.

An objection seems necessary. Certainly the type of the supreme being must be placed separately and above the so-called cultural heroes. Most emphatically the question should be raised whether this supreme being was worshiped. If he was not, he is only an "efficient cause" or, if one will, a postulate of causal reasoning. This would make him a figure that is not a god in the proper sense of the word.

It is true that the creator-god occurs a number of times as a *deus otiosus*. After his creative act he withdraws to the sky and apparently does not make himself felt in the world. As described by Van der Leeuw, he is rather like a traffic policeman on his platform: he watches as the regulations are observed. Here and there it has been established that the creator-god does not receive offerings and that no prayers are addressed to him. This is the case sometimes but certainly not the rule. The opinions of scholars vary with their preference for one series of witnesses or the other. Either the sky being was a venerated supreme god who faded when other religious forms appeared (animism, ancestor cult), or he was a dim *Urheber* from the start, who was granted a certain amount of cult only in favorable circumstances.

Apparently it is hard to escape biases in dealing with this sort of question. Söderblom needs ethnographic data to prove his thesis. He chooses information especially from Central Australian tribes, while Father Schmidt prefers information from those of Southeast Australia, for he believes the latter represent a very ancient culture and the former are quite a recent people. Consequently, Schmidt reproaches Söderblom for neglecting completely the ethnological age of the various tribes. Söderblom does not mention the most ancient strata—such as the Pygmies, Ainu, and Fuegians—and gives only several lines to the Southeast Australians; but the Central Australian tribes alone have sixteen pages of text and thus make up the core of Söderblom's factual material.[21]

It is difficult for someone who is not an ethnologist to judge in these matters. Söderblom was an historian of religions who utilized ethnographic materials for his theses. Father Schmidt, on the other hand, was an ethnologist, thoroughly acquainted with these materials, who demonstrated his knowledge of the age of cultural phenomena by constructing a scheme of cultural development (the so-called *Kulturkreislehre,* or "theory of culture circles," which we shall discuss more elaborately later).

Beyond all doubt, a supreme celestial being exists among peoples at the lowest level of civilization. The question is only in how to define it. One scholar wants merely an *Urheber* (a "primal instigator"), while another insists on using the predicate "God." And there are other interpretations. In 1922, the Italian historian of religions Raffaele Pettazzoni (1883-1959) published the first volume of his *Dio, Formazione e sviluppo del monoteismo nella storia delle religioni* ("God; Origin and Development of Monotheism in the History of Religions"). This volume deals with the primitive beliefs in a supreme being. In the introduction Pettazzoni summarizes his main thesis:

> Thus it seems to me that this supposed primordial monotheism, which all by itself would be tantamount to the first

and original moment of human religion, must be reduced
to the more modest proportion of a belief in a Supreme
Celestial Being, conceived as a personal form of the sky in
accordance with the mythical thought which determines all
forms of primitive religiosity.[22]

Pettazzoni begins by assuming that of all the parts of nature
that primitive man could have meditated on none was more conducive to a sublime, majestic thought than the sky. This assumption seems quite unfounded to me. There are nations who observed the sun or the moon with special interest and reverence.
The Panbabylonists developed a theory that deemed the Pleiades
the inspiring constellation *par excellence.* There is an extrava-
ganza of phenomena in nature, as the thunder and daybreak
mythologists knew. But what supports the thesis that primal man
assembled all these celestial phenomena in the sky and that this
really rather abstract presence moved him to become religious?
It is even questionable whether nature in the first place inspired
man to a religious sentiment. Could it not have been his awareness of his personal self and the problems contained within it?
Furthermore, how could Pettazzoni's theory harmonize with the
conviction among those primitive tribes that the supreme being
withdrew to the sky after the creation? Does that not imply that
perhaps the god was not originally celestial?

Of course, Pettazzoni had to deal with the question that has
puzzled so many: how does the observation of the sky lead to a
cult of a personal being? Pettazzoni's answer is simple. Personification is an activity of the imagination or, rather, of imagining
and intuiting or, even more precisely, of that form of intuition
that is mythic. What really happens is this: the supreme being
personifies not only a first cause (and so basically a logical conception) but a perceptible element of nature—the sky.[23]

This reasoning is refined but not very satisfactory. The transformation brought on by that mystifying "mythical thought" does
not help matters. As Pettazzoni admits, the sky seems really much
less fit for personification than, for example, the sun or the moon.
The following explanation by Pettazzoni can hardly be called
clear: the personifying apperception of the sky was reduced to
applying a personality to a being that is at work behind the
celestial phenomena and that is in itself a center of the many
phases of atmospheric life. This reasoning suggests that what is
personified is something at work behind the sky that sums itself
up in the life of the atmosphere. This, however, is an abstraction

and verges on being an allegory: it is hard to imagine that it would give rise to a real religious figure.

Once the supreme beings attracted attention, there were plenty of endeavors to work them into a fashionable system of interpretation. Each scholar seemed to work them into his own train of thought. Thus Emile Durkheim (1858-1917), who considered totemism the most ancient form of religion, tried to deal with these beliefs in a high god:

> Far from being derived from a different source than the regular totemic beliefs, they are, on the contrary, only the logical working-out of these beliefs and their highest form.
> We have already seen how the notion of mythical ancestors is implied in the very principles upon which totemism rests, for each of them is a totemic being. Now, though the great gods are certainly superior to these, still, there are only differences of degree between them; we pass from the first to the second with no break of continuity. In fact, a great god is himself an ancestor of especial importance.[24]

This exposition taxes the reader's patience. It virtually bypasses the ethnological facts. The most primitive tribes, who worship a creator-god, are marked by the absence of clearly pronounced totemism.

After studying the phenomenon of the supreme being, Robert Harry Lowie (1883-1957) concluded that Father Schmidt's logical premises were acceptable but that it is impossible to reconstruct a monotheistic phase of religion on the basis of what is found among the primitive peoples.

> On some of these tribes, such as the Tasmanians and the Congolese Pygmies, information is practically non-existent, hence they must be completely disregarded. In the case of the Andamanese, for whom our accounts are most satisfactory, individual and local variability is so great that only certain features can be assumed to represent the proto-Andamanese creed, and they are precisely not in harmony with the monotheistic theory.[25]

At this time, there is no final word on the matter. When Adolf E. Jensen (1899-1965) speaks of supreme deities,[26] he grants their importance, yet establishes the fact that they always exist among other forms. Furthermore, he points out that they are abstract and out of touch with events on earth. Jensen's exposition is not quite convincing either. We know even the most primitive tribes only from a recent phase of their development. Further, the other religious forms found alongside a supreme being are not that important; what matters is the existence of such a being, which cannot be deduced from those other forms. Admittedly, he is often a *deus otiosus,* but there we may be seeing the degeneration of a belief; there are also examples where he is worshiped.

The consequences of primordial monotheism are so farreaching for religio-historical theory that the opposition to it is understandable. Thinking in terms of evolution is quite ingrained, and it is hard to give it up. Yet the line dynamism—animism-fetishism-polytheism—proves to be a mere fancy of ours. Apparently, there are many cases where it makes more sense to speak of degeneration than of evolution, for if there is some form of monotheism at the beginning—beside this high, moral, and abstract God—all the other forms almost seem to be a "fall" of man. It is exactly this impression, resembling Jewish and Christian theology, that makes many scholars hesitate to defend a primordial monotheism.

We should also note here that Father Schmidt spoke of a "primordial revelation" *("Uroffenbarung").* Coming from a Catholic clergyman this is important. It may provide an opening for certain dogmatic inclinations. Naturally it evoked a reaction, often sharp, from agnostic ethnologists and historians of religion. Nevertheless, I do not think that *Uroffenbarung* should be made a point of discussion. Schmidt introduced the notion, but he said expressly that he wanted it to be considered as a personal opinion. One *might* explain a primal monotheism in this manner, and such would be an acceptable solution for a Catholic theologian, but it is not more than an assumption. Schmidt is not really trying to reveal the genesis of primordial monotheism; he only tries to prove that it exists, specifically on the most primitive level of religion. Undoubtedly, we are faced at this point with fundamental questions. As soon as a primal form of religious awareness is designated, our intelligence demands an explanation for it. Such an explanation can only be hypothetical. Whether its source is intellectual or personally religious is irrelevant. The hypothesis preserves its hypothetical nature. It would be deplorable if further research fixed itself on Father Schmidt's personal assumption; then a scientific problem would be obscured by cloudy controversies about world views.

The Mother Goddess

In more differentiated religions the skygod has a female partner, Mother Earth. This pair is so familiar that our inclination is to attribute them to a very early stage of religious development. But if we presume that a masculine deity was venerated at the beginning, the question occurs as to when and in what circumstances a mother goddess appeared at his side. Or perhaps—there are various possibilities—we assume that each of the two belonged to his own "culture circle" and that the two autonomous deities were joined only later to form the illustrious couple.

There are many signs that even long ago a mother goddess had a dominant role in the cultic life of many nations. We find her cult well established in a vast area around the ancient Mediterranean and further to the east in Babylon and Assyria. We read about it in classical sources. Herodotus informs us that the Assyrians called Aphrodite by the name of Mylitta, the Arabs by Alitta and the Persians by Mitra. The last, of course, is the well known masculine Aryan divinity; Herodotus is thought to have meant Anāhita, who is usually called Anaïtis by the Greeks. In Lydia, in the first century of our era, a goddess Artemis was known, but hers was merely a Greek name for the indigenous goddess Nanaïa. These original names occur among nations outside the Indo-European group and hence are not Indo-European names; they suggest a divinity that may have been venerated in the east from time immemorial. In Syria, the great goddess occurs with the name 'Atar'ata; in Arabia, Athtar; in Babylon, Ishtar; in Phoenicia, Astarte; and in Carthage, Tanit. All in all, it seems not only that a similar type of mother goddess was known to all these nations but that her names are somehow related and are perhaps derived from a common root. It is possible to conclude that in these lands she has been among the most divine powers, as we said, since time out of mind.

By nature a mother goddess grants fertility. Woman, who gives birth, is the prototype of all generation. Even in prehistoric images we can observe the constant emphasis on the breasts and the organs of generation. She is most intimately connected with all realms of nature—the animal kingdom and the plants. We know her in ancient Crete as the *potnia thèron* or the mistress of animals; she is depicted between two animals, usually lions or panthers. Sometimes the animals are peaceful and seem to be in her service; sometimes she seizes them violently and apparently wants to tame them. The famous lion gate of Mycenae shows the same imagery—only in this case, as in many others, the goddess herself is replaced by an aniconic symbol—the pillar. In short, the mother goddess has a double relation to the beasts, and presumably she was related to the wild animals before she was related to the domesticated. She probably was the motherly deity who guaranteed abundant offspring in animal life—which was vital in those days when hunting was the chief mode of subsistence. The cult of this goddess may have been important in the domestication of animals. Perhaps some wild creatures were not killed, but dedicated to the mother goddess and set aside in sacred places for her cult. When the domesticated animal began its crucial role in man's existence and when cattle breeding developed, the goddess must have become more significant. Instead of the lion or panther, the images began to show the domestic cow and horse.

The time of agricultural expansion was very differently oriented from the hunting and pastoral days. Yet in this period, too, the mother goddess retained her significance and perhaps even reached the peak of her power. She became the mother of vegetation. How important this development is can be seen in the Greek figure Demeter: the tremendous distance in time from the lion-goddess of Crete to the goddess of the Eleusinian mysteries suggests also a distance in refinement and depth of religious experience. The cultic climax of the Eleusinian mysteries was the celebration of a *hieros gamos* ("sacred marriage") of hierophant and priestess.

The assembly waited in darkness. Suddenly a light shone and the hierophant exclaimed: "The divine one gave life to a holy child, the powerful goddess to a powerful god!" And he showed the assembly an ear of grain. The Eleusinian mysteries are far from transparent in meaning and in terms of historical components. Yet, some points can be suggested. This sacred marriage reveals how the mother goddess was introduced into a cult in which a masculine deity was predominant. The ear of grain relates to the slow transformation from an animal-centered culture to one where grain was crucially significant.

One is inclined to say that the mother goddess is a benefactor, granting well being throughout the cultural stages. This is not quite true. The goddess is ambivalent. She is the feminine power who, on one hand, bestows her blessing and, on the other, strikes with destruction and death. The Greek concept of Artemis as kindly disposed and harsh at the same time is typical of this ambivalence of nature. The cruel mother goddess was often venerated in bloody and cruel cultic acts—so the Greeks related of their neighbors, the Carthaginians, for instance. We are told of priests called Galli who wounded and castrated themselves in ecstasy. In the nineteenth century, the British administration in India abolished the gruesome sacrifices of hundreds of humans to a demanding mother goddess.

The mother goddess is mistress equally of life and death. The striking image of both these reigns is the seed that dies, only to be born again. Kore is kidnapped by Pluto and rules as Persephone in the netherworld, visiting the surface each spring to make the grain prosper. One might think this simply a poetic metaphor, but the figure of the mother goddess must always have functioned as a symbol, weaving life with death. Possibly there is some indication of this in a burial custom that goes back into prehistory—burying the dead in a crouching position. Even in early Sumer and Akkad, graves contained a squatting corpse; this custom suggests an imitation of the foetus in the womb. Thus, the corpse was deposited in Mother Earth, symbolizing the certainty of a new life.

In a cultural phase when the mother goddess is central in the cult, it seems natural that in social life women will dominate. One thinks first of matriarchy, the institution whereby some scholars infer that at one time women were heads of families and inheritance was matrilineal. The name of Johann Jacob Bachofen (1815-87) is linked with the study of and speculation in these problems. His book *Das Mutterrecht, eine Untersuchung über die Gynaikokratie der alten Welt nach ihrer religiösen und rechtlichen Natur* ("Matriarchy, a Study of Gynecocracy in the Ancient World, According to its Religious and Legal Nature"), published in 1861, made matriarchy a current and much disputed hypothesis of ethnology and sociology. This book belongs to that group of imposing works that do not become antiquated because they contain the breath of life imparted by a great and sensitive scholar. However one may judge the hypothesis he unfolded (with great erudition) one cannot help admiring Bachofen's warmth and earnestness as he tries to discover the lasting values in the mythical structures. He has been called a belated Romantic.[27] It may be true, but at the present time that might well be considered a title of honor again, for this scholar, at work in a world of rationalism, shares with the Romantics a precious gift: fundamentally it was a true interest in religion that impelled his scholarship.

Bachofen noticed elements in Greek religious life that for long had been nearly imperceptible and yet were of paramount significance. For this reason, later research has never been able to ignore completely his points of view. Whether his formulation of *Mutterrecht* ("matriarchy") was fortunate is of less importance. The corrections his theory needed came from facts observed among primitive peoples. It is quite certain that nothing, or hardly anything, is known about societies in which women wield real power, in the sense of central political power. Everywhere we look the maintenance of authority is the burden of men. Only—and in this respect Bachofen's work was an eye-opener— it makes a difference whether a man has this authority on the basis of his patrilineal or his matrilineal descent. In matriarchy, the descent from the female determines the child's family group or clan. Not the father but the mother's brothers are responsible for the child's education.

What concerns us most, however, is not the essence of matriarchy. What we look for are the unmistakable signs—no matter how they are defined—of the cultural and religious significance of woman in her role of procreator. In a culture that acknowledges this significance the part of women is of considerable importance.

The cult of the great mother is doubtless behind these signs of matriarchy. Clearly, the social systems of this order were once wide-spread in Europe, too. This can be established by studying certain peculiar features of many nations whose overall structure is patrilineal. Among the Germanic tribes, there is a hint in the significant function of maternal uncles. There are several traces among the Celts, and such features among the Picts were known even to the classical authors. There is evidence of this kind in India, also. Thus, it seems that wherever they settled the Indo-Europeans found a more ancient population with some cult of a mother goddess and, accordingly, some sort of matriarchal organization. Such traces extend from western Europe to Indonesia.

The question arises, how ancient exactly is this ancient veneration of the mother goddess? Jean Przyluski's book, entitled *La Grande Déesse* (*The Great Goddess*), was published in 1950 after his death and is very knowledgeable and original in constructing the history of the goddess cult. Przyluski believed it may have existed in the Palaeolithic era. After all, that era has its odd little statues of women, characterized by an accentuation of certain parts of the body. The figures appeared in France (Brassempouy, Lespugue, Laussel) and immediately took the fancy of archaeologists and art historians. The Venus of Willendorf is usually referred to as the prototype. This figurine from lower Austria is made of limestone and is colored red. It is a naked woman, with large hanging breasts, broad hips and a big belly. Her arms, which are trifling in proportion to the whole image, are placed over her breasts. The date assigned to the Venus is the period 25,000-20,000 B.C. Since attention was first drawn to this type of image, many examples have been found, some as far away from Europe as Siberia. In most cases they are made of wood, and we may assume that we have found only a small fraction and that most of them have perished in the soil. It is established that in general these figurines are not found in cult sites but—as in middle and eastern Europe—in homes, sometimes in a special recess in the wall.

What did primitive man have in mind with these plastic images? Shortly after the first ones had been discovered and at a time when an exaggerated significance was given to examples like the Venus of Willendorf, they were interpreted as profane artistic products. Karl Schuchhardt definitely rejected the thought that this Venus could represent a fertility goddess.[28] He rightly noted the position of head and arms; the head with its odd coiffure is bent down deeply, and the expression conveyed by the hands as they cover the breasts is one of devotion. It seemed apparent that this was an image of devotion rather than the posture of a powerful goddess. Still, were other interpretations possible? Could this be a divine personage giving all its attention to maternity? The bowing head seems to say that the eye of the goddess, and so of the devotee as well, is turned in reverence to the mystery of motherhood. The hands on the breasts may mean the same; there are images elsewhere in which the goddess seems to press her breasts with her hands; this can only call to mind woman the nurse. There are few who agree any more with Schuchhardt.

But who is this goddess, if she is a goddess? We should bear in mind that these figurines belong to the ancient Stone Age. Man was living by the hunt of big game; there was nothing resembling agriculture. Thus, the presence of a great goddess, who occurs as a central force only in agricultural societies, becomes problematic. Przyluski, too, wrestles with the problem and suggests shifting the discussion from religion to magic. He says the figurines are not idols but objects that could be used for fertility magic. Thus, these Venus figures would not yet be images of the mother goddess but would anticipate her cult.

In my estimation, Przyluski's hypothesis is wrong in taking for granted that magic precedes religion. It is as if he is afraid to see a goddess venerated in such an ancient phase of culture. It is true, of course, that Palaeolithic man practiced magic. It is enough to think of the animal pictures he drew with such marvellous realism on the walls of caves. He drew the animals he hunted (mammoth, bison, reindeer), and the pictures probably related to hunting magic: the arrow drawn on a body must certainly be a symbolic sign of hunting luck.

But the magic explanation is not satisfying in this instance. A figurine like the Venus of Willendorf is carved with too much care and craft to be only a serviceable tool in fertility magic. K. J. Narr,[29] the most recent investigator, considers the possibility of its having a religious function and we are inclined to follow him in the matter. Still this does not constitute a final solution. What could the adoration of a female deity mean in a Palaeolithic hunting culture? One might like to recall the *potnia thèron* ("mistress of the animals"), the more so because the Siberian hunting tribes have a lord of animals who oversees success in the hunt and the welfare of the game. But he is a lord of animals and not a *potnia* ("mistress"). Moreover, what is meant by the emphasis on the female organs? On Crete there is no such emphasis in the images of the mistress of the animals. Is it possible after all, Narr asks, that we have found a goddess of fertility, and could it be that women were rather important in the economic constellation of the Old Stone Age? We cannot answer these questions, he concludes.

I am inclined to see in these figurines the image of a mother goddess—one who was venerated for the sake of fertility and specifically for the preservation of game. There is no reason to believe that woman the life-giver is linked only with the new role women assumed in the preparation of plant food at some early date. I should think, rather, of an attachment, felt even then, between the human and the animal world. Fertility of woman meant fertility of the animals. It is not out of place to think of a similar correlation in higher agricultural civilizations between woman and the grain crop. The sexual relations of the farmer and his wife on the freshly sown field enhanced the growth and ripening of the grain.

The fact that male figures are almost totally lacking in the Palaeolithic finds does not entitle us to draw conclusions. An absence usually does not prove much. There are no birds among the game of the rock paintings; would that prove that birds were not hunted? This raises the problem that one thing is depicted and another is not. Who would dare answer such questions? The presence of a creator-god in Stone Age religion is not overruled by the fact that no pictures were made of him. The very nature of this deity, on his celestial throne, stands in the way of plastic representation. It is very well possible that the Ancient Stone Age knew a creator-god and that the big game hunt gave birth to his divine life-giving partner.

While the idea of a mother-goddess cult in the Palaeolithic period remains problematic, the extraordinary significance of such a cult in later ages cannot be overestimated. The most ancient mother figurines in Egypt are believed to date to at least 3000 B.C. In Mesopotamia they occur as early as the Chalcolithic period. But these are lands where agriculture was very early. Obviously, this was the origin of the constellation of fertility powers. Agriculture—at least in its earliest form of gardening— marks the growing importance of women in the economic and social structure. Men continued to hunt, but women, predisposed by nature, became the guardians of the plants. Gradually, agriculture grew in importance, and the prestige of women gained accordingly. Thus, the worship of a fertility goddess is not difficult to explain.

The arguments Przyluski levels against Father Schmidt are quite insufficient. Following previous attempts, he suggests that primal monotheism among primitive peoples displays the influence of higher cultures and even of Christian or Muslim sources. It has been sufficiently demonstrated that this cannot be true. Przyluski's reasoning at this point is a mere subterfuge to silence a witness who might confound his own theory. Indeed, is there any reason to put a creator-god and a mother goddess in such sharp opposition? They had their cults, in their proper time and place. The intriguing question for the history of religions is how their paths crossed and how they united in a common cult.

It is also important to examine traces of the cult of a mother goddess in the polytheism of Indo-Europeans and Semites with their strictly patriarchal organization. In these cases a more an-

cient population stratum may be discerned that can fairly be
called matriarchal. But the work of indicating these cultural
amalgamations requires caution. The equations of names that
Przyluski forces (Indra and the hermaphroditic [?] Hittite Inara
or, even worse, Mars and Artemis) can only bring such studies
into disrepute. It seems unlikely that indubitably masculine gods
such as Indra and Mars could derive from ancient mother goddesses.

If the cult of the mother goddess relates especially to the practice of agriculture, this suggests a relatively recent age, since agriculture is a rather recent stage of civilization. Future research
will learn more accurately the relation between the *potnia thèron*
and the mother goddess properly so-called.

Totemism

The word "totem" occurs in the language of the Ojibways, a
North American Indian tribe. It refers to a class of objects, whose
name is borne by a clan or a group that feels kinship and soli-
darity with the object and deals with it in a special way. Once
these totems were noted, the same and similar things were discovered all over the world. Expectably, the Ojibway word was
used for other—not always identical—phenomena, and the concept of totemism became more vague. This development explains
various attempts to return to a more accurate definition.

Arnold van Gennep was aware of the careless usage of the concept of totemism and gave his own definition under four points:[30]

1. belief in a relationship between a group of people akin to
    each other and a species of animals or plants or certain
    objects;

2. in religious life this belief is expressed in a number of
    positive rites to ensure one's relationship to the totemic
    group and negative rites (prohibitions);

3. socially totemism affects certain marriage regulations: re-
    stricted exogamy;

4. the totemic group bears the name of its totem.

For Father Schmidt the main features of totemism are the following: the belief that one stems from the totem or at least that

one is akin to it (because of this, marrying within the totemic group is forbidden); often, though not always, the injunction that the totem animal or plant must be neither killed nor eaten by the members of its own group. It is circumstantial whether the kinship system is determined as patriarchy or matriarchy.[31]

Finally, G. van der Leeuw defines totemism as follows:[32]

1. the group bears the name of the totem;
2. the totem is accounted its ancestor;
3. the totem involves sundry tabus, such as
   a. the prohibition against killing or eating the totem, except in specific cases or under special conditions;
   b. the prohibition against intermarriage within one totem group (exogamy).

Van der Leeuw is careful enough to observe that all these features need not occur in all instances.

These definitions give some common denominator to numerous religious and social forms. Obviously, the relationship of man and totem is expressed in very different ways. As observed by F. Graebner,

> It is often believed that the ancestors of a clan were born from the animal group, but sometimes the other way round, that at one time the animals belonged to the human clan. There is probably an animistic signature when people are believed to turn into their totem animal upon death. Often the totemic relationship seems quite indistinct: the totem animal is regarded as a friend or companion of the clan. The rule however is a prohibition against killing or eating the animal, and also exogamy.[33]

In short, totemism has a religious and a social aspect. The mystical relation between clan and totem is religious, the clan organization and exogamy are social by nature. The question may be raised as to which of these aspects is the primary one. For a sociologist like E. Durkheim the answer is not hard. Totemism, which he calls nothing but the symbol of the clan's community, represents for him the foundation of all religious forms. In a totem he sees the sign by which a clan makes itself distinct. Since a totem is also the manifest form of a totem god, Durkheim draws the following forced conclusion: if a totem means at the same time a deity and a community, are not that god and the community the same thing?

Giving such weight to the fact that the clan is named for its totem, one does not get beyond a nominalistic explanation of the sort given by Max Müller, Andrew Lang, Lubbock, and Spencer: according to his characteristics, an ancestor was given the name of an animal; when the ancestor was forgotten, his animal name was preserved and people thought they had descended from a real animal! It is amazing that such superficial explanations ever convinced serious scholars.

In the meantime, it is important to pay close attention to the religious element. First of all, can totemism be called a religion? Sir James Frazer says it cannot. He argues:

> If religion implies, as it seems to do, an acknowledgement on the part of the worshipper that the object of his worship is superior to himself, then pure totemism cannot properly be called a religion at all, since a man looks upon his totem as his equal and friend, not at all as his superior, still less as his god.[34]

But it must be said that everything depends on one's definition of religion. For our part, we can only agree with Van der Leeuw when he says:

> But it is a failing of modern thought that, in connection with the term religion, it must immediately think of "gods." Totemism, however, needs no gods; it implies submergence in the power of some animal.[35]

Thus Van der Leeuw links totemism to the animal worship that developed in hunting cultures, and he compares it to phenomena, like those in Germanic antiquity, in which an animal was the ancestor of a heroic or royal race. He also wants to compare it with werewolf lore and with the ancient Germanic "Berserker" (warriors who, in a religious frenzy, became bears).

Animals have played a vital role for primitive humanity, and their role has differed among the civilizations. But this does not imply that, whenever there is a close connection between an animal and a god in higher forms, such as polytheism, there must have been an earlier stage with theriomorphic deities. Although Athena is owl-eyed, she is not an owl that has assumed a human shape. When Germanic tribes, like the Cherusks or the Hundings, name themselves after animals, this does not have to be understood as animal totemism.

It does seem probable that animal totems are more ancient than totems of plants or objects, but this fact does not explain totemism. It may be good to ask if here, as in so many cases, a religious phenomenon has been explained too easily. Rightly, Adolf E. Jensen stated:

> No one will claim that this sociological phenomenon is "understood" as it stands. The fact that man feels himself related to animals, that clan members will regard themselves related in the absence of close consanguineal ties, that marriage within the group is forbidden, though one may marry a close blood relative just as long as he or she belongs to another clan—none of this is self-evident.[36]

It is strange to realize that at one time the notion of totemism was regarded as a scholarly miracle; it seemed to provide the key to the origin of religion. The French historian of religions Salomon Reinach (1858-1932) even believed that totemism itself was the earliest religion, and he never wearied of pointing out its traces in all religions, including the highest. This was not difficult, since he identified totemism very vaguely and used it for all sorts of animal worship without further qualification. At last, in 1908, without giving up his devotion to his theories, he could not help admitting that totemism was an "overridden hobby." [37]

In overestimating totemism, Reinach had a predecessor in Robertson Smith (1846-94). Smith also put totemism at the root of all religious development, and being an Old Testament scholar he sought its mark especially in the religion of the Semites, most especially in the religion of Israel.

Today the tide has turned. Pinard de la Boullaye observes:

> . . . [Now] that totemism has proved to be not *general*, not *uniform*, not *religious* (at least, not in essence) and not *primitive*, . . . it has lost much of its importance.[38]

As noted before, the study of totemism became unnecessarily complicated because all instances of relationship to animals were considered totemic. This led to a huge but confusing accumulation of facts. For example, clan and individual totems were lumped together. Nowadays, individual totems are kept quite distinct as "nagualism" (named after Central American Indian beliefs) or "manituism" (after North American Indian beliefs).

What is meant here is that an animal can be closely related to a single individual. A young Indian enters the jungle, where he fasts and mortifies himself, hoping for a vision in which his totem animal will reveal itself. This animal is an individual guardian, identified by some scholars with the soul that is manifest outside the body. The correctness of this identification is open to serious doubt. Another explanation is possible: the belief in clan totems may have suggested to individuals that each associate himself with a totem. In that case, the nature of the vision one had in a trance determined the animal, while the clan totem was fixed by tradition. It is equally possible that this nagualism has no more in common with totemism than the fact that in each case an animal functions as protector. Precisely because the totem is revealed in a trance, one may suspect an explanation in the area of shamanism. The shaman, too, invokes the help of animals in his voyages to heaven or the netherworld.

It is wrong to think that all peoples at some time had totems. Totems occur only in certain parts of the world. They have been found in Australia, Melanesia, and Polynesia, and in central and south Africa. A totemistic pattern is discernible among various Indian tribes in North and South America, but it seems to lack some characteristic features. Could totemism perhaps be a religious form linked to a certain cultural stage? Indeed. Totemism belongs to cultures with patrilineal exogamous clans that live by hunting big game. This type of culture has nothing to do with primal forms of culture, although it must be said that it is primitive. It is not unthinkable that the Ancient Stone Age in Europe, with its rock paintings and numerous animal pictures, also had totemic images of some sort. At any rate, totemism could prevail when hunting was the method of subsistence; a later stage was nomadic and pastoral, when man—who at first killed animals—tried to make them his helpers. The dog was probably tamed before any other animal; it is likely that in the last phases of pure hunting life man learned to use this intelligent and faithful animal.

Animals have an extraordinary place in the thought of hunters. The men know all the ruses and customs of the game with which they are in daily contact. To ambush an animal they may cover themselves with skins and so identify with the beast. In rites to ensure their hunting luck and the procreation of the animals they dance wearing animal masks. There are many times when man identifies with animals; the real source of totemism may lie in this fact.

The life of hunting societies led to the domestication of certain animals (yak, buffalo, reindeer, deer). Pastoral people kept a close association with the animal world. This might suggest some religious relationship to the animal, some survivals of totemism proper, yet one must realize that it is not real totemism. In addition to the Ural-Altaics, the Indo-Europeans and Semito-Hamites are nomadic pastoral peoples. Such peoples were so wide-ranging that it is not astonishing to find a continuing closeness with the animal world even in the historical period, long after the Indo-European nations had passed over to agriculture.

All these considerations are still far from explaining totemism. Like so many primitive religious ideas and symbolisms, it remains an enigma for moderns. No wonder new solutions are ventured again and again. Thus H. Petri made a novel proposal on the basis of Australian totemism.[39] Among various tribes, such as the Wondjina, the totemic ancestor is at the same time a man and an animal. To Petri this suggests an early stage when the line between man and beast wavered. Petri's thought is that those totemic ancestors basically have the same character of the dema-divinities who also belong to a bygone phase (and whom we shall discuss in Chapter 16). Petri concludes that totemism as we know it must be considered in spite of everything a late form, one that occurs in a rigidified social structure.

Chapter Sixteen

SOME OTHER
TYPES OF GODS

BESIDES distinct gods and powers that ethnology uncovered, there are further sorts of deities to which later research drew attention. A classical philologist outlined one specific type that on closer investigation proved to be a misunderstanding. Another type was formulated by an ethnologist and seems quite promising for future study.

Momentary and Functional Deities

In 1896 the classical philologist Hermann Usener (1834-1905) published a book entitled *Götternamen, Versuch einer Lehre von der religiösen Begriffsbildung* ("Names of Gods, Essay on the Formation of Religious Ideas"). His point of departure was a number of peculiar deities mentioned by Servius in his commentary on Vergil's *Georgica*. At the sacrifice on the field the *flamen* (one of a category of priests ordained for the service of specific deities) invoked not only Tellus and Ceres, according to Fabius Pictor, but also twelve other deities—Vervactor for the first plowing of the fallow land, Reparator for the second plowing, Imporcitor for the third and last, Insitor for the sowing, Obarator for plowing over the the seed, Occator for harrowing, Saritor for digging out weeds, Subruncinator for weeding, Messor for harvesting, Convector for bringing in the harvest, Conditor for piling up, and Promitor for distributing the grain. The farmer's every act, from the first plowing to the use of the crop, was guarded by a special power. And there were comparable powers, Sterculinus for manuring, Nodotus for the formation of the stalk joints, Volutina for the development of the ears before they open, Patella for the ears opening up, and several others.[1]

As Usener himself observed, these divine figures are vague, but he suggests that the farmer may still have given special weight to the litany chanted by the *flamen*. Usener is backed up by the fact that Lithuanian beliefs recognize a great many such gods who have a very limited activity. These are a handful of examples: Austheia, goddess of bees; Birzulis, god of birch foliage; Eratinis, god of lambs; Gotui, goddess of young cattle; Karvaitis, god of work on the field; Raugupatis, god of beer-yeasts.[2]

Usener gives a theory of the genesis of these special deities. To begin with, man is subject to momentary experiences that make him realize a divinity is present. He has such experiences not only with objects but also in accustomed situations or when surprising things happen. As soon as such a moment gives the value and authority of divinity to that object, situation, or happening, the "momentary deity" (*Augenblicksgott*) is experienced and created. Immediately, with no intervention of anything at all, each phenomenon is divinized. No generic category, no matter how limited, plays a role in this process: only that specific something that happens, and nothing else, is the god.[3]

Later the nature of these gods changes. Since the same momentary deities appear at each occasion of certain activities they assume continuity; they belong no longer to the moment of performance but to the activity as such. That means that men do not see at every harrowing Occator suddenly at work, appointed and named for the occasion, but that they are aware of this Occator all the time, although he is manifest only when the field is harrowed. Occator has become the harrowing deity and is not just the divinity in the moment of harrowing. Upon this transformation, Usener speaks of "functional deities" ("*Sondergötter*")—gods of a certain activity or a certain something (bees or heifers, for example).

It is interesting to see how Usener imagines the further development of these gods. First, he emphasizes that not all functional gods were equally valued; the guardian deity of hearth and home was much more important than the harrowing god. From the start there was a hierarchy. He then turns to Apollo, whom he wants to call "the danger-averting god." When the Greeks ceased to feel the connection between the name Apollo and *apellein* ("to avert"), the tie with the "functional concept" ("*Sonderbegriff*") was broken, and Apollo could become a personality. It is startling to read—for here suddenly Max Müller's old theory emerges:

> The law we can formulate is simple and transparent. The condition for the birth of personal deities is a process of language! When the name given an important "functional god" loses its coherence in the living language, through phonetic change or the decay of a word stem, and is no longer understood, it becomes a proper name. When fixed with a proper name, a god becomes fit and inclined for a personal unfolding in myth, cult, poetry and art.[4]

This ingenuous theory has been remarkably successful. The ideas of momentary and functional deities have entered the repertory of the historian of religions. In our opinion, the career of the theory is undeserved. The ideas could only be persuasive when the fashion was to search for the very simplest divinities on an evolutionistic bias. What is simpler than a god who appears the moment an act is performed and fades when it is over? But how should we imagine this sort of thing? If the Roman farmer, while he harrowed, was aware of something divine, surely he must already have known of divinity. If he created a beneficent god in the midst of activity, he knew beforehand that divine power exists and must be invoked. Then why should that god be so ephemeral? When the farmer harrowed in the next year, did he really call up a new Occator? Would he not have had in mind the first whom he asked once for a blessing and with a good result? Strictly speaking, one can find a momentary deity only once—at the moment an act is first performed.

It would be more precise to say Usener's momentary god was latent before it appeared. The momentary god is actually the functional god in the form he takes the moment his help is needed. But there is nothing special about this. It is impossible to regard the momentary gods as a primitive state of the idea of god. In fact, they never existed.

But what of the functional gods? There are many examples of gods who are interested in one well-defined human activity. We may recall Asklepios or Hygieia, Damia or Auxesia. They rank below the great gods; not one of them has evolved from a principal deity. It is quite possible that in a civilization becoming more complicated and where techniques were multiplying a need grew up for gods with very particular spheres. It must be added that these limited gods were more accessible than the great heavenly powers. But one should consider these functional gods as derivations from the gods proper and not as their ancestors.

The examples Usener used for his thesis are not felicitous. Those gods called on by the Roman farmer at the sacrifice on the field do make a very modest impression; no wonder the Church Fathers liked to use the little list to expose the worthlessness of the pagan gods. Besides, there is nothing really primitive about deities such as Subruncinator or Patella. Only the scrupulous caution of the Roman could produce such extreme things as these functional deities. In every religious act the Roman was afraid he omitted some deity. He protected himself with the formula *sive deus sive dea* ("Be it a god or a goddess!") added to every invocation. It is no wonder that the Romans eventually had a god for almost every occasion. Such deities as Nodotus and Patella convey the juridical scrupulousness of the Roman mind. They are recent abstractions. In all likelihood the priest, not the farmer, invented them.

The Lithuanian gods are no better as examples of Usener's theory. They are not nearly as specialized as the Roman deities. It is not surprising to have gods who bless the useful domestic animals. There is no reason here to speak of the type of the momentary deity. There is, however, the more serious fact that the Lithuanian divine names come from a muddled source. It was particularly the clergy, in their Reformation endeavors, who tried to destroy pagan religion. In their fight against the "demones," or the *ignominiosa phantasmata,* as they are called in the *Collatio episcopi Warmiensis* in 1418—before the Reformation —the clergymen mention the Lithuanian deities. Did these zealous pastors exert themselves to learn exactly what the pagans meant with all those barbaric names? Is it not quite possible that those names were originally those of Catholic saints and patrons and had become part of the popular religion under indigenous titles? If we had an accurate picture of the way they were invoked, and especially of their cult, we should be able to form an opinion about them. In any case, these names cannot support such farreaching religio-historical constructs as Usener's.

Usener observes somewhere that a great many Christian saints took the place of the *indigitamenta* deities (those listed in the ancient invocation prayers). This is only partly true, for one would look in vain for saints like Subruncinator or Occator. Moreover, Usener should have made his comparison with saints cautiously. The saints are a type of functional gods, yet they were never able to play the role that Usener gives to his functional gods. They live in the presence of a real God; they bring divine grace to those living the common life.

We can only say that with a number of definitely secondary religious phenomena, which he borrowed from the Roman commentators, Usener constructed a theory that the *indigitamenta* are too weak to support. Philosophical data alone cannot solve the problems of the history of religions. In such cardinal matters, the materials of the ethnologist are richer and more dependable.

Dema-deities

Adolf E. Jensen, a pupil of Leo Frobenius, pointed out a curious kind of deity that he found among the so-called early cultivators.[5] Such gods occur even today in almost all tropical regions. In addition to gathering fruits, those early cultivators burned out forest patches and then cultivated tuberous plants on the sites. They did not know grain cultivation or plowing or fertilizing. Their livelihood was not the most primitive (the primal) level, but it belongs to the lowest cultural stages we know of.

Of course these tribes have beliefs concerning spirits and manes; only those beliefs were detected in the heyday of animism. Jensen, who made painstaking researches into the culture of the tribes living on Ceram (in eastern Indonesia), found other religious forms behind that rather general belief in spirits; what he found can really be regarded as a religion, distinct and clear.

The mythological tradition itself supports his find. Among the Wemale tribe, Jensen discovered a triad of goddesses: Satene, Rabie, and Hainuwele. As soon as these figures were defined, they could be discerned in other parts of the world—for example, among the Uitoto in South America and the Bantu tribes of the Congo basin.

In primordial days, according to the myth, there was a species who were not yet people, who were not generated and did not die. Jensen gives those beings the customary name of the Marind-anim on New Guinea: dema. The human world evolved after the dema-deity had been killed by the dema themselves. In the myth of Hainuwele this happens at a dance, the maro-dance, which moves in a ninefold spiral movement. Once, while that dance was performed, during the ninth night of dancing, Hainuwele was slowly closed in on by the narrowing spiral and at last pressed into a hole that was dug in the center. The dema covered her body with earth and trampled it firmly with their dancing. The next morning, Hainuwele was missing, and her father went out to find her. He found the spot where she was buried, dug up her body and cut it into small pieces, which he hid in the earth around the dancing place. These pieces of Hainuwele changed into tuberous plants, which have sustained the people ever since.

Then another dema-goddess, Satene, furious at Hainuwele's death, built a great gate in the shape of a ninefold spiral. She took her place on a log next to the gate, holding in her own hands the arms of Hainuwele. Then all the primordial beings were summoned by her and compelled to go through the spiral. The successful ones became people, but those who failed to pass through the spiral became animals or spirits. Thereupon, Satene became the goddess of the netherworld. But she also became the moon, whose phases symbolize the continuous renewal of life.

This myth reveals how man came to his present mode of being. The myth takes up the problem of life and death. Birth is made possible by death. Death, the enigma that man has always wrestled, is made the result of a "primordial sin." But the myth also shows the connection between death and life. This holds not only for man's own physical death. He himself must kill in order to stay alive. He must hunt animals, and the plants he raises for eating he must cut from the earth. The tuberous plants grew from the parts of Hainuwele's body; thus, she too had to be slain and cut to pieces, so that people could live. We shall return to this important myth to explain the institution of sacrifice.

The myth indicates that man originated from the dema-beings. The people who now populate the world go back directly to those dema via a long line of ancestors, and when they die, they will return to the dema-community. Jensen thinks this reveals the real nature of ancestor worship, which is prominent and clear exactly in the religion of these early cultivators. But we also noticed that when Satene divided the dema-beings at the ninefold gate, those who could not pass the test became spirits. At this point a totally new explanation offers itself, quite different from the idea of psychic phenomena in dreams or trances: ancestors are not worshiped because they are "ghosts" but because they are parts in the chain between the present man and those primordial beings.

Jensen stresses that it is possible to extend a line from the dema-deities to the real gods of polytheism. The significance of the ancestor cult is especially that it satisfies man's need for salvation. But it is precisely this yearning for salvation that may have made man search for a satisfaction beyond the dema-deities, for properly speaking, dema-deities had been active only in the primordial period, which was irrevocably ended. There may have been a growing desire for gods that were present and could always turn a hand to human life.[6]

Jensen also observes that the gods of polytheism have a curiously double nature. They are really the dema of primordial days, who performed the first killing, but they are also real gods, who are in need of sacrifices. They are distinct from the dema-deities in that they never withdraw to some realm of the dead but remain near, omnipresent. The striking thing is that omnipresence is also what characterizes the supreme being. Jensen draws a conclusion:

> . . . the ambiguous nature of many polytheistic gods was brought about by the blending of two originally separate concepts of deity. One would be the idea of the deity that reigns in heaven, to whom the creation of the world is attributed, who is ever present, holds human destiny in his hands, and can reward or punish; the other would be the primeval divine being through whom the things of this world came to be as they are and thus bear the mark of their divine origin for all times.[7]

If Jensen is correct, it makes no sense to think of direct developments, one thing from another, in the terms preferred by the older theories. In the course of time, civilizations flourished —the hunters, the early cultivators, the nomads, and the agricultural peoples. These cultures were not in everlasting isolation; they intermingled. This means that religious imageries distinct by genesis and by nature could conjoin and produce new and higher forms.

This sequence of ideas is most interesting, and the complex of religious images symbolized in the beautiful myth of Hainuwele appeared to introduce a totally new element in the discussion of the origin of religious forms—a discussion that had slowly reached a deadlock. It is odd that a century of thorough research into the religious ideas of the Indonesian peoples did not come upon this type of dema-deity but that it was discovered only in the twentieth century. It appears that ethnographers have sometimes examined the primitive world wearing blinkers. Animism was anticipated, and animism was found.

It should be emphasized that the myth of Hainuwele is a commentary on a whole series of religious phenomena. I have already mentioned its explanation of man's mode of being and also of sacrifice. The symbol of the ninefold spiral points far beyond Indonesia, as far as the Cretan labyrinth; it refers to the realm of the dead. The myth is reflected in ritual acts that are still performed: the maro-dance and the initiation ceremonies. If we keep in mind that even now such completely new facts can come to light, facts that lead to wholly different interpretations, we can only repeat Marett's words, that the time for writing a history of religion has not yet arrived.

Chapter Seventeen

PSYCHOLOGICAL EXPLANATIONS

RELIGION is, to a great extent, emotional in character. Of course, religion is not feeling alone; it is directed toward a supernatural world that must first be recognized as something more elevated—indeed, something supreme—before it can become an object of veneration. Thus, religion is as much a matter of reason as of emotion. A myth like Hainuwele's shows that primitive man wanted a coherent account of the mystery that envelops human life.

It is difficult to say whether reason or emotion is at the root of religion. In fact, the question itself is probably inaccurate. The human spirit is not halved into hermetic compartments. Whatever moves man's reason affects his emotion; what touches the emotion also touches the power of reason. There is something rational about all forms of belief. We may observe that every religion tends toward rationalization: dogmas are rational statements meant to fix the content of beliefs. Further, philosophy attempts to explain the consequences of those statements of faith with ever greater subtlety.

An idea that had occurred even to the Greeks is that religion originates in fear. This makes sense with respect to beliefs in demons, and whoever assumes such beliefs as the beginning of religion has no difficulty in accepting the idea. But the beliefs in a supreme being, which we have found even among the most primitive tribes, are certainly not a fearful inspiration. If they were, how could the creator-god ever be portrayed as good and just? The same one-sided reasoning is applied to the ancestor cult, and too much emphasis is laid on the fear among many nations of everything related to death. But one forgets that the love and honor given to a man in life do not suddenly cease upon his death.

Frequently, feelings of wonder and admiration have been regarded as roots of religion. If, as Max Müller did, one deduces religion from man's response to the daybreak, one assumes the primitive was captivated by that phenomenon just as any of our contemporaries with a rather poetical nature might be Eduard von Hartmann posits yet another type of wondering as the basis of religion—man's wonderings about evil and sin. According to Von Hartmann, man is always aware of weakness and misery in his being and his life, and this is the source of an unquenchable desire for happiness. This happiness prevails only in dreams, in another world. Thus, man strives for liberation through the figments of his imagination.

It is significant that Von Hartmann calls attention to the role of the unconscious. He thus inaugurates an important type of research in the nineteenth century. Wilhelm Wundt in particular devoted himself to conscientious psychological researches and established the science of psychophysiology. It aroused interest in the old and the new worlds and yielded meaningful results for the study of religion. Without special concern for the content or the value of beliefs, these investigators tried to explain religious phenomena purely biologically.

Psychopathological Explanations

In the spiritual life of a religious man there are phenomena that are not necessarily products of his religion. Especially the agnostic sees in things like consolation and fear—which are related to religion—resemblances to other phenomena of hallucinations, ecstasies, and visions. The psychiatrist observes these things particularly in neurotics and among lunatics.

No wonder many have been reminded of hysterical symptoms

in the observation of religious phenomena. Psychopathological explanations originated in clinical observation. The psychologist who examines a case of stigmata or of faith-healing does not consult a theologian, let alone consider with him the possibility of a supernatural origin; he simply records cases of autosuggestion. The histories of many religions present cases of morbid exaltation; sometimes whole periods are marked by such exaltation—such as the dancing manias in the Middle Ages. Similar statements can be made about specific religious types, most clearly exemplified by the shaman. However, all these are borderline cases of a neurotic nature; they do not constitute the essence of a normal religion. Doubtlessly, they are interesting because they reveal certain religious elements that usually remain dormant but can come abruptly to the fore. All these cases prove how strong emotion is in religious experience. The way in which man relates himself to the supernatural is always marked by intense affectivity. This is clear in the responses evoked in adherents to certain traditions by whatever is considered "mana" or "holy." In some circumstances—sacrificial feasts, initiations, burial rites—the abundance of emotion can lead to excesses that suggest mental disturbance.

Such cases show first and foremost how man's psyche in its entirety can be moved by religious experiences. Religion is certainly a matter of man's total life, mind, and heart. Hence the interplay of mind with emotion, of experience with knowledge. This situation does not, however, give us any reason to derive the phenomenon of religion from psychopathological mental conditions. These conditions are important only because they enable us to study—as if through a lens—normal phenomena through abnormal excesses.

Psychoanalytic Explanations

Sigmund Freud (1856-1939) and his pupils did not bypass religious phenomena in their study of the unconscious life of the psyche.[1] One can only say that the results are deplorable. It is superfluous to recall in detail how researchers contrived to find the famous Oedipus complex existing everywhere in myth and in primitive religion. No wonder that Clemen, in some critical essay, calls it an *idée fixe*! Indeed, for Freud religion is a kind of neurosis.

In Freud's expositions, the unconscious is the storage place of the residue of conscious experience. Memorial images that can be raised above the threshold of the unconscious can be reproduced whenever we need them for our conscious thought. They can be remembered. There are other images which men tend to consign to oblivion. They are repressed into the unconscious. But they allow themselves to be forgotten only at a price; they claim man's complete attention when they assert themselves. To make their claim, they undergo distortions, which often express their disagreeable or dangerous nature. They then manifest themselves in troubling dreams. Such repressed elements of the mental life may cause neuroses, many of which Freud was able to study in his psychiatric clinic.

This much about the negative side of the unconscious. On its basis it is impossible to find an explanation of something as positive as religion. However, if one is able to develop another standpoint, the unconscious sheds a great light. The Swiss psychiatrist Carl Gustav Jung (1875-1961) emphasized the positive side. Though a product of Freud's school, Jung was able to open wholly new avenues for psychoanalytical study. He too found his materials in the dreams and visions of his patients. But in addition to the Oedipus complex and the rest of the Freudian sexual symbolisms, he found matters of great significance and value that opened his eyes to the structures of the unconscious.

Jung believed that the analysis of the dreams of his neurotic patients revealed true mythical images. He concluded that these dream images give definite answers to our questions concerning the origin and essence of myth. It is undeniable that these dream images resembled mythical figures that date back to a dim past. Freud noted the same thing with respect to the Oedipus complex. In any case, the dream images were certainly not novel figures in the unconscious of individual patients. The same ancient mythical symbols were reappearing to neurasthenics who could not have heard of them, directly or indirectly. Therefore, Jung called these symbols "archetypes." They were primal images that had never lost their hold on man. Since they could not have emerged from the psychic experience of individuals, they could only come from an even more profound, apparently preindividual psychic layer. According to Jung, the images showed an unconscious psychic activity that persisted through millennia unchanged and undiminished and that could suddenly enter the dreams of modern man when his soul was in peril. And not only then. The images can also occur to normal people in normal times when the moment favors them; there is, for instance, the creative thought of poets, in which such symbols can be a powerful force. This is perhaps Jung's most noteworthy conclusion. He goes on to speak of the "collective unconscious," an unconscious life present in all people but not acquired during their lifetime; therefore, it is one that must be considered prenatal. The collective unconscious is enigmatic, but of course this does not mean it must be illusory. Jung's thesis brought sharp objections, especially from the positivists, yet it seems that the facts Jung dealt in are taken more and more into consideration today. Their role in clinical work increases. The theory has opened new perspectives for the study of religious phenomena such as symbols. What matters is that Jung's reasoning gives a greater significance to the unconscious and considers religion an affair of supreme importance. Religion is no longer regarded as a neurosis but rather as an age-old mysterious experience of life and world expressed in undying symbols. These symbols are alive in every soul. When the time is ripe, they show themselves to men in their full significance; then a religious awareness can be reborn.

The "Völkerpsychologie"

In addition to the psychology of individuals, scholars began in the mid-nineteenth century to give their attention to a collective psychology, or what is usually called by the German name *Völkerpsychologie*. This new branch of psychology was practiced first in Germany. The ethnologist Adolf Bastian (1826-1905) observed that two very different nations, which could never have been in contact, could show similarities of culture. He was led to believe that such similarity expressed the structure of the human mind and that, despite different spiritual conditions and different conditions of life, various people resolve in the same way the experience thrust upon them by existence. *A fortiori*, this must be so for nations. Bastian calls these similar solutions "elementary ideas" (*"Elementargedanken"*). However, these elementary ideas are not universal, for there are obvious differences in human culture. The distinctive determinants in various traditions were explained by Bastian as products of the geographical setting. He spoke of *Völkergedanken* (national or collective ideas). These names do not give an explanation, of course, but they point up certain facts. When we find the same religious imageries in Australia and North America—as those of a creator-god—we need not puzzle over where the beliefs first occurred and how they could become disseminated from one side of the world to another. Instead we can register the fact and call it an elementary idea. The solution seemed plausible but carried the danger that students would be satisfied merely with recording ethnological data that actually called for some explanation. There were so many cultural phenomena, such as specific technical abilities and inventions, that had definitely been diffused over great distances that "elementary thought" could not be their sole or principal explanation. In fact, men traveled across incredible distances in the earliest prehistory. If the Australian population migrated in a dim past from southeast Asia via the Indonesian chain of islands, and if the American Indians journeyed from eastern Asia across the Bering Straits, it is possible to explain their comparable cultural and religious features on the basis of a genetic coherence. Hence, ethnology has made reluctant use of the elementary idea—only as an *ultimum refugium* and always in the hope of eliminating it after continued research.

In 1859 Heymann Steinthal (1823-99) and Moritz Lazarus (1824-1903) founded the *Zeitschrift für Völkerpsychologie und Sprachwissenschaft* ("Journal for Ethnopsychology and Linguistics"), which was to serve as a forum for the psychological study of historical and social phenomena with a collective character, such as language, art, ethics, and religion.

The first to try to give a solid foundation to this science was Wilhelm Wundt (1832-1920) with his ten volume work, *Völkerpsychologie (Ethnopsychology)*. It had become clear to Wundt that such complex and long-lasting phenomena must not be studied from the point of view of the individual alone but that they demanded an explanation in terms of communal life. He thought of a community not as the sum of a number of people but as an autonomous reality. Whatever is produced in a community is a creation *sui generis,* qualitatively different from every individual creation.

He wanted to establish in all objectivity the firm rules that create and govern social phenomena. Nations with a higher culture did not suit his aim, for in them there are always creative individuals who influence or even disturb the evolution of collective life. The primitives presented the most fitting study; in Wundt's day the opinion still prevailed that the primitive peoples had an exclusively collective nature or, at least, that it was impossible to find among them pronounced individual characters.

Wundt explains in a curious way the origin of a religion. Since the primitives did not seem to possess any clear concept of causality, at least in a scientific sense, he assumed that the object and subject of perception merged so thoroughly that they attributed the qualities of the subject to the object. Thus, he said, the primitive believes that all things have feeling and life like man's. This is some sort of animism. Nothing displays rational deduction; all these views of primitive man are the products of his imagination. They are incorporated in myth, and it is myth that leads into religion. Myth expresses the lessons of experience through the prism of imagination. In the end, when facts and relations are more accurately known, this process should lead to science. Religion begins with a mythical conception of the world in order to deal with practical life. Let us pass Wundt's further elaborations—how polytheism evolved from primitive animism through fetishism and totemism. These elaborations are purely theoretical, and they have been rendered obsolete by ethnological facts.

Moreover, there is reason to question Wundt's point of departure. Could religion really have originated as he describes it? It is hard to believe that religion, with its ultimate importance for humankind, would go back again to an illusion—the confusion of the object and subject of perception. The presence of "supreme beings" among very primitive peoples implies that causal thinking of some significance must have existed even at a very early date. Further, religious experience remains always and everywhere an individual matter, in spite of the fact that every religious system is to quite an extent a collective product.

Wundt's system gives the impression of a disregard for the results of ethnological studies. Whatever did not fit his system he rejected or belittled. Through Andrew Lang, he knew about the concept of a supreme being among extremely primitive tribes; but, for Wundt, Lang's findings only show that such an idea appeared with the influence of Christianity. It must be said that Wundt himself knew very well that he had presented only a hypothesis, and ultimately, like many others, this hypothesis was discarded.

Two American Psychologists

In 1902 the psychologist of religion William James (1842-1910) published a series of lectures he had presented in Edinburgh in 1901-02. The book, *The Varieties of Religious Experience,* was reprinted a number of times, and great value was attributed to it. Actually, the author deals with experiences in the higher forms of religion; the primitive peoples are mentioned only in passing. Of the monotheistic religions it is principally Christianity that is discussed and even then only Protestantism in detail. It is not surprising that James is interested only in the subjective side of religion. Whatever is institutional —cult and sacrifice, theology, church organization—is left aside. As a psychologist, he occupies himself with religious feelings and impulses and particularly with such well developed subjective phenomena as occur in the writings of quite self-conscious individuals, hence in religious treatises and autobiographies. This means that he wants to treat only the psychological phenomenon of religion and gives no thought to the religio-historical and anthropological aspects. Such a procedure is hardly defensible or even possible. It is too one-sided to concentrate only on the inner religious experiences that developed in Christian and particularly Protestant circles.

The results of his investigation are surprising. A psychologist living in the heyday of psychoanalysis must give a lion's share to the unconscious. What James has in mind is not the subconscious self to the extent that it is made of incomplete memories, inhibitions, and other "disintegrating" elements. Rather, in James's opinion, on the deepest level of the unconscious are origins of genius and the seed of mystic experience and conversion.

> At the same time the theologian's contention that the religious man is moved by an external power is vindicated, for it is one of the peculiarities of invasions from the subconscious region to take on objective appearances, and to suggest to the Subject an external control. In the religious

life the control is felt as "higher"; but since on our hypothesis it is primarily the higher faculties of our own hidden mind which are controlling, the sense of union with the power beyond us is a sense of something, not merely apparently, but literally true.[2]

James further observes:

The further limits of our being plunge, it seems to me, into an altogether other dimension of existence from the sensible and merely "understandable" world. Name it the mystical region, or the supernatural region, whichever you choose. So far as our ideal impulses originate in this region (and most of them do originate in it, ·for we find them possessing us in a way for which we cannot articulately account), we belong to it in a more intimate sense than that in which we belong to the visible world, for we belong in the most intimate sense wherever our ideals belong. Yet the unseen region in question is not merely ideal, for it produces effects in this world. When we commune with it, work is actually done upon our finite personality, for we are turned into new men, and consequences in the way of conduct follow in the natural world upon our regenerative change. But that which produces effects within another reality must be termed a reality itself, so I feel as if we had no philosophic excuse for calling the unseen or mystical world unreal.[3]

I find this line of reasoning contestable. After the experiences of the faithful are presented as invasions of the unconscious, they are said to relate to reality only because they have results in the real world. But so do dreams. We know many sagas in which a king dreams that he is threatened by a son who has yet to be born. When the child is born he is killed or abandoned. Hence, the dream has very real results. Granted that this is a saga, does it not correspond to a reality? Are dreams deceit? Do not many people listen attentively to what a dream "reveals"? If the supernatural world—and God in particular—must be proved with such reasonings, then it is indeed poorly off.

Further, James's exposition does not help us much in our problem. When a believer undergoes "invasions" of the unconscious he experiences an indisputable reality because he relates the invasions to his conviction that the supernatural world is real. In other words, the experience does not occur because the subject knows reality or his invasions from a psychological point of view. James might have had a different view if he had known of the archetypes of Jung, for the archetypes let us speak of realities mysteriously pictured in the soul.

But what do these invasions mean with respect to the origin of religious images? Must we assume that a person who had not found supersensual powers in, let us say, a perfectly natural manner would get to know them now because ideas, which he must call real on the basis of psychological laws, appear to his unconscious? Then where do these laws come from? Are they imaginary images of the unconscious or do they relate to some reality too? We are in a vicious circle. Did not even Tylor explain the origin of religious ideas by dream experiences? Have we gained much if instead of dream experiences we now speak of invasions of the unconscious?

It is no wonder his compatriot J. H. Leuba called James's supernaturalistic explanation a fiasco. It is evident that in this explanation every direct intervention by God is eliminated. The higher manifestations are understood to be determined by spiritual powers that work through the unconscious. Of course, we can assume that God would exert his own power by means of this unconscious, but why would he be forced to move along this line alone? This psychologizing of faith leads to the questionable conclusion that faith might be no more than the illusion of the unconscious.

Leuba's own point of view is pronouncedly positivistic. A few sentences from his book *A Psychological Study of Religion,* published in 1912, will show this:

> The reason for the existence of religion is not the objective truth of its conceptions, but its biological value. This value is to be estimated by its success in procuring not only the results expected by the worshipper, but also others, some of which are of great significance.[4]

Or elsewhere:

> The general fact of man's entering into relations with certain hyperhuman agents needs no other explanation than is afforded by the lust for life.[5]

Man—with the possible exception of the western Europeans and Americans of the last few centuries—cannot live without religion. Religion is, in a special way, a necessity of life. The urge to live is clear because man procures food and makes clothes, tools, and weapons—in short, provides for life in all material things. Next to these essentials the creation of religious values seems a secondary function. This point has been elaborated on by Paul Radin. It is exaggerating to say that man has grasped for religion because it served his urge for life. The religious imageries, the myths, and the rites meet another need—his wish for a place in the cosmos, which is the problem of his human existence. He arrives at transcendental solutions because the answers to these needs are not present in the material world and cannot be found with worldly talents. Once the supernatural powers have been posited, they are expected to be efficacious. Their transcendental character gives such a distinctive signature to their power that it must surpass everything else. But man did not create divine powers of fertility in order to give himself a prosperous harvest. The dema-deities depicted by Jensen did not have such an origin. But once the tuberous fruits are born from the parts of Hainuwele's body, it is natural that abundance is awaited from her at each new harvest. Why no offerings are brought to her we shall see later when we speak of the nature of sacrifice.

Leuba also begins with preanimism as one of the most ancient forms of religion. Like a child (sic), primitive man inferred from various natural phenomena (wind, smoke, clouds) that there are spontaneous powers that generate motion and change. It is hard to see what is really religious in this conception. After all, these powers were not personal to begin with. Since their efficacy cannot be predicted or guided, they often cause fear, but when man can use them, they lose their mysterious nature and become familiars. They are not clearly conceived of as an intelligent will, and therefore man's attitude toward them is essentially different from the belief in personal and invisible powers. The former generate magic, the latter religion. It is plain that this view does not agree with the concept of mana formulated by Codrington.

Leuba's merit lies in his disregard of the attempt to connect primitive religious ideas evolutionistically. On the contrary, he emphasizes that the same images can have totally different origins. He mentions the following:

1. dreams and trances engendered the belief in gods and spirits with a human appearance and human attributes;

2. the personification of natural objects led to the belief in deities of nature, often conceived of as animals;
3. the problem of creation brought belief in one or more creators who are thought to have human form.

He is content to have established that religious images of this nature develop in normal spiritual processes. But is there much space left for religion itself? Is the belief in a creator-god really only a more or less rational answer to the question of who made everything? Do not these gods of the most primitive peoples have ethical qualities of a higher order than expected? Do they not provide justice in history? Are they not prayed to fervently? Finally, if they were the mere result of "normal" psychological processes, would they not vanish in the same normal processes? When we consider Leuba's three roots of religion it seems clear that scientific man will give a different and completely rational answer in all three cases. Does this mean the total defeat of the transcendental?

Finally, we may mention that Leuba considers religion exclusively a phenomenon of the emotions. Yet there is an intellectual element from the beginning that is no less important. This element is the will to account for the mystery which surrounds the essential situations of life, and which exists for primitive man just as it exists for us. The answer primitive man gives often contains a bold hypothesis—let me recall the dema-deities —but precisely because such accounts give definitive information on the critical situations of life they are strongly emotional at the same time. What answer can we, who pride ourselves in the victories of rational thinking, especially in the results it has had in dominating nature, make to the existential questions?

Rudolph Otto

Although *Das Heilige* (*The Idea of the Holy*), published by Rudolf Otto (1869-1937) in 1917, is more a phenomenological than a psychological work, we want to conclude this discussion with it. The success this book has had—twenty-five editions in less than twenty years—indicates the impression it made on Otto's contemporaries. I think I may assume that his ideas about the holy are known.

Disregarding all moral facets, Otto's major idea can be described as the *Ganz Andere* (the totally other), the Numinous, a category meant to explain and evaluate the holy and also to convey its strong numinous mood. Otto distinguishes two aspects: the *tremendum* and the *fascinosum*. Confronting the numinous, man feels a shudder of anxious fright, the feeling of the *Unheimliche*—the eerie—is evoked. When the *tremendum* broke through, an epoch began. In this are rooted demons and gods and whatever else the "mythological apperception" or the fancy have made of this feeling. Next to this element is another element in the *numinosum*. For the numinous does not only make one shudder, it also appeals, it charms, it is a *fascinans*. This contrast / harmony occurs in the whole history of religion, at any rate since the phase of the *dämonische Scheu* (the anxiety over demons). Then the *mysterium* is no longer only fraught with terror but is also something wondrous. Thus, in the deity wrath and grace are revealed side by side—the *tremendum* and the *fascinans* at the same moment.

The Protestant theologian Otto illuminates his thesis mainly with examples from the Old Testament. These examples are felicitous, and the contrast / harmony he indicates in the religion of Israel also emerges in Christianity.

Nevertheless, all this shows no more than the emotion of man when facing the "totally other"; we end up again in the realm of psychology. Rudolf Otto's further exposition on the evolution of the numinous is most unsatisfactory. There is no sign that he ever consulted the ethnological data with any care. In a brief survey of the historical development, he states:

> It must be admitted that when religious evolution first begins sundry curious phenomena confront us, preliminary to religion proper and deeply affecting its subsequent course. Such are the notions of "clean" and "unclean," belief in and worship of the dead, belief in and worship of "souls" or "spirits," magic, fairy tale, and myth, homage to natural objects, whether frightful or extraordinary, noxious or advantageous, the strange idea of "power" (orenda or mana), fetishism and totemism, worship of animal and plant, daemonism and polydaemonism. Different as these things are, they are all haunted by a common—and that a numinous—element, which is easily identifiable. They did not, perhaps, take their origin out of this common numinous element directly; they may have all exhibited a preliminary

stage at which they were merely "natural" products of the naïve, rudimentary fancies of primitive times. But these things acquire a strand of a quite special kind, which alone gives them their character as forming the vestibule of religion. . . .[6]

Consequently, in Otto's opinion, what preceded real faith (by which he means Judeo-Christian faith) is merely like a "vestibule." There is no reason yet to speak of true religion.[7] The poor pagans did not just wander in the night of their ignorance but, worse still, had no religion in the "real" sense of the word. Myth is pitilessly treated the same way.

What does Otto say about "primal monotheism"? Here we are asked to think of anticipatory presentiments, which are not surprising because they developed under the pressure of a continuous and strong *innervernünftige Ideenlage* ("natural intellectual structure"). In fact, their sudden appearances are quite expectable. This is an easy way to get rid of a troubling problem. It would have been laudable if precisely in the vestibule Otto had tried to show the slow maturation of the numinous. But all this material is discarded as not being belief in the proper sense. No doubt the book has its importance for the interpretation of the Judeo-Christian idea of God, yet this idea is somehow related to more ancient imageries, reaching back to the most ancient past. For us, who would like to be enlightened at this point, his book is disappointing.

Chapter Eighteen

SOCIOLOGICAL THEORIES

RELIGION is a social phenomenon, at least in one essential aspect. We cannot say it is only social, for a certain part of religious experience is always individual. Yet religion presupposes a community of adherents, and that implies an organization, a "church."

In a primitive stage religion can be thought of only as a constitutive part of a community. Again, this does not exclude the personal experience, as with the young North American Indian, who, in solitude, fasting, and self-castigation, awaits the appearance of his manitu. Religion's social character is expressed, first, in the communal and regular cult. It is also expressed in initiation ceremonies, bringing the young men into the sacred mysteries of the tribe. Moreover, it is clear from the social structures that are anchored in religion, as with totemistic or matriarchal cultures. The organization of polytheism in the form of a state with one god ruling (Zeus and the Olympic deities) is not so much a replica of human society as it is a prototype and hence the guarantee of its sacredness. We shall see later how this can be shown very typically in the pantheon of the Indo-European peoples.

The so-called *Völkerpsychologie* of Wundt took as its point of departure the social nature of all civilizations. In this context, mention should be made again of J. J. Bachofen, who was the first to detect and formulate the social phenomenon of the matriarchate. On the basis of mythology he uncovered the features of a matriarchal organization, which are faintly indicated even in the very patriarchal organization of the Indo-Europeans. He concluded that an ancient matriarchal structure must have preceded the patriarchate, and it is pardonable that he considered this matriarchate the most ancient social structure. However, matriarchy is not a universal phenomenon; it is related to certain forms of culture in which women have been elevated because of their part in the economy of the tribe.

In the meantime, the matriarchal traces Bachofen found in the Greek myths convinced him of the fundamental significance of mythology. This was not a collection of fabrications about gods but a truthful tradition handed down from most ancient times. "In all high things," he says, "the most ancient people had correct and great thoughts, as may be expected from those who are still close to their eternal origin." [1] Naturally, his idea led him to the great religious significance of symbolism, for only symbolism and the elucidation by myth can convey man's intuitions about life and death and the high expectations of novices.

Although Bachofen was aware of the social structure reflected in religion, his ideas suggest that he did not like to regard the social element as primary. This whole state of affairs in scholarship was soon to change. When Bachofen published his book in 1861, the academic discipline of sociology was in its infancy. Wundt's systematic work on *Völkerpsychologie* served as a first foundation, but sociology reached a high point around 1890 in France. Here Emile Durkheim (1858-1917) devoted himself exclusively to this science and attracted a circle of scholars like Hubert, Mauss and Lévy-Bruhl, who had their forum in the journal *L'année sociologique,* published since 1896. We shall limit our attention to Durkheim because his work demonstrates the method—and especially the results—of this sociological school very clearly. Let us focus on his *Les formes élémentaires de la vie religieuse (The Elementary Forms of Religious Life)*, published in 1912.

Durkheim demands in sociological study a complete objectivity. He makes a rule that social facts must be regarded as any other materials and hence as objective facts; all prejudice and subjective interpretation must be avoided. The facts must be classified

by certain external, typical features held in common. When this
sociological method is applied to religion, one runs great risks
immediately. The objective facts alone do not make a religious
phenomenon understood, for much more significant is either the
individual interpretation of the fact or the metaphysical meaning
given to it by the community. If one wants to examine a phenomenon of religion, these two psychological matters cannot be
eliminated at the chance of substituting another explanation
that could be equally subjective. This last point is made abundantly clear by Durkheim's own thesis!

To determine the most primitive form of religion, Durkheim
continues, it is necessary to define "religion." This is how he does
it: "A religion is a unified system of beliefs and practices relative
to sacred things, that is to say things set apart and forbidden—
beliefs and practices which unite into one single moral community called a church, all those who adhere to them." [2] But this
formula makes it necessary to ask what is meant by sacred and
church and also if they have, in fact, a religious meaning. The
circumscription "set apart and forbidden" no doubt refers to
the well-known phenomenon of tabu. But not every tabu is
religious. We know many tabus in our own society that have a
strong social sanction but certainly need not be considered religious. Sacred things can become forbidden and be set apart from
the profane world, but what is intriguing is to find out just what
characteristic element necessitates this setting apart. The word
"church" is altogether misleading; it suggests a special religious
fellowship. In spite of the best scholarly intentions, the word is
quite inappropriate for primitive communities that exist on a
sacred foundation. All that is left of the definition now is that
certain things are declared tabu and such rules are valid for a
community. This is a thin picture of religion.

It stands to reason that, for a sociologist, totemism is an appealing religious form. It has exogamous totemic groups in the
clan and hence positive forms of social organization. It is here,
if anywhere, that religion is tangible as a sociological phenomenon.

Thus the totem, Durkheim infers, is at the same time the
symbol of the god and of the clan.

> So if it is at once the symbol of the god and of the society,
> is that not because the god and the society are only one?
> How could the emblem of the group have been able to

become the figure of this quasi-divinity, if the group and the divinity were two distinct realities? The god of the clan, the totemic principle, can therefore be nothing else than the clan itself, personified and represented to the imagination under the visible form of the animal or vegetable which serves as totem.[3]

Along this line, Durkheim arrives at a truly astounding conclusion:

Before all, it is a system of ideas with which the individuals represent to themselves the society of which they are members, and the obscure but intimate relations which they have with it. This is its primary function; and though metaphorical and symbolic, this representation is not unfaithful. Quite on the contrary, it translates everything essential in the relations which are to be explained: for it is an eternal truth that outside of us there exists something greater than us, with which we enter into communion.[4]

This is juggling with words. Man may communicate with something greater than he is, but how many different things can this something be! Durkheim himself thinks it is the community, the burgher thinks it is the king's majesty, the faithful think it is God. Yet for Durkheim this vague definition suffices, and it identifies God and community without further delay and brings religion to the level of a cult of the idea of community.

With these premises it is not difficult to trace the evolution of religion. Totemism is a group of religious ideas that may be considered very primitive.[5] Totemic cult in its proper form does not relate itself to certain animals and vegetables—not even to one particular species—but to some unclear power diffused in all things. Even in the highest forms that sprang from totemism (like those of the North American Indians), this idea does not disappear. On the contrary, it becomes more self-conscious; it is expressed with new accuracy and therefore reaches a higher, more general pitch. It dominates the whole religious system.

This is the *materia prima* of all beings of every sort that have ever been adored. Spirits, demons, genii, the gods of whatever rank—they are all concrete and individual shapes of this energy or potentiality. They all came into being through fixation on a specific object or a specific point in space or by concentration on some fictitious and legendary being, which, however, is real in the popular imagination.

Clearly. what is lacking in this theory is precisely the idea of religion. The totem is the hypostasized community, and everything else is illusory. Indeed, if one considers the social facts *"comme des choses"* ("as things") and classifies them only *"par certains caractères extérieurs"* ("by certain typical external features"), it may happen that what is essentially religious vanishes in the process.

It hardly needs to be said that Durkheim's point of departure also is incorrect. He believes totemism is a very primitive and general form of religion. Actually, it is neither. One may even ask whether totemism, known to us as a social structure, is really a form of religion, even granted that religious elements are mixed with it.

One might expect that the supreme beings would endanger Durkheim's theory. This is not at all so; those beliefs are fitted into it beautifully. In his opinion, this type of god is the logical result and the highest form of totemism. The idea of mythical ancestors is implied in totemic principle, for each of the ancestors is a totemic being. Although the great gods may exceed them, there are only differences of degree; there is a transition from one group to the other and no discontinuity. A great god is only a preeminent ancestral spirit.[6]

What helped the Australian aborigines, Durkheim continues, to go from a plurality of ancestral spirits to one tribal god was the insertion of a middle term—the civilizing heroes. Actually, "the fabulous beings whom we call by this name are really simple ancestors to whom mythology has attributed an eminent place in the history of the tribe, and whom it has, for this reason, set above the others." [7]

As one can see, the argument is closely reasoned. Nevertheless it is a paper system, the fiction of a fabricating and obviously agnostic mind that arranges facts to its own satisfaction. Ethnographic data are cited in abundance, but they are selective and beg the question.

In the conclusion of this study Durkheim states:

> . . . we admit that these religious beliefs rest upon a specific experience whose demonstrative value is, in one sense, not a bit inferior to that of scientific experiments, though different from them. . . . But from the fact that a "religious experience," if we choose to call it this, does exist and that it has a certain foundation—and, by the way, is there

any experience which has none?—it does not follow that the reality which is its foundation conforms objectively to the idea which believers have of it. The very fact that the fashion in which it has been conceived has varied infinitely in different times is enough to prove that none of these conceptions express it adequately.

. . .

. . . this reality, which mythologies have presented under so many different forms, but which is the universal and eternal objective cause of these sensations *sui generis* out of which religious experience is made, is society.[8]

Sensations *sui generis*, indeed. But this class is not sociological but irreducibly religious. Whoever believes he can derive religion from this concept of society confuses what is accidental with what is essential. Of course, we must admit that no religion exists without the community of believers—disregarding exceptions like ecstatics and mystics, although we know of them too only in social frameworks—but the same can be said of art, jurisprudence, and moral codes. Yet these are certainly not treated fairly if they are called hypostasizations of society, for they are expressions of an aesthetic or ethical sentiment. Durkheim erred by his fixation on totemism, whose social character is quite pronounced; but to explain all other forms of religion as sociological forms on that basis is staggeringly lopsided and shows little understanding of any serious religious awareness.

Chapter Nineteen

PRIMITIVE THOUGHT

THE primitive religions present imageries and mythical narratives that could only strike the modern investigator as fanciful and abstruse. Evolutionism fostered the assumption that a line ran straight from the simple and naïve to the complicated and abstract. It was startling when in many cases the very opposite was established. Compared to the transparent modern languages with their logical structure, the languages of many very primitive peoples are complex to the point of being impenetrable. The social forms, with involved clan systems and almost incomprehensible marriage restrictions, present an equal image of complexity. It all seems in flagrant contrast to the evolutionistic ideas.

The outsider, watching magic imageries and acts, is astonished at such lack of simple logic. What is done by the magician seems quite inadequate to what he intends to achieve. He blows tobacco smoke toward the sky and expects rain clouds to form. Magic looks like hocus pocus for a childish mind.

Still worse is the impression that the most elementary, natural notions never occur to the primitives. Several times the opinion has been advanced—we find it confirmed by Malinowski—that peoples on the lowest stage of culture do not make any direct connection between the sexual act and pregnancy. The Arunta in Australia believe that a woman becomes pregnant when an ancestral spirit, who is present at certain places, succeeds in penetrating her body. Frazer concludes that primitives are completely ignorant concerning the world's most natural process, although they may have learned from observing animals that no birth takes place without a preceding coitus. Lévy-Bruhl says in this context[1] that the savages do not raise questions about the necessary antecedents of birth but look for its cause in a mythical event. This would demonstrate once more that primitive man is not even interested in the workings of natural law. Nevertheless, as Jensen observed,

> Our supposed satisfaction with knowledge of the natural law, to which we would refer in the given example, would not account for the fact that pregnancy does not attend each sexual act or that it never does so in the case of a barren individual. Scientific thought would never stop at the mere correlation between the procreative act and pregnancy but would search for additional causation. Assuming even that all concomitant causes had been fully established, what would the whole celebration have to do with the question raised by the event itself? Are the conception of a living being, pregnancy, birth, not miraculous events indeed? [2]

Perhaps the Arunta are not entirely wrong in thinking that a coitus alone does not suffice to explain a conception; something else must happen as well before a conception succeeds, and it is not so foolish if this unknown is thought of as mythological. Nevertheless, there is an element in the thoughts of the primitives that eludes us. The same is true of their work. They are able to fashion all sorts of tools; their eye for the properties of materials and their technique are excellent. And still, in making a house or a boat they consider it indispensable to go through magical or religious acts, which alone, in their opinion, are responsible for the successful completion of their work. To modern considerations, primitive behavior mocks the simplest laws of logic, and this has to be explained. The explanation is found in the "primal stupidity" of primitive man!

Lévy-Bruhl

When the curious thought occurred to Frazer that magic was some sort of primitive science, he had to find out why magic stemmed from such strange premises. Frazer thought primitive man tried to think causally but applied the rules of thought incorrectly; when he considered an association, a similarity or a contiguity, in space and time, he imagined an identity, and this was the basis of magical practices.

An analogous theory was developed by the French sociologist and philosopher Lucien Lévy-Bruhl (1857-1939). He called the associations cited by Frazer "participations" and believed that primitives turned them into identifications without further ado. Another primitive error, he felt, was to have no sense for the mutual exclusiveness of two different things. Finally, primitives did not comprehend the laws of causality. Generally, observers of primitive thought have established that the primitives detest logic and that this is not so much the result of a lack of intelligence as of their overall habits of thought.

This led Lévy-Bruhl to conclude that the primitives use their intellect in a very different way, and he calls their mentality "mystical" or "prelogical." "This fundamental characteristic," he says,

> permeates his whole method of thinking, feeling and acting, and from this circumstance arises the extreme difficulty of comprehending and following its course. Starting from sense-impressions, which are alike in primitives and ourselves, it makes an abrupt turn, and enters on paths which are unknown to us, and we soon find ourselves astray. If we try to guess why primitives do, or refrain from doing, certain things, what prejudices they obey in given cases, the reasons which compel them with regard to any special course, we are most likely to be mistaken. We may find an "explanation" which is more or less probable, but nine times out of ten it will be the wrong one.[3]

Lévy-Bruhl supports his theory with numerous examples. They were not hard to find; they abounded on the pages written by missionaries and ethnographers. We feel no strong objections to his decision to call this thought mystical. But why does he call it prelogical? Why not simply a-logical? The word he selected suggests that the primitives are *not yet* familiar with the normal function of logical reason. This is truly a primitive mental condition. Apparently, Lévy-Bruhl's theory seeks some middle ground between animal instinct and normal human logic; this middle must precede logical thought and be characterized by mental short circuits.

Whoever protests that the savage thinks just as we do in many of his daily routines would have Lévy-Bruhl's accord. He says himself that he does not intend a commentary on primitive technical skills (invention and perfection of tools and weapons, domestication of animals, construction of houses and boats, cultivation). Indeed, things like the outriggers of the Papuas are a marvel of ingenuity and technique.

In this respect Lévy-Bruhl fully recognizes primitive man's logical soundness, and he grants a knowledge of "secondary causes." Then why should we insist any further that primitive mentality is prelogical?

It seems absurd, and yet his clear expositions and abundant documentation had a powerful influence on his generation. They were also very well suited to the popular conceptions about primitives. The scholarly fashions of preanimism and magical practices were completed by the theory of an undeveloped intellect. It will become evident that this whole theory is based on a series of misconceptions and misinterpretations. At this point we want to mention only that Lévy-Bruhl himself, at the end of his life, gave up a good deal of his thesis. He declared in 1938 that his conception of prelogical thought was inaccurate; the notes he jotted down, revising his theory, were published posthumously in his *Carnets*.[4]

We might let the theory be, since its author abandoned it.* But the theory has influenced many a study of primitive religion and mentality. Thus, G. van der Leeuw's *Religion in Essence and Manifestation* takes as its point of departure prelogical thought as a solid fact. A scholar like Karl Beth concludes that after Lévy-Bruhl's thorough study of the primitive psyche it can no longer be denied that primitive man is incapable of drawing a logical conclusion and is little inclined to relate himself rationally to his environment.

Before dealing with the criticism leveled against this hypothesis we want to note Van der Leeuw's observations in a suggestively written book, *La structure de la mentalité primitive* (*The Structure of Primitive Mentality*), published in 1928. He begins with Lévy-Bruhl and, like him, establishes the idea of a singular mentality. He would like to call it "asyntactical" rather than prelogical, but he does consider it subject to the law of participation.

---

* At least, in its pristine form. The *Carnets* are not a complete recantation. —TRANS.

This mentality is dominated by emotional elements, on the one hand magically and on the other mythologically. However, the importance of Van der Leeuw's study is not the modification and emendation of a definition.

He shows that the same mentality is still ours in certain realms of spiritual life. It is not too important that we find it in dreams, in the psychology of children, and in schizophrenics, for these have not reached our admirably modern and logical world view, or have regressed. But a primitive in the true sense is the poet and certainly the religious man. Once this is clear, there is no reason to look down on that heterological mentality. Obviously, the human spiritual development cannot be construed as a simple evolution from a primitive prelogical stage to modern reason.

Van der Leeuw rightly indicates[5] that we can know the world from many points of view. All of these are related to structures in our soul. A structure can be aesthetic, economic, scientific, or, also, mythical. It follows that these structures reflect a like number of aspects of the world and exist side by side. He emphasizes in particular that primitive man thinks as logically as we in cases where logic alone suffices. The only difference is that we apply this method in a much wider sphere than does the primitive.

Van der Leeuw makes an example of the conception of time. Our time is linear; the time of primitive man is cyclical. (However, cyclical time is certainly not restricted to the primitives; it occurs in much higher cultures and among ourselves.) One remark made by Mircea Eliade in his *Cosmos and History* sums this up; he says that the idea that time is irreversible and always produces novelties must be regarded as a "recent discovery." [6] Because of this recent discovery we have an idea of history that is foreign to primitive man. For him, each act becomes real only when it is a repetition of an archetype. We shall return to the significance of this when discussing sacrifice.

Van der Leeuw's expositions enable us to understand that there is no line to draw between the modern western mind and the primitive mind. We celebrate our rational thought and its constant victories in the natural sciences and technology. Still, it would be improper to forget that in some circumstances we are no less prelogical than the Australian savages. In times of war, revolution, and epidemic, modern man is the toy of his passion.

Magical practices, soothsaying, horoscopy, and somnambulism flourish in certain circles and under favorable conditions, against all expectations of rational sobriety.

Man has always been like that. Primitive or modern, he behaves reasonably today, well aware of the rules of causality, and tomorrow his emotionality governs him. It may be more accurate to say that modern man, having gained his present attitude of mind from western European rationalism, is the exception to mankind as a whole. Does he not show a hypertrophy of reason because the whole supernatural world has lost its significance for him?

If we want to understand prelogical thought, we must study the situations it occurs in. When an aborigine builds his prau, he brings to bear all his skill. Yet he also performs magical acts and finds the latter even more important. Why? Any medieval man would have understood immediately, for he too would not fail to implore God's blessing on his work. On how many unforeseen circumstances does the success of an act depend! The axe a savage uses to fell a tree slips and wounds his foot. He constructs his prau as well as he can—but will the boat be seaworthy or capsize in the first storm? Craftsmanship is useless unless a man is "lucky" in his work. But he does not have this luck at his fingertips.

A. E. Jensen makes some apt observations; apropos prelogical ideas of birth and death, he says:

> Scientific research has not diminished the mystery of either by any statement of higher rationality. Man's spiritual and physical existence contains many mysterious enclaves. The growth process, metabolism, maturation, all are in a way mysterious happenings. Questions of cosmogony and creation, the relationship between the animate and the inanimate world, between plants, animals, and man only multiply the examples. *Exactly in this sphere, however, we encounter most of that which seems strange and incomprehensible to us.* It all has a common element: *the basis of our existence is involved.* Significantly, concerning such matters no answer has ever been devised by rational thought that would transcend cultural boundaries.[7]

It is unfair to reproach primitive man for his logical insufficiency in problems where logical thought would fail in any case.

Among the primitives, as among ourselves, thought occurs on two levels. When a Melanesian, in Codrington's account, is confronted with a disease, he asks if this disease is natural. If it is not, he tries to learn whether it is caused by mana or ghosts, by spirits or gods. If the disease is natural, the ordinary medicines are administered. It is well known that primitive peoples are thoroughly familiar with medicinal herbs and plants through experiment and observation. But if a disease is incomprehensible, there must be causes beyond the confines of a logical treatment. After all, not long ago in Europe it was generally believed that demons possessed an epileptic and could be exorcised.

It will be best to drop the unfortunate term prelogical. Certainly Lévy-Bruhl's other word, "mystical," is more in keeping. We must assume that human reflection on the riddles of existence, to which Jensen draws attention, is different in kind from logical reasoning; logic has no access here. Is it possible then to say anything in detail about the "mystical"?

Lévy-Bruhl emphasizes the law of participation. Who would deny that in the perspective of the cosmos things show a mutual participation? According to Preusz, the Huichol in Mexico believe there is an identification of stars, deer, and the peyote cactus. (The rationalistic explanation Preusz proposes had best be left alone. We, at least, have no easy accounting.) There are in fact numerous interplays—as between the moon and vegetation—whose real sense escapes us and which as logical people we should like to ignore. At any rate, all men are prelogical in circumstances where logic is insufficient. Whoever does not suspect another world exists beyond the one that is logically defined—a world that can be entered by intuition, vision, and imagination—still has no reason to regard others, who do have such suspicions, as primitive.

Ernst Cassirer

In his *Philosophy of Symbolic Forms,* Ernst Cassirer (1874-1945) discusses *Mythical Thought* in the second volume. For the sake of a proper perspective, he juxtaposes it with scientific thought, although strictly speaking only the latter is considered the correct mode. For the man of science, in the final analysis the "truth" of the phenomena is the totality of the phenomena, not in their concrete reality but transferred to the form of a coherence of thought—that is, a coherence that is based on both logical connection and logical distinction.

Myth too envisions a coherence, but it does so quite differently. While science discovers ideal relationships, structuring the world according to the governance of laws, myth fuses all that exists and occurs into tangible and vivid details. At this point Cassirer registers a difference in principles of thought. Myth attempts a unity that does away with distinctions of moment and place. The relationships established by myth become identities and, thus, more than parts that correspond in terms of ideas.

> Things which come into contact with one another in a mythical sense—whether this contact is taken as a spatial or temporal contiguity or as a similarity, however remote, or as membership in the same class or species—have fundamentally ceased to be a multiplicity: they have acquired a substantial unity.[8]

Cassirer therefore characterizes mythical thinking as subject to the law of the "concrescence or coincidence of the members of a relation."

Of course one need not say that mythical thinking is undeveloped thinking as measured by scientific logic. Rather, a definition depends on a point of view. It may be strange for us to see a man identify himself with his totemic animal. Yet one does not understand the identification as long as one considers it a mythical coincidence of two members that works by making absolute a presupposed relation between the two. One must begin with the idea that the two are essentially the same. If one insists on calling this a mythical participation, he must bear in mind that what the two participate in belongs to the essence of both. The essence, however, is one thing in a scientific sense and another in a religious sense.

Cassirer states:

> [The basic mythical conceptions of mankind] are not culled from a ready-made world of Being, they are not mere products of fantasy which vapor off from fixed, empirical, realistic existence, to float above the actual world like a bright mist; to primitive consciousness they present the *totality*

of Being. The mythical form of conception is not something superadded to certain definite *elements* of empirical existence; instead, the primary "experience" itself is steeped in the imagery of myth and saturated with its atmosphere. Man lives with *objects* only in so far as he lives with these *forms*; he reveals reality to himself, and himself to reality, in that he lets himself and the environment enter into this plastic medium, in which the two do not merely make contact, but fuse with each other.[9]

Cassirer demonstrates this mythical thinking in terms of space, time, and number, and applies it to the phases of religious development (preanimism, animism). He makes remarks that are to the point and cause the typical features of mythic thought to stand out clearly.

However, it must be said that mythical thought is religious thought and more so than Cassirer seems willing to admit. Myth expresses the world in symbols; it does so because reason alone gives insufficient leverage on the reality in which man finds himself. Symbolism expresses reality. But, while it reveals it, it also conceals it. This fact is not terribly significant for Cassirer. He is interested only from the point of view of the *logos,* which unfolds fully in science. The road to that *logos* was long and difficult; before starting out on that road humanity had to wander in the darkness. In fact, however, myth is not darkness and error but a manner of thought *sui generis*. When Cassirer discusses what is truly religious and sacred, it appears to him only as a method of creating a cosmos out of the ephemeral stream of perceptions. However, the problem is not how our present intellectualism may judge the method. The real problem is that all of humanity has chosen this singular way to build from ephemeral phenomena a cosmos in which it can live and be safe.

Paul Radin and A. E. Jensen

It is crucially important to us to understand primitive thought, no matter how abstruse we find it. Since the primitives weigh and act logically in technical matters and are then perfectly able to apply cause and effect, why should we assume they err completely in the area of mythical thought?

There used to be a special fondness for comparing primitive man's development with that of children. This suited the catch-thought that ontogenetic evolution repeats the phylogenetic evolution. Yet a child is soon ripe enough for logical sequences of thought. A little girl, not five years of age, asked: "If there is no egg, where does the chicken come from? I mean, at the time when there was no egg yet, where did the chicken come from?" This sort of question could well have produced the image of the cosmic egg. Moreover, the question shows keen observation and thought and yet can be properly answered only by myth!

However that may be, the comparison with the spiritual ca-pacity of a child is uncalled for. Primitive man is an adult who has undergone life, who knows the struggle of existence, and who has had his part of joy and pain. What special reason could there be to compare him with the child in the parental home, making its first feeble steps toward experience.

It is a prerequisite for understanding primitive man to re-frain from considering him childish. We must abandon the idea of a split between his logical daily activities and his religious life (in which he would suddenly think differently, "mythically"). If he is not led astray by the "concrescence or coincidence of the members of a relation" in the first case, while building his prau, why should he be led astray in the second?

Missionaries have often asserted that primitive man can not think in a well-organized and discursive way. Coincidentally, the fact has been established that he is extraordinarily capable of apprehending things that can be learned mechanically. And still in the same breath we are told there is not a trace of mental in-dependence. "Among us," a missionary relates, "little children do nothing but ask: Why? But a Mossi on the River Niger never asks: Why is this as it is and not different?" Why should he? After all, no adult among ourselves would go about asking such questions! Among the Mossi, as among us, most questions of that sort have been answered satisfactorily for a long time.[10]

In the meanwhile, the same missionaries can be amazed by the sagacity of the primitives in debate. They are never at a loss for words when it comes to a lawsuit or the palaver of a public meeting. Their animal stories show a keen power of ob-servation, their poetry an imaginative and creative mastery of the language.

Paul Radin (1883-1959) was among the first to picture the intellect of the primitives in a new way. With a certain irritation he writes:

> Lévy-Bruhl did anthropology a great disservice when he introduced into it the conceptions of *mentalité prélogique* and the *loi de participation*. It has only been equalled by the disservice Ernst Cassirer rendered by his conception of *mythical thought (das mythische Denken)*.[11]

One of Radin's books, *Primitive Man as Philosopher,* indicates even by its title that he attributes philosophical thought, and *a fortiori* rational thought, to the primitives. The error of most observers was that they measured the intelligence of the primitive tribes by that of their average member. If the intelligence quotient of western man were determined on the same basis, things would look sad among us as well. As a rule, the majority of people do not excel the intellectual capacity of a high school pupil of fifteen or sixteen. Our high civilization, in which we so pride ourselves, is created and carried on by an extremely small elite. It is precisely the same among the primitive tribes. Priests and shamans are the guardians of the magical and religious traditions. Customs and legal traditions are preserved by older men who guide the tribe. Those who are talented produce the literary works. It is always these individuals who create the mythical images and attempt to explain the enigmas of the world. If only one listens to them carefully, they prove to have profound understanding.

Consequently Radin can say:

> It is a matter of common experience that in any randomly selected group of individuals we may expect to find, on the whole, the same distribution of temperament and ability. Such a view, I know, has certain terrors because of national and class prejudices, but I do not think it can be really seriously questioned. Certainly not for temperament. But, you might ask, is this true for primitive peoples? Is not their mentality, is not their whole emotional nature utterly different from our own? Most laymen, all sociologists and many ethnological theorists are of that opinion. Nothing in reality is wider from the mark. Perhaps I need hardly insist upon this after the examples of logical and speculative thinking I have given you. Primitive people, as a matter of fact, are quite as logical as ourselves and have perhaps an even truer sense of reality. There is not the slightest indication of the existence of any fundamental difference in

their emotional nature as compared with ours. I think we may, in fact, confidently assume that the same distribution of ability and temperament holds for them that holds for us. Indeed I think there is ample reason for believing, granted that chance mating has existed since man's first appearance on earth, that the distribution of ability and temperament never has been appreciably different. What has differed is the size of populations with its corollary of a larger proportion of men of a certain type of ability and temperament.[12]

Hence Radin strongly opposed the fashionable idea that mana was an impersonal and universally effective power that came to be personified later on.[13] The opposite is true. From the beginning, supernatural power is the attribute of a deity. It may be appropriate to add that this fact was already abundantly clear in Codrington.

Radin continues:

The fact that the formation of religious values is only a secondary function of life has important consequences. One of these is that man of the primitive communities, who is religious only at specific occasions—hence like the vast majority—does not concern himself very much about a clear image of his spirits and gods. He is interested almost exclusively in their doings. To understand this fully, we need only compare the vagueness in the appearance of spirits and gods and their often contradictory features with the unmistakable definiteness of their activities. Only in politically and economically more advanced primitive civilizations, especially where a class and caste system exists, do things change.[14]

Then why does this mythical thinking seem so strange and inadequate to us? We have already noted A. E. Jensen's observation that primitive man expresses himself mythically in the critical situations of his life—that is, situations in which a rational solution is impossible and in which we too could never provide one. But we should bear in mind:

that these [primitive] religious teachings are concerned with a true cultural creation; this means that an eternal truth is "recognized" and given a shape and that a pronouncement about man's nature has been made that is irrefutable and is certainly not due to a "wrong application of the notion of causality." [15]

Jensen also indicates that our modern conceptions show a hyperdeveloped intellect. Now, it is not true that the culture of an epoch or a people is determined by the quality and quantity of intellect. There are aspects of every civilization where intellect cannot apply, such as art and music. There is nothing inferior about these. All that is knowable begins in perception and evolves to matters beyond perception. In this respect the primitive peoples have not progressed as far as we have. But this still does not relate to what makes culture. Culture consists above all in an expressive recognition of reality, and in these matters the criterion of progress is irrelevant. What matters is the content of the cultural form. These contents depend on so many things that one could not list them in a study of cultural history.

> Important, however, is man's capacity for experiencing and representing the grandeur and nobleness of life. The presence or lack of this capacity is not a variable, dependent on technical means, but depends on the magnitude and nobleness of the formed and forming experiences. In this respect no difference exists between older and younger cultures. From this point of view, cultural change is nothing but a change of Weltsicht, of the attitude toward the environment. Man has again and again asked questions bearing on the foundations of his existence; he has sought answers to the changing aspects of the reality about him and has thereby produced the documents of culture history which, at the same time, are a self-realization of original creativity.[16]

This prompts a respectful approach to the mythical traditions of the primitive peoples. If we do not understand, it is because we cannot assume the vantage of primitive man. The myth of Hainuwele shows us that between its limits of birth and death man's existence can be explained meaningfully. It may also fill us with admiration for the unity and completeness of its world view.

Chapter Twenty

THE THEORY OF
CULTURE CIRCLES

BY THE end of the nineteenth century, simplistic evolutionism began to lose its appeal. There were so many theories that projected an ascent of humanity from primordial man to the zenith (modern man in western Europe and America) that it became difficult to believe in any of them. There was reason to doubt that one could speak with meaning of a natural evolution toward a technical age. This particular path was possible, but not necessarily best, in cultural history. With different criteria, one might certainly call Greek civilization an unequalled summit.

Was it really self-evident that humankind progressed along the same cultural lines all over the earth? Culture does not unfold automatically, as if obeying an immanent law. If culture means the manner in which man asserts himself within nature, it is mandatory that one take into account the world in which the man lives. The hinterland of the Asian continent has another potential for culture than have the vast archipelagoes of the Pacific. Fertile river valleys like those of Mesopotamia and Egypt force a mode of life different from life in a desert. There are tremendous differences in climate, which stimulate or hamper culture. Finally, there are differences of race in disposition and temperament.

Among the first to note this fact of geography was Friedrich Ratzel (1844-1904). He studied the relations among land, people, and history. The effort to view man so closely in relation to his setting may have been one-sided, but the principle of this branch of study was justified and proved fertile. Ratzel's pupil Leo Frobenius (1849-1917), who was more concerned with ethnography, accepted and continued Ratzel's views: he would study the primitive civilizations in light of the geography on which they arose. Culture is a fabric of the most diverse threads. It begins with the struggle for existence and creates tools, weapons, and garments. It soon leads to the building of dwellings and of boats and other vehicles. By the nature of his existence, man must make social forms: family, horde, clan, tribe, nation. Such organization needs norms of justice and morality. Finally, there are religion, art, and knowledge, which crown the civilization of man.

A civilization is not a loose and arbitrary linkage of all these elements. It is a "wholeness" in which every detail functions specifically. Religion is in tune with the economic life and at the same time with the forms of social coherence. It always belongs to a particular people of a particular period; it is not a stage in itself through which all mankind passes. Cultures are expressions of a time and place. Each culture has its own possibilities and its own right to exist.

The ethnologist, therefore, must try to determine not only the character of the civilization he studies but also its sense in the region where it unfolded. Frobenius—who felt particularly drawn to the study of Africa—successfully distinguished certain cultural areas and delineated them precisely. The cartographic method was most suitable for his purpose. By marking down and comparing the geographical extension of elements of culture (bows, vessels, and bellows of specific shapes; agricultural forms; types of dwellings; boating techniques; religious customs; images; myths), he obtained a map of a culture. Although certain elements overlapped the borders, the map portrayed rather precisely a cultural area complete in itself.

Frobenius could take pride in the fact that he had been first to formulate the *Kulturkreislehre* ("theory of culture circles"). Extending his comparisons to phenomena in other parts of the world, he found elsewhere certain elements of the African cultural regions. This proved as true of religious phenomena as of tools and weapons. The initiatory imagery of the boy devoured by a monster or demon and resurrected occurs on New Guinea and in northern Australia, but it also occurs on the west coast of North America, in Tierra del Fuego, and in some spots in Africa.

Some questions inevitably arise. How can such widespread yet seemingly sporadic occurrences be explained? Thinking of Bastian's "elementary ideas" one may suppose universal self-assertion of the psyche. However, one may also assume some cultural coherence, in the sense that a tool or rite originated in one place and was carried from there to other parts of the world. In that case either a migration from the region of origin or another connection—commercial, perhaps—must be supposed.

The cartographic picture of the initiation rite is particularly striking and puzzling, but as an example of cartographic processes it is not typical. Frobenius made careful efforts to depict extensive areas of civilization by tracing cultural elements, and his cartograms enabled him to show a number of large and definitely coherent cultural provinces. The method revealed coherences over tremendous distances in all parts of the world. But the results could only be schematic, and Frobenius, who was always inclined to see things in giant perspectives, in the end was accused of superficiality and hasty generalizations.

More painstaking study of distinct regions of civilization provided a great improvement. A continent like Australia is by no means homogeneous; it is populated with ethnic groups that came from outside in waves, each with a culture of its own. Although this continent has remained extremely primitive, it too has had its history. Fritz Graebner (1877-1934) drew attention to this fact. In 1906 he published a study of the social systems of Australia;[1] his very detailed investigation uncovered two completely distinct forms existing side by side. The older was a local totemism, with numerous patriarchal clans but without marriage groups; the more recent had two exogamous marriage groups matriarchally organized. The combination of the old and recent forms gave rise to two systems with totemic classes and patrilinear or matrilinear rights of inheritance.

Graebner's study settled one important issue: it is impossible to derive the patriarchal organization from matriarchy, as general opinion had done since Bachofen. In Australia two forms, originally independent, interpenetrated; the result was the typically totemic system. The study also made it possible to distinguish three cultural levels. The first was Negritic and included the extinct Tasmanians. The second was West Papuan, from the northwest and north, and covered the Negritic level or pushed it back to the utmost limit. Then from the east an East Papuan civilization penetrated to the middle of the continent, and in some places reached the west coast.

It is not necessary to pursue the details. The main concern is that the culture pattern, even of such a very primitive population, is complex and involves important historical movements even in the most ancient days. It is no longer possible to speak of "the" totemism of the Australians, for there are varied types.

This example also shows what a painstaking task must be performed in all parts of the world in order to gain an understanding of the structure of existing cultural forms. The scholars who have undertaken this labor are associated mainly with two schools: Graebner, Ankermann and Foy with Cologne and W. Schmidt and W. Koppers with Vienna.

The observation of the elements of culture (first the way of life and subsistence, second the social structures and religion) led to a new classification of cultures—not in successions but as neighbors who flourished in proximity and by mixing made novel and higher forms.

It has become clear that matriarchy and patriarchy must belong to very different types of civilization. Matriarchy belongs to peoples who practice the most ancient form of agriculture— the earliest care of cultivated plants; patriarchy belongs to nomadic pastoral cultures. This is reflected in the fact that primitive agriculture is carried on by women, while for obvious reasons the care of large herds of cattle is the man's work. The moment one goes beyond such main lines and tries to draw the whole human cultural development, one meets great difficulties and relies heavily on personal judgment.

One example of this is the scheme presented by W. Schmidt. In addition to the primal culture, he distinguishes three higher degrees of civilization, which he calls primary, secondary, and tertiary. The ancient civilizations of Asia, Europe, and America are tertiary, and we shall leave them out of our discussion.

The mark of the primal culture is that man hunts small game and gathers only the fruits presented by nature. Of course, the hunt is man's work and food gathering is woman's.

The most ancient primal culture known is that of the Pygmies in Africa and the Negritoes in Asia. It is characterized socially by monogamy with local exogamy and religiously by primal monotheism and hence by beliefs in a creative supreme being who instituted forever the juridical norms. Another type of culture mentioned is found on Tasmania, in southeast Australia, and Tierra del Fuego; the society is also monogamous but with a totemism related to the sexes; along with the supreme being, animism and magic are strongly evident. The arctic peoples live by (small) fishing and among them shamanism is found. The highest type of the primal cultures occurs in parts of Australia, Africa, and North America and has the beginnings of a rather powerful tribal organization. Here the supreme being yields to the tribal ancestor, and a lunar mythology develops.

The primary culture circles are more developed in all respects. Their principal mode of subsistence is big game hunting, primitive gardening, or breeding and herding cattle. The hunting peoples are known in Australia and New Guinea, India (the Dravidas), North Africa, and northeast America. They are structured in exogamous totemic clans, in which the father has the most important place. The highest god is a solar deity; there are ancestor cults and a strongly developed magic. A second group in these primary culture circles, the peoples whose women cultivate certain plants, is dispersed all over the world: in Melanesia and Indonesia, Indochina, southeast India and certain parts of Africa, and North and Central America. Understandably, they are matriarchies; the men organize themselves in secret societies. The principal deity is the moon or a mother goddess; animism is strongly developed; masked dances are important in the cult. Finally, there are pastoral peoples, organized in large patriarchal families with right of primogeniture. In addition to the sky god, various gods and spirits are known to them. This type of cult occurs among the Ural-Altaic peoples, the Indo-Europeans and the Semito-Hamites.

The secondary cultures are all amalgamations of the ones mentioned. Our discussion does not require a detailed list. I will mention as an example the cultures that emerged from the mixture of matrilineal gardening peoples and patriarchal pastoral peoples—those in Melanesia, New Guinea, and Indochina, among the African Bantus, in the southeastern part of North America, and in the northeastern part of South America. The social organization is marked by large families guided by the grandparents and by a more or less matriarchal tendency. Usually there is a sky god and an earth goddess linked with a cult of skulls.

Obviously, all these expositions are schemes, and every new study will modify them, but this is not too important. What matters is that the history of religions will have to account for the findings of this "theory of culture circles." After all, it shows that particular religious types appear in different parts of the world in association with specific social structures. For instance, we may find a cult of celestial bodies, but it makes a difference whether the sun or the moon is adored. It is evident that in matriarchally persuaded civilizations the moon comes to the fore; the phases of the moon are the prototype of the natural birth, growth, death, and new life. The moon's period is clearly related to woman's; it is often said that the moon has its menstruation during the three new moon's days when it is invisible and for that reason that women in the same circumstance must isolate themselves.

The place assigned by W. Schmidt to the Indo-Europeans is a ready occasion to come back to their beliefs, which for so long were the pivot of all considerations concerning religion.

Chapter Twenty-one

INDO-EUROPEAN POLYTHEISM

THE enthusiastic efforts of the early nineteenth century to determine the mythology of the original Indo-Europeans ended as a fiasco, and further attempts of that sort were abandoned. The reason for the debacle, as mentioned before, was twofold. The self-contradicting naturalistic explanations became unsatisfactory. What was worse, reconstructions of the Indo-European religion were seriously mistaken in the linguistic comparison of the names of gods. The science of linguistics was in its infancy, and as it grew thoughtful and accurate and used more precise phonetic laws, the glamorous comparisons proved to be false— or dubious at least.

One comparison remained tenable—that of the sky gods Dyaus-Zeus-Jupiter. It was concluded that the other gods arrived after the Indo-European linguistic and ethnic differentiation. This meant that most of the pantheon of Indians, Greeks, Romans, and Teutons was rather recent. I have mentioned before the results of these opinions in interpretation: gods such as Wodan and Donar become borrowings from elsewhere; in the beginning there must have been a belief in spirits and demons, as current ethnology suggested.

Although the early attempts to determine the Indo-European

mythology proved disastrous, there followed a period of more constructive study. It was hard, after all, to deny the resemblances between such gods as Donar and Indra; some relationship must exist. All Indo-European peoples knew a pair of gods of the Dioscuri type. Wodan (Odin) was not as isolated as had been assumed; he shares many features with the Indian Rudra. Cosmogonic imageries bore similarities; it is difficult to separate the Indian Yama and the Iranian Yima from the Old Norse Ymir.

Names alone should not tell the story of gods in the various traditions, since names can be replaced without the deity changing. Other criteria in relationships had to be found.

First, the personal traits and adventures of the gods required consideration. Donar and Indra both play the thunder; moreover, both are warlike. The Nordic god Tyr lost a hand, as did the Irish god Nuadu. The myth of the divine drink, to which Adalbert Kuhn had devoted an excellent study, was treated anew in 1924 by the French scholar Georges Dumézil (b. 1898) in a book emphatically subtitled a "Study on Comparative Indo-European Mythology." [1]

Before this new comparative research could really come into its own, an old prejudice had to be destroyed. The idea had too long persisted that in the beginning the gods were divinizations of the powers of nature. As cosmic beings of course they were related to material phenomena. Zeus hurled lightning and opened the rainclouds. Indra could do the same things. The *vajra,* his weapon, was like Thor's hammer "Myollnir" and symbolized lightning. Yet this aspect of the gods was not paramount. Zeus ruled the Olympus; he was more a powerful king of gods than a god of thunder and lightning.

Indeed, the Olympus as depicted by Homer appears as a well-organized state. It had been thought that this was a rather recent development, but in India and among the Germanic tribes, too, we find that the gods inhabit a community very much like the community of men. It would be odd if unrelated nature deities of all the Indo-European nations had formed similar divine states.

In 1907, in Boghazkoy, a village of north central Asiatic Turkey, a discovery we have mentioned before (see page 69) was made in the archives of a Hittite king. Several texts were found of a treaty concluded by this king and the king of the Mitanni around 1380 B.C. Each monarch named his own gods to guarantee the treaty. Among the gods of the Mitanni occurs one series who were immediately recognized as identical with Indian gods: Mitra-Varuṇa, Indra and the two Nāsatyas. In 1926 the Dane A. Christensen established that these gods were the principal deities of the Aryan community. This was an important piece of scholarship, for the Aryan community precedes the date we can assign to the Vedas. It would be no exaggeration to place it some 2000 years B.C. Finally, in 1945, Georges Dumézil decided that those gods, functioning as warrantors of the treaty, must be understood to bind the whole nation and hence to represent it in all its parts.

If this is so, we must learn the meaning of these gods in the religious system. In other words, we should forget about a haphazard group of nature deities and see the Indo-European pantheon as representing the divine help the community calls for in all its endeavors.

Dumézil, who has certainly been influenced by the sociology that flourished in France, sought an explanation along these lines. The Indo-European society was divided into classes; this is perfectly clear in each of the Indo-European peoples. In India the classes became extremely set in the fixation of caste. This development is relatively recent and limited to India; yet somewhat more flexibly we find the same class system among the Greeks, Romans, Celts, and Teutons. The king is at the pinnacle, and he is directly supported by a militant nobility. The base is made up of the bulk of the population—farmers, herdsmen, and craftsmen. The question that arises is whether this social structure is reflected in the pantheon.

Since 1934, Dumézil has worked with this problem. A clear summary of his views, which had been presented in a growing number of complementary and mutually corrective studies, was published in 1958 in *L'idéologie tripartite des Indo-Européens* ("The Indo-European Ideology of Tripartition").[2] He brought out the fact that the "third class" is reflected in the pantheon in the first place by the divine twins (the Dioscuri type) but, in addition, by a whole series of female divinities whose influence, expectably, relates to fertility in all realms of life. It is interesting that in the exclusively patriarchal world of the Germanic peoples even these deities of fertility are male: the gods Nyord and Freyr. The nobility (or warrior class) is represented by a god, Indra to the Indians, Mars to the Romans, Donar to the Germans. Thus the "nature" character of a thunder god would seem to be secondary. Through thunder and lightning a tremendous power, which is the celestial equivalent of the rage of a noble warrior class in battle, becomes clear.

Kingship has a double aspect in all Indo-European traditions. This is shown most lucidly in the Indian divine pair Mitra-Varuna, who are almost always mentioned together in a grammatical dual form. Corresponding to these are the Roman Jupiter and Dius Fidius and the Germanic Tiwaz and Wodan. This pair represent the highest authority, which was twofold. In many respects the two gods present contrasts. Mitra is the god of agreements and contracts; he is a friend of men. Varuna the magician is violent and pitiless with anyone who has transgressed. Mitra is the guardian of law, prosperity, and peace, and Varuna is the patron of war and conquest. Although they contrast, Dumézil interprets them as the two faces of authority, protecting and preserving the social order and maintaining the law, but also as a revolutionary power, erupting through a fossilized order and creating new forms. While Varuna incorporates authority in a secular sense, Mitra does so spiritually. For that reason, in the Indian texts the *brahman* or priest and the *kṣatra* or warrior often play their parts side by side.

A crucial matter in Dumézil's exposition is a certain myth that occurs in various Indo-European versions and is clearest perhaps in Scandinavia in the struggle between the Aesir and the Vanir. The Aesir are the gods of the two great classes; the Vanir are the gods of fertility and the guardians of the third class. Thus, the tensions between the aristocracy and the multitude, that in the course of history have often led to conflicts, are cast in a mythical war. That war ends with a treaty of peace, establishing the harmony of the classes. In India, too, a myth relates that initially the Aśvins did not belong among the real gods but became accepted after a violent conflict. Dumézil compares with this type of conflict the war of the Romans and Sabines, which occurs early in the history of The Eternal City.

Throughout Dumézil's work, this scheme of functions assumes greater and greater proportions. He has paid special attention to the lesser gods in the retinues of great deities and sought to relate some of their functions.

It is interesting that the supreme god of the pantheon, the sky god, is sometimes—as in India—placed outside the rest of the system. It is not true, though, of the Roman Jupiter or the Germanic Tiwaz, both of whom correspond to Mitra in India. Zeus is a typical god-king, but for the rest the Greek pantheon deviates considerably from the Indo-European pattern because of the influence of the ancient Aegean cultures.

This new interpretation by Georges Dumézil found favor in some quarters and stirred criticism in others. We shall not judge it here; time will tell how much is tenable and useful. It speaks well for Dumézil that many mythological traditions—until now virtually incomprehensible—suddenly were solved through his functional system.

If we compare this system with the culture circles theory as to the structure they attribute to Indo-European religion, the difference is evident. The culture circles outlook emphasizes the sky god almost to the exclusion of the other gods.

Still, the theory designed by Dumézil does not detract from the sky god's high position. The figure of Zeus (Jupiter) Tiwaz, corresponding to Dyaus-pitar, is the direct descendant of that sky god who occurs among the nomadic peoples.

Dumézil's system presupposes a cultural stage at which the Indo-Europeans had either accepted agriculture or established themselves as rulers over an agricultural indigenous population. At any rate, they created in that day a firm social and political organization of the same type we find in historical times among the various nations.

We may infer that the typical Indo-European pantheon with its functions developed only in the last phase before the separation into nations and tribes. We must assume a long prehistory —previous to this development—which held the germ of that firmly fixed and admirable system. The known traditions of the various Indo-European nations may be regarded as the final phase of that long history.

This means that at least two specific problems remain. The first is whether we can reconstruct the historical prototypes of the Indo-European pantheon. It seems clear that the "original" Indo-Europeans must have been a nation rigidly organized under an hereditary kingship and hence already rather highly civilized. Our problem then is how to extend the line of development back to an earlier, perhaps simpler stage.

The second question concerns the subjected peoples. Wherever the Indo-Europeans settled, they found an earlier population, sometimes primitive but sometimes quite civilized. Rulers and subjects together gradually made a single nation. This implies within the broad cultural amalgamation an interpenetration of religious elements that may have altered in meaning and lost their source. We may think of matriarchally organized agricultural peoples with cults of female powers. Is it possible that remnants of such cultural and religious complexes survived in the many female deities of the third class? Does a struggle like the Aesirs' and the Vanirs' portray a historical struggle between Indo-European invaders and an earlier, peaceful agricultural population? The answers to these questions will decide whether Dumézil's theory is tenable in the form he gave it and to what extent the functional, tripartite system itself must be regarded as a product of an earlier development.

Part Four

SOME SPECIAL
PROBLEMS

Chapter Twenty-two

MAGIC AND RELIGION

THE relationship of magic and religion has been in controversy for the past half-century. Of course, it is agreed that they are fundamentally opposed from a phenomenological point of view. According to W. Otto, religion, more than being man's idea of a higher power, is the cult he creates always involving the beginnings of morality.[1] Magic is more audacious and tries to coerce the powers to do the will of men. This is the boldest contrast of magic and religion—the pose they strike in relation to the power beyond them.

Yet the two go as brothers through the ages. Over and over magic threatens religion; over and over reverence gives way to cajolery and the will for control. Even the holiest Christian acts can turn into something magical. The question is asked many times: which—religion or magic—is earlier and more original?

Let us start with Sir James Frazer's view, expressed in *The Golden Bough*.[2] He distinguishes two kinds of magic: imitative and sympathetic. In the first, the magician mimics the result he would like to achieve: he blows smoke toward the sky so that rain clouds will appear there. The second magic works against victims by manipulating objects connected with them: what is done to the object will happen to the person. To inflict sickness or death, the magician performs certain acts on his victim's hair or nails or something else representing him. These feats work because one thing follows inevitably from another. There is no intervention by any kind of spirit. The magician works by a law of cause and effect, as does the scientist. They both calculate lawful, unchanging sequences of events. Thus Frazer calls magic a sister of science; it knows laws and acts in accordance with them. But it is an infant science; it forms all kinds of wrong presuppositions and is greatly mistaken about the character of the laws it desires to apply. The relation between astrology and astronomy or between alchemy and chemistry seems to confirm Frazer's views.

Faith contrasts with magic, according to Frazer. He calls faith the attempt to propitiate and reconcile powers that are higher than man and that are believed to move nature and human fate. This service to superhuman beings may so move them on man's behalf that for his benefit they change the course of natural events. Since religion begins by believing that the conscious powers who rule the world can be persuaded, it is fundamentally different from both magic and science, which judge that the world is subject not to the will or mood of personal beings but to unchanging mechanical laws.

On these grounds Frazer decides that magic may be older than religion. Magic rests upon the simplest spiritual activity—the association of thoughts on the basis of a similarity or relation in space or time—but religion presupposes conscious and personal powers. This is a more complex idea. If one inquires into its genesis, Frazer suggests that man found that magic was far from complete and nature would not always yield to it. If magicians did not compel the world, there must be even mightier beings. Those who reflected more deeply on this issue caused the great transition from magic to religion. Thus, religion results from the realization that magic does not suffice. It originates only when reasonable people gain this insight and reflect on the consequences.

Obviously, this is all just a mental construction of Frazer's. Magic is not primitive science but a technique for obtaining results. The technique is correct because the results follow. The sorcerer does not act at random. When it is dry and he wants to "make" rain, he acts at a moment when he is led to suspect that a change in the weather will indeed follow his act. If we look on magic as a formal technique, it does seem that the sprinkling of water causes the rain to fall. But the man who performed this act for the first time had no causal law in mind, not even incorrectly. Primitive people had not come that far, and such logic would have been quite outside their sphere of interest. They took to magic in emergencies. This is all rather suggestive of a psychological pattern that we will speak of later on.

Frazer's theory of the development of religion from magic is also quite unsatisfactory. As is so often the case with the nineteenth century, we find the notion that religion functions where the intellect becomes insufficient. There is a border that magic and science cannot cross; beyond the border is irrational religion. The man of magic perceives that his method fails and gives it up; the man of science is steadfast and knows that research will enlarge his scope and press back the boundary of religion further and further.

It is not at all clear how Frazer thinks religion was born. Working his magic in vain, man became convinced that there are superior powers. Has he simply fancied these, assumed their possible existence in order to complete his world view again? Frazer proposes invisible spiritual beings who would be a preliminary to religiously worshiped beings. Had these been altogether inactive while magic was supreme? In that time their influence was not possible or necessary, and it would follow that the powers man has always worshiped are mere intellectual constructs! Or had they been active, indeed, in certain experiences of man—dreams and trances? But then there would be no need for us to say religion originates at the point where magic falters.

Marett correctly points out that, in general, experience precedes a theory; if magical theory exists, it is derived from experience that accumulated in magical behavior. Marett seeks to explain magic in terms of inner emotions. When I shake my fist in fury at someone who is not present, I am filled by the will to hurt him. If my emotion is strong enough, I can even be convinced that my gesture itself will hurt him. Magic enters when such symbolic performances assume the force of a mime that actually brings about what it portrays.[3] According to this view, the oldest kind of magic is a method of harming an enemy. All the other forms supposedly grew out of this black magic. Here we find the mistake of all explanations that reduce a set of phenomena to one basic form from which all the others developed. It is less far-fetched to presume that man seized on magic in the most diverse spheres—and for purposes other than inflicting harm.

The French sociologists Hubert and Mauss have developed another theory of magic.[4] They define it as every rite that is outside the organized cult and therefore private, secret, mysterious, and tending to be illicit. This is a very arbitrary delineation of magic. Many magical rites no doubt have these qualities, but many others favor the entire group—rainmaking, hunting magic, fertility magic—and often occur in the presence of the tribesmen. The two French scholars go on to say that the rites of magic are traditional—if they are not repeated, they are not magic—and the whole group must believe in their efficacy. How can this be reconciled with the earlier assertion that by its nature magic is private and secret? And yet, the whole community is convinced of the practicality of the magic act? And would acts have to be repeated to be magical? The magical acts of a mere individual do not fulfill these provisions. Thus it would seem that the first man who performed a magic rite did not in fact act magically. Also, where is the demarcation from religion, since the mass, for example, is an act repeated over and over in a manner prescribed by tradition? Scholars consider collective acts, like rainmaking, "quasi-religious." They are making a rather forced sociological distinction between the individual's magic and the social character of religion. Surely the difference is not social but psychological, resting in the individual's attitude: magically he wants to govern; religiously he feels reverent. As late as 1910 Irving King still sought the difference in the social nature of religion and in the individual nature of magic.[5]

An ethnologist like Preusz understandably has a totally different conception of magic.[6] He assumes a preanimistic phase. Dead bodies emanate danger; a corpse will bring down calamity on its surroundings. Preusz equates this influence of the dead with *Zauber* ("magic charm"). It is aimed first at the one who caused the death and then at the dead man's closest relatives. Thus, the notion of magical influence arises from feelings of fear. We may disregard the other exaggerations Preusz is guilty of, such as reducing language, art, and religion to magical suppositions. Of course, every human activity can be given a magical flavor. Language can be used magically; art can have magical effects as certainly as it has had a religious function. But there is no reason at all to speak of an *origin* in magic. What we miss in Preusz's presentation is the volitional element that is dominant in every magic act.

In 1914 Karl Beth published a voluminous and wide-ranging treatise on the relation of magic and religion.[7] He assumed man's desires to be the starting point of magic. The hunting tribes who occupy the oldest phase of culture developed methods of catching game. The hunter imitated the sounds of animals; he wrapped himself in their skins in order to approach them. More or less magical acts evolved from these procedures.[8] Therefore, the primitive hunter took parts of the animal's body as magical objects, after first having used them to decorate himself. The underlying desire here perhaps was for a successful chase; the hunter hoped that carrying the animal's organs would have the same effect as wearing its skin. In this way, his desire for success in hunting led to a more general application of what was originally only a method, hunting, and this general application separated the hunting method from the hunter's real experience.

All kinds of objections should be raised. According to this presentation, magic began in a misapplied abstraction. But was the course of events as Beth suggests? The very idea of a transition from hunting ruses to more or less symbolic acts is most unclear. Another development of magic seems more probable to me. The hunter makes his preparations for the hunt. He wraps himself in an animal skin. He knows the significance of it; he has learned from experience that in this way he can approach the animal unobserved and that his success in the hunt depends on that. In his anxiety—for if he has no luck he and his family will go hungry—the donning of the animal skin gives him the feeling that he will be successful, and he has a passionate desire for success. The act of wrapping himself in the animal skin is thus associated with powerful emotions suggesting that he has already come close to his game or has already reached it. We may put it this way: putting on the animal skin symbolizes the success of the hunt. This in itself contains a magical idea: the animal skin brings about success. The same thing can be said of the hunting dance. The hunter mimics the movements of the animals; he copies the animal in all details, for then the game will see him as a brother. Before he sets out, he makes all these gestures in great excitement, again with the feeling that they will guarantee the success of the hunt. These emotional acts at every preparation for the hunt become a custom; here in fact is the tradition that prescribes that such must be done to assure hunting luck. All this is behind the hunting magic depicted in the cave paintings of southern France.

Beth's suggestion that parts of animals were used as ornaments first and then as charms is dubious; indeed it is possible that the opposite occurred and that the ornament was a secularized charm. If man wants to hunt deer, he puts antlers on his head; if he wants to hunt birds, he puts feathers in his hair. Whatever serves as hunting magic can easily become a hunting trophy. The hunter returning with his bag feels proud of those animal parts that gave him most of his success.

In all these cases there is not the slightest reason to speak of abstraction. Rather, one should speak of anticipation. The emotion that precedes the hunt could instigate a complete imitation of the hunt. More often than not success followed, and therefore the gestures of anticipation were repeated time and again. In this manner a really magic ritual may have come into being.

Beth says we must assume that when magic began it was possible for those primitive people to establish beforehand the "results" of magical acts. In hunting magic, as I observed, the reverse probably happened: results preceded magic. Only the success of the anticipatory mime turned it into a magic act.

With time, magic became a mass of abstruse and seemingly meaningless acts. We must begin with those that are somewhat clear to us and that we may suppose to be very old. Beth thinks it may be that weather magic was even older than hunting magic —which I think we must doubt, since it belongs more to a culture concerned with the growth of plants—but that it too began in abstraction. But could it not have been in anticipation? When the first cloud formed after a long drought, the whole tribe was filled with expectation. Would the cloud disappear again by evening? Would it grow and darken? Would the thunder come? Man had in view what he passionately hoped for. Smoke was blown into the air, or water was sprinkled on the ground, to see at once what was only anticipated: the dark cloud and the gushing rain.

It is clear that in questions of origin one always deals with guesses. Beth guesses when he wants to begin the history of religion at preanimism and speaks of *manaistische Frömmigkeit* ("mana religiosity"). Here he gives himself a chance to demonstrate the bifurcation of magic and religion.[9] The preanimistic piety he speaks of may be called a religion of fate. Belief in fate has in general a religious nature, but it is often magical as well.

This magic resides in the effort to fathom and direct fate beforehand. Therefore, Beth argues, religion and magic were separate attitudes from the beginning.

> We learn from the religio-historical materials that the psyche recognizes both magic and demons but is directed at the same time by its experience of an abstract power. This power becomes manifest and tangible in both man's magical and religious behavior, and both have persisted through time, so that religion is always forced to combat magic.[10]

Beth's final conclusion is that:

> Religion did not come from magic or from rational thinking. The "august supernatural" always faces religious man. It has become clear that religion originates in religious *Anschauung* [vision], religious life in religious experience. This expresses the idea that religion is an autonomous sphere of the human psyche.[11]

Beth moves still deeper into the origins when he visualizes a stage both premagical and prereligious, when experience first taught man that his power and skill are bounded and insecure. The human reaction to this knowledge was an egocentric sense of power leading to magic and at the same time a sense of a higher power leading to religion. However, we shall not follow this writer in his further discussion of the path leading into the post-animal stage of mankind.

Paleolithic man practiced hunting magic, and I have tried to show how we should visualize this fact. At the same time paleolithic man had a religious awareness, as may be inferred from the Venus of Willendorf. But the scholars part ways again: one says magic, and the other says religion. Why should it not be both? Man is at the same time reverential and filled with emotion. He knows from experience that he can exert a mental influence. A scowl can make another man shrink back. A threatening hand can cause him to flee. A man knows the power of his eye and uses it when necessary. The evil eye is part of all magic, in all nations and at all times. Always in moments of great excitement, that feeling of possessing the power to coerce someone or something by a look or a gesture occurs in man. It means that he can revere but also coerce the higher powers. When this happens we may say that man forgets his place. Yet may we not assume that primitive man was subject to emotions more often than we? He was less protected and more helpless against the whims of nature. There were risks on all sides. This natural anxiety may be seen in an animal, who always lives with fear. The sound of a leaf may mean danger, and the head turns anxiously in the direction of the noise. Certainly primitive man was not less anxious. This also explains the keen emotionality of his life. He cannot always be patient; he must exert his power; he assumes a pose that we now call magical.

Finally, I want to cite G. van der Leeuw's explanation in *Religion in Essence and Manifestation*.[12] He begins with the participation that Lévy-Bruhl says is a constitutive element of primitive thinking. Things participate mystically in each other; the world and I are joined in a fellowship where the natural and the supernatural merge. Thus the world and I can influence each other. Van der Leeuw speaks of a conflict between the two; this conflict is typical of the magical attitude; he calls the truce afterward the mythical-creative attitude. There is no reason to make magic and religion antithetical, as do those who consider religion a successor to religious magic. It seems to me that Van der Leeuw errs in his next step, when he posits that magic is religion because it has to do with powers. He loses sight of the great difference between the two in their behavior toward those powers. The black mass is not religious at all, although it may copy the ecclesiastical mass. Still, one may agree that religion and magic exist side by side, and the question of which came first is therefore the old question of the chicken or the egg.

It must also be granted to Van der Leeuw that magic does not need the supernatural. If the savage shoots an arrow at an enemy who is far out of range, this constitutes a magic act with no supernatural intervention presumed. Perhaps it can be said, though, that another power is acting beyond the hand and the bowstring, for what power sends the arrow from the string with so much more force than the arm could have mustered? It is none other than that peculiar power that is the *will* of man to hit his enemy. In the grip of this power he cannot imagine anything but hitting his mark.

Van der Leeuw points out that in magic acts man protests the limitedness of a mere animal life. In the will to coerce nature lies a first feeling of freedom and even a seed of idealism. I will not consider his other observations because I want to concentrate on the relation of magic and religion. I myself would begin on the basis that the human conception of the world, wherein magic takes its place, has a more or less religious character. In any case, magic manipulates powers that are not natural. To work with such powers one must know them; to know they exist needs a disposition one must call religious. The act of the magician—I think of one who really wants to coerce supernatural powers—is audacious, because he bends to his service what the community venerates. There are only a few in a tribe who dare to deal so with the supernatural.

In many cases priest and sorcerer are the same person. In fact, they are the only ones who know how to deal with supernatural beings. They know both how to worship them and how to coerce them. The transition between the two attitudes is unclear. A cultic act, if rightly performed, must yield the intended outcome: the deity grants his grace, or his wrath is averted. This sets the priest apart. It seems to the community almost as if he directs the supernatural. Is it astonishing then if he does something illicit, if he tries to make the gods grant their favors in ways other than that of the official cult? This other disposition of the same person explains the correlation of magic and religious acts, which stands out more and more clearly with the advance of civilization.

Chapter Twenty-three

THE PROBLEM OF
SACRIFICE

ALMOST all religion involves sacrifice. Among deities, the supreme being of primal monotheism alone seems to be beyond
sacrificial requirements.

There are various sacrifices, and usually supplications, thanks-
offerings, and expiatory sacrifices or peace-offerings are distinguished. Everything is suitable to be sacrificed, from the smallest
coin or poorest piece of cloth to man himself. Human sacrifice is
the most difficult to understand, yet we know that in the Aztec
empire thousands were slaughtered on the altar of the sun god.
Animal sacrifice seems more comprehensible, although it may
perhaps involve the death of hundreds of oxen, as it did among
the Greeks. Many like to believe that the animal is a substitute
for man. Classical tradition knows an earlier age in which only
milk products and plants were offered; this recollection testifies
that once life was more frugal and man's sense of life purer.

The Greeks themselves were puzzled about the meaning of
slaughtering animals in honor of the gods. The very idea that
the aroma of roasted meat would waft to the gods and please
them betrays a humanist frame of mind. The well-known myth
of Prometheus dividing the sacrificial animal, tricking the gods
into choosing the worthless part, seems to be trying to explain

an anomaly: why are the bones reserved for the gods and the meat for the people?

At one time sacrifice was interpreted as a gift to the gods. That is how Tylor saw it.[1] According to his view, the purpose of sacrifice is to win favor or avert wrath. Herbert Spencer, in line with his theory of the origin of religion,[2] finds a beginning in the food offerings left for the dead on their graves. When the ancestral souls evolved into gods, these gifts to the dead became real sacrifices to deities.

None of this illumined human sacrifice. W. Robertson Smith did not succeed in this either, although he broke new ground.[3] He began with totemism, which in his day was regarded as one of the oldest forms of religion. In general, a totemic animal is tabu for the members of its clan, yet at sacred occasions the animal is eaten. The ritual ceremony ends with a sacramental meal that ensures the unity of clan and totem and hence the clan's well-being. Robertson Smith infers from this that an animal sacrifice is essentially a communion through the flesh and the blood of the sacred animal. The higher forms of sacrifice have retained some of their sacramental character; the people commune with the god through sacrifice, and this communion occurs because the people share food and drink in which the god is immanent. Parallel to this type of sacrifice, an offer of pure veneration originates, in which a gift is presented to the gods. It is plain that this hypothesis does not encompass human sacrifice. Moreover, totemism cannot support a general explanation of sacrifice; after all, peoples that have never known totemism do sacrifice.

F. B. Jevons also begins with totemism.[4] He thinks the totem's blood is spilled in the totemic ceremony in order to ensure the totem's presence. When man learned to tame the totem animal, its character changed, and its function became nourishment. Then the sacrifice was merely a gift. Jevon's very inadequate theory is typical of the manner of rationalists who intend to make a clear explanation of sacrifice but in fact do their utmost to reduce an extremely difficult problem with sophisms.

Of course, Salomon Reinach, a life-long devotee of the totemistic theory, declared himself in favor of Robertson Smith's explanation.[5] Even in 1920 the same opinion was set forth in *Hasting's Encyclopaedia of Religion and Ethics*.[6] The example selected is the "intiuchiuma" of the Australian Arunta tribe. The intiuchiuma was the favorite topic of ethnologists and his-

torians of religions for a long time. It is a ceremony meant to
increase the species of the totemic animal and create a sacramental relation with the totem, thus establishing some kind of
blood-brotherhood with the animal. The kangaroo killed at this
occasion strongly resembles a sacrificial animal, although it does
not follow—as it did for Robertson Smith—that the slain animal
was a mediator between man and the totem species. The mana
in the sacrificial animal (especially in its blood) pours from the
body and makes the communicant powerful; it neutralizes his
weaknesses by absorbing them. This artificial theory too is far
from satisfactory. It remains a total mystery how the species of
a totemic animal can be preserved or increased by eating one or
more samples of it. Apparently, the idea of communion, known
in the Christian religion, was accepted from the Old Testament
scholar Robertson Smith and supplemented by the concept of
mana.

Still another interpretation is given by Sir James Frazer in
The Golden Bough. He seeks the origin of sacrifice in the ritual
murder of the king. The king was a sacred person, whose power
(mana!) assured the well-being of the people. When he became
weak and old, his mana weakened, and the tribe ran the risk of
decline. Then the king was killed, usually by a kinsman who
then succeeded him. Sometimes, however, the loss of a king's
power was avoided by limiting the period of his reign; at the
end of his time the king was killed. The meaning of this killing
has nothing to do with sacrifice, and besides, this type of sacred
kingship occurs only in some parts of the world—Africa in particular. Obviously, one cannot build a general theory upon it.

Edward A. Westermarck assumes that those sacrifices that must
be considered gifts are connected with the anthropomorphic
transformation of the gods, for when the gods became like humans they assumed human needs. They needed to be fed and
to have their thirst slaked, so man had to see to that! The
reason for human sacrifice is that the sacrificial victim is a
substitute for someone else whose life is endangered. In the
course of time animals were sacrificed instead of people.[7] Westermarck's explanation is forced, but it shows clearly how difficult
the problem of sacrifice is; here—if anywhere—beautiful theories
fall short.

The French sociologists Hubert and Mauss called sacrifice a
religious act that, through the consecration of the sacrificial

animal, alters the status of the sacrificer or of something that vitally concerns him.[8] Like Robertson Smith, they believed that a sacrifice makes a relationship between the human and the divine. This occurs through the mediation of the ritually slain animal and participation in the sacrificial meal.

It was an old idea that man makes a gift to the deity and expects a gift in return. The two sociologists could relate this view to a gift they had studied with care: the potlatch of the North American Kwakiutl exemplifies man giving everything with the conviction that the counter-gifts will more than compensate him. When scholars relate these observations to sacrifice, the old *do ut des* formula turns up. *Do ut des* ("I give that thou mayest give") has a certain notoriety, since it has suggested to many that sacrifice was actually a matter of negotiating with a deity. In Brahmanic ritual we even hear a plain pronouncement: "Here is the butter—where are thy gifts?" However, if blunt negotiation is made the principle of interpretation, it yields a most humiliating picture of the way man honors his god. It is unthinkable that it sums up sacrificial procedures. Otherwise, how could the Edda poet say: "It is better if no sacrifice is made than if too much is sacrificed, for a gift always demands a gift in return"? From the standpoint of the *do ut des* formula it would rather seem that man can never make his hecatombs great enough.

A study by Marcel Mauss[9] provided another view. In giving, an object is not merely passed on. The object has, so to say, a relation with its owner—one could speak again of "participation" in this matter. Customary terms can express the transaction: the owner's mana is conveyed to his possession. When the object is given away, the new owner shares in this mana. The gift creates a mystical relationship between donor and recipient, and the recipient enters the influence of the donor's mana. If the mana is strong, the situation may be dangerous. There are striking examples in the Icelandic saga literature where a gift is refused out of fear for the consequences of accepting.

This explains the sense of the saying from the Eddas: "A gift requires a gift in return." It is not to be understood as the counterpart of "Scratch my back, and I'll scratch yours." It is not a barter. The gift creates a bond. Better still, it makes power flow both ways to connect the giver and receiver. Our saying "Gifts preserve friendship" reflects a similar thought: friendship is imagined as an active interplay between two persons. But the interplay must remain vital, and that is best effected through a gift, a new impulse.

It is better if not too much is sacrificed, for the sacrificial gift has the same meaning as the gift between man and man! With his offering, man releases a flow between himself and the deity. He may expect that the god will reply, but the gifts of a god are incalculable. Through sacrifice man places himself in a power field that he can not survey or predict the effects of.

Rightly Van der Leeuw observes:

> [Sacrifice] is no longer a mere matter of bartering with gods corresponding to that carried on with men, and no longer homage to the god such as is offered to princes: it is an opening of a blessed source of gifts.[10]

However, I cannot go along with him when he continues by saying that the central power of the sacrificial act is neither giver nor god but in the gift itself. This has a little too much of a magical flavor. Actually, the sacrificial gift is always a means toward the relation between god and man; when the relation is realized, man is responsible, since he released the stream. He is the one who offers the sacrifice, charged with his mana—his wishes, desires, and needs.

"Do you know how one should send?" asks another Edda poet. To direct the offering correctly to the gods is an art known only to sacrificial priests.

All this is a reasonable explanation of sacrificial gifts in the higher polytheistic religions, but it does not suggest why animals and human beings must be slain. The bloody sacrifice cannot be explained with anthropomorphic gods who eat and drink like men; the gods are not cannibals. Yet we know that in Rome, in times of emergency, people were buried alive to propitiate the gods of the netherworld. Why did it occur to men to try to pacify the deities with such a barbaric rite?

In his interpretation of bloody offerings Van der Leeuw concurs with Robertson Smith: the bloody sacrifice originates with the communal meal, where the god is either a participant in or identical with the sacrifice.[11] This interpretation takes us right back to totemism. Karl Beth goes further in the same direction, still within the limits of totemism.[12] The oldest rite we know of, he believes, is the one at which the members of a clan cut their arms and pour blood on a shield or on the soil of their totemic place. This early custom presages sacrifice, because it is a "giving away of the homologous" to vivify the totemic energy. Since, supposedly, the blood is not even the most important element in the procedure, Beth even speaks of a *homöopatische Zuwendung* ("homeopathic application") that serves to introduce or stimulate a natural process.

Not only is Beth's theory a mere construct, but it fails to explain human sacrifice. The fact that, at a certain moment, man decided that murder would please the gods remains an enigma. As civilization progressed, religious acts seemed to become more barbaric.

Despite the best efforts, it appears impossible to find a positive sense in slaying humans and animals as an offering to the gods. Greek and Roman sacrifice has the aspect of an atavism, a primitive survival. The question is whether we are able to point to any culture within which such sacrifices are meaningful.

As we saw, totemism is no aid; it is restricted to certain regions. But it does seem possible to reach an explanation in early civilization, in the very first practice of gardening. In such a culture, woman, who is the gardener, plays an important part in tribal life. The people are mild tempered as a rule, but at certain times of the year an incomprehensible cruelty obsesses the tribe; then there is head-hunting and cannibalism. A prisoner can be subjected to gruesome torture, killed, and eaten in a communal meal. None of this has to do with totemic animals.

The fact that this rite occurs at a very primitive stage—the first beyond so-called primal culture!—may suggest that an explanation of the bloody sacrifice can be found here. A. E. Jensen tried to solve the problem along this line.[13] Things look promising, for in this case we know the myths from the basis of the sacrifice.

The myth of Hainuwele recorded on Ceram has been mentioned before. It typifies many myths; in it the world of men is introduced by the murder of a dema-deity at the end of the primordial days. Hainuwele is forced into a hole and trampled under. Her body is cut to pieces and from those parts come the tuberous plants on which people have existed ever since. Another dema-goddess becomes the realm of the dead and also becomes identified with the moon. With these primordial events the world assumes its present shape. Birth and death are man's lot; certain plants become his food. When people eat plants, they really eat Hainuwele. Since the goddess also transformed herself into a pig, the slaying of a pig is actually identical with the death of the dema-deity.

When a pig is consumed in a ritual, Hainuwele's death is repeated. There is no "offering" at all. There is only the recollection of something that happened in primordial days, and the recollection actualizes that event. Here we discern a thought that is present somehow in almost all later forms: it is not enough that a primordial event came to pass; it must occur over and over for its benefit to radiate undiminished throughout the tribal community.

In this sense all feasts and offerings revivify a primordial event. When the year is nearly over, a new source of power must be tapped for the new year. In Rome they celebrated the Saturnalia, during which established social relations were utterly abolished: slaves were masters and the masters served slaves. Elsewhere such a time of transition is characterized by sexual promiscuity. The meaning in both cases is that the order of the cosmos has receded and that chaos has set in. The world was created in chaos; this temporary chaos, too, will be the condition for the creation of a new cosmos.

The royal ritual in Babylon, which began the new year, identified the king with Marduk. A priest recited the creation epic, the Enuma Elish, which relates how Marduk slew the chaos monster Tiamat and created earth and sky from the huge corpse.

Nothing and no one is sacrificed at any of these occasions. All that happens is that a primordial act is imitated or, rather, repeated. What happened at that time (*in illo tempore*) happens here and now (*hic et nunc*) with all its happy consequences. The so-called human and animal sacrifices—including headhunting and cannibalism—are simply a festive commemoration of the fact that eating cultivated plants is really eating the deity from whose body the vegetation sprang.

Thus, a meaning is shown in this ritual killing. It did not, however, retain the meaning when it was transmitted to or borrowed by higher civilizations. In the first place, a so-called *Herrenkultur* ("culture of rulers") developed in various parts of the world—as in Colombia, Polynesia and Indonesia, West Africa and Southern Rhodesia. Under its influence the practice of human sacrifice continued into the archaic higher civilizations. These higher civilizations must have accepted a good deal from the early cultivators. Actually a myth like Hainuwele's does not fit their cultural pattern; yet the ritual death of people and animals is preserved. It is no longer a commemoration and renewal. Borrowing the felicitous formulation by Leo Frobenius, we might say that an "application" (*Anwendung*) takes the place of "expression" (*Ausdruck*); the application is the meaningless repetition of a traditional custom.

The occasion of the sacrifice, however, is generally the same as in early cultivation: the building of a house, especially of a temple; rainmaking; the stimulation of fertility; the expiation of a moral offense. Nevertheless, it has lost its precise, original meaning, and its various reinterpretations are each insufficient.

Let us consider the expiatory sacrifice. How can guilt be expiated by killing and eating an animal? Could a god be cruel enough to demand it? It becomes understandable, though, if we bear in mind that a sin offends the moral order, which was divinely established at the beginning of the world. The transgressor offended because he lost sight of the rules of the world. He forgot at the moment of his sin. His awareness of the moral order must be restored. That can be done only by repeating the primordial event, bringing it clearly to life. All guilt is basically a matter of having forgotten.

The *Bauopfer* ("institutional sacrifice") is equally problematic. Why should a man, a child, or an animal, sometimes dead or sometimes alive, be immured in the foundations of a temple or a bridge? The theory that the mana of the sacrifice is conveyed to the construction is most unsatisfactory. But it is worth mentioning that the *Bauopfer* occurs particularly in headhunting cultures. And indeed, the Hainuwele-mythologem explains it, for when her body is divided the dema-goddess transforms herself into the dwelling-place of the dead. The temple, the sacred place, is a copy of that elementary place. Hence an immediate connection between constructing a temple and human sacrifice: only the death of Hainuwele could build the realm of the dead. When a structure is erected that is especially important or sacred, it is necessary to enact the primordial drama.[14]

Thus, sacrifice in higher cultures is a survival without meaning of a sacred act that was once lucid through the creation myth. Sometimes there are clear traces of the ritual of the ancient cultivators in the archaic civilizations. Herman Lommel gave an interesting example.[15] The Indian gods Mitra and Varuṇa oversee the orderliness of the world, but they step out of character in a myth that relates the establishment of sacrifice. The sacrifice performed by men has its prototype in the sacrifice performed by the gods. Now in order to perform their sacrifice, the gods must slay the god of the "mead," Soma. They do so jointly, sharing the horrid murder. Mitra alone refuses—showing a pang of conscience belonging to a later, perhaps more humane, period. It is no use, however; he is forced to be an accomplice in the sacred crime, the beneficial murder.

If we recall that Soma is a primordial being, that he was on earth before all other life, we can clearly see the features of a dema-deity. He is related to the bull, to a plant, and to the moon; this is analogous to the myth of Hainuwele. His death brings forth life, vegetal and animal; the pressing of the Soma plant, the reenactment of his slaying, produces the potion of immortality. Lommel concludes:

> In the Indian Soma-sacrifice, the highest and most solemn of sacrifices, the main point was clearly not the offering to the gods, but a copying and repetition of the primeval sacrifice which the gods performed.

There is another striking example in a Scandinavian myth. The myth relates how the god Thor stays at the home of a farmer and kills one of his male goats, but impresses on the partakers of the meal that they should not fracture the bones to get at the marrow. The next morning Thor lays the bones on the goatskin, swings his hammer over them, and the goat is restored to life. But one leg is lame; the farmer's son was unable to resist splitting a bone with his knife. The same story survives to this day as a popular saga in the Alps. On certain nights of the year, mountain spirits visit the herds of the farmers and kill one animal, which is eaten in a common meal, and by a rite similar to Thor's they revive the animal the next morning.

These sagas seem to correspond to a procedure in which bones and skin were carefully collected so that the sacrificial animal could be restored to life. Why? Must it reach the gods alive? Did the ritual slaying not really destroy the animal? The whole matter seems inexplicable.

An unexpected light is shed on it by the customs of a very ancient culture—even more ancient than that of the primitive cultivators: the primal hunting culture. The hunters of that early culture lived on game and had no scruples about killing animals. Their main concern was the abundance of game. A strict ritual was observed in the slaying and eating of the game; after the meal the bones were laid out on the skin in the design of the skeleton, in the expectation that the "Master of Animals" would restore it to life and thus maintain the animal stock.

Obviously, killing itself presented no problem to the hunting peoples. It did to the ancient cultivators. Why were they more "sentimental"? The first thing to point out is that the regular eating of vegetables made hunting secondary. No matter how important it remained, man's cruel occupation was in sharp contrast to the peaceful work of women. Here, perhaps, are the germs of problems to which the myth of Hainuwele presents a clear answer: all human existence stems ultimately from a killing. In life there is an antinomy; it persists by destroying other life.

The early cultivators must have felt that deeply. For them even the gathering of fruits was a way of killing; plants as well as animals had to be destroyed to keep man alive. Why is the world made that way? The animals devour each other, and man devours animal and plant.

This question, which arises in a way from guilt feelings, is answered by the Hainuwele myth. The myth gives the prototype of human life: this is what happened in the primordial day; this will happen forever. The mythic deed justifies humankind's "sinful" existence.

The myth does not tell us what brought on Hainuwele's murder. Would it have been able to? The myth does not really permit questions. The killing is inscrutable. There was no alternative, and the act was absolutely necessary. The most one can say is that Hainuwele had to be killed because killing is the condition of human existence.

It is clear that the original meaning of killing was gradually lost. The Greeks did not understand why the gods were given the worthless parts of the sacrificial animal, so they made up the myth of Prometheus. If we think of the ritual of the ancient hunters, however, the apportionment of the Greek animal sacrifice is at once clear. The meat and the good parts went to men, but the bones and the skin were carefully kept for the "Lord of Animals." It seems that the Olympic gods were given the poorest share; but the more archaic idea was that the power of life was present in those hard and indestructible bones.

Precisely because the meaning of sacrifice was lost in higher civilizations, sacrifices could become grandiose. Granted that headhunting needed many victims, it did not require the extravagance of the sacred feasts of commemoration. In later times, however, the significance of the sacrifice was calculated by the number of victims. To those later and more civilized men it was as if hundreds of slaughtered oxen pleased the Olympian gods that much more than a single ox. The sacrifice of the Gauls, in which people and animals were burned alive in a network of branches, was atrocious. In ancient Mexico thousands were slaughtered in honor of the sun god. This is what happened when "expression" became "application." The theory of sacrifice as a gift is unapplicable here. It would be trying to make some sense of an act that had in fact lost its meaning.

The ancient formula of *do ut des,* although it was not a common barter, was a way to implore the gifts of a god. But it is dangerously easy to move from this religious act to mere magic. A sacrifice may be made to implore a deity or to coerce. Ever greater sacrifices must eventually impress the obstinate gods. We can only guess the thoughts of the priests while they performed those hecatombs.

The early cultivators must have been different. In their ritual they did not ask for anything. They did nothing but sanction existence by remembering how human life received its final form and its precarious nature.

Chapter Twenty-four

THEORIES ABOUT MYTH

UNTIL the middle of the nineteenth century the history of religions was principally an explication of mythical traditions.
Only ethnology put an end to it: primitive forms of religion were
discovered in which myth played no part or, more accurately,
did not seem to play a part. Animism and then preanimism
contained little material for the study of myth. As research delved
further into the past, myth lost importance as a constituent of
religion. It came to be considered a later element, and the opinion
arose that it was significant only in the more highly developed
polytheistic religions.

Myth was also regarded as a child of the imagination. Hence
Wundt derived myth from the mythological fairytale and the
mythological saga. The birth of Mithras from a rock in the midst
of herdsmen and flocks has the mark of a fairytale birth; his
struggle with the primeval bull is a fable after the example of
Heracles and other heroic sagas. With all this, Wundt sets things
upside-down. Many heroic sagas are, in fact, secularized myths.
Myth is doubtlessly primary; heroic songs adapt it.

Wundt goes so far as to trace the gods as personal beings back
to saga heroes. Somehow the heroic saga seems to him a saga of

gods as well, and his more ancient mythical fairytale mentions all manner of demons but the gods not at all.[1]

Although the ethnologists neglected myth and pushed it aside as a fancy, their studies led in the long run to a better understanding of myth. Preusz emphasized the relationship of myth to the practical applications of magico-religious beliefs.[2] In his view, myth owes its existence to the desire to explain traditional customs. This remained the accepted interpretation: myth explains ritual. As late as 1946, Cassirer elaborated:

> Myth is the *epic* element in primitive religious life; rite is the *dramatic* element. We must begin with studying the latter in order to understand the former. Taken in themselves the mythical stories of gods or heroes cannot reveal to us the secret of religion, because they are nothing but the *interpretations* of rites. They try to give an account of what is present, what is immediately seen and done in these rites. They add the "theoretical" view to the active aspect of religious life.[3]

Myth thus becomes an etiology of a rite, and indeed there are times when this is so. In all probability, the story of Prometheus' ruse in dividing the sacrificial animal was invented to explain why the best parts fell to people and the worthless parts to the gods. It was previously illustrated that these cultic acts have their analogies in acts of the ancient hunting peoples where they are meaningful; it was natural that the Greeks of historical times no longer understood the custom they followed. But will a similar reasoning apply to the mysteries of Eleusis in their relation to the myth of Demeter?

What sense can a ritual have if it must be explained with an afterthought? Why then is it performed at all? The problem was easy as long as one assumed that earlier mythless magical acts were continued in the religious cult in the framework of a belief in personal deities, but this is certainly inaccurate. The confusing term magico-religious is used frequently by those who would not dare draw a sharp line between the two. But a thing is either magical or religious, not both.

When Preusz lived among South American tribes and observed their religious life, he formulated his ideas precisely.

> Ritual and myth re-enact a primordial happening that is essential to the preservation of cosmic and social order. Therefore it must be repeated again and again, in the rite

as act, in the myth as narrative. The two are inseparable. The rite would be ineffective if its meaning were not made manifest; the myth is not fruitful if it is not transformed into action. The old idea that myth is etiological is at the same time right and wrong, but the myth certainly explains the rite in the sense that it presents its meaning.[4]

This elaboration implies that a myth can only be approached by observing it in a community that has preserved myth and ritual intact—that is, among primitives. At the close of the story that narrates the theft of fire-making by Maui, the cultural hero of the Maori, Maui orders the people to sing the song of the fire god when they light a fire to ensure the spark's success.

Malinowski confirmed Preusz's ideas after observation of the natives of the Trobriand Islands. He says emphatically:

These stories live not by idle interest, not as fictitious or even as true narratives; but are to the natives a statement of a primeval, greater, and more relevant reality, by which the present life, fates, and activities of mankind are determined, the knowledge of which supplies man with the motive for ritual and moral actions, as well as with indications as to how to perform them.[5]

In a particular act it is not enough to master the external skills. A skill becomes effective through active recollection of its first success, in a divine act, once upon a time. In a discussion of classical cultures, Ortega y Gasset used the image of a diving-bell: it is as if ancient man had a way of diving to the divine ground of being, to prepare himself for his activities by becoming fully conscious of the primeval symbols.

Thus there is a close association between myth and the social life. Malinowski says:

. . . once we begin to study the social function of myth, and so to reconstruct its full meaning, we are gradually led to build up the full theory of native social organization.[6]

The actual, given forms of society are determined by a primeval event. Finally, in view of mythologies of the higher civilizations, he observes:

I believe that the study of mythology as it functions and works in primitive societies should anticipate the conclusions drawn from the material of higher civilizations. Some

of this material has come down to us only in isolated
literary texts, without its setting in actual life, without its
social context. Such is the mythology of the ancient classical
peoples and of the dead civilizations of the Orient. In the
study of myth the classical scholar must learn from the
anthropologist.[7]

Earlier mythologists were not aware of this primary requirement. If they had been, many mistakes could have been avoided.
Logical analyses alone, however subtle, fell short; they might
elucidate origins and histories, but they never revealed the function of myth. Yet for those who have learned to use their eyes,
the function is obvious.

In the light of Malinowski's observations, we understand why
the whole Enuma Elish was recited at the Babylonian new year.
Certainly this creation story was not composed to "explain" the
ceremony. The new year's festival was a micro-creation whose
power derived from the original and total creation of the world.
This is how Theodor H. Gaster expressed it:

> The purpose of ritual is to present a situation formally
> dramatically in its immediate punctual aspect—as an *event*
> or *occurrence,* something in which present and actual in-
> dividuals are involved. That of *myth,* on the other hand,
> is to present it in its ideal, transcendental aspect—as some-
> thing transpiring (rather than occurring) concurrently in
> eternity and as involving preterpunctual, indesinent beings
> of whom living men and women are but the temporal in-
> carnations.
>
> · · ·
>
> *Au fond,* therefore, Myth is consubstantial with Ritual.
> They are not—as is often supposed—*two* things artificially
> or schematically brought into relationship with each other,
> but *one* thing viewed from two different angles or through
> two different prisms.[8]

This also makes clear the distinction between myth and narrative. Once it was customary to set apart from the true elements
of religion narratives or sagas concerning the gods. Gaster under-
lines the distinction between myth and narrative:

The difference lies not in their subject matter nor in the credence that is accorded them, but in their function and motivation. A myth is, or once was, *used;* a tale is, and always was, merely *told.* The former presupposes an actual or original counterpart in cultic performance; the latter does not.[9]

Myth and cult both relate to the same aspects of the world. Myth has its own way of expressing them. One may speak of "mythical thought," as long as that does not mean prelogical, and certainly it should not mean such a thing as primitive laws of participation. The myth of Hainuwele is not wanting in logic, although its events are very far from commonplace. We must recall that this myth, like so many others, has a bearing on the critical situations of life—birth and death, man's destruction of animals and plants for the sake of his own existence. Here we meet enigmas that we cannot resolve through reasoning any more than the primitives can. Only symbols provide illumination or at least reconcile us.

It is fantastic to see a myth solve the puzzle of human life. Things—as they are or are meant to be—are ordained at a divine time by divine powers. A true mythologem reveals an everlasting source of life. Hence Pettazzoni says:

> . . . human thought is mythical and logical at the same time. Neither is religion pure rational thinking which knows nothing of myth, as Andrew Lang supposed. Like magic, so also myth is already religion. The idea of the creative Supreme Being among primitive peoples is nothing but a form of the myth of beginnings and as such shares in the character of myth, at once magical and religious. This character is, as we have said, the very truth of myth, an absolute truth because a truth of faith, and truth of faith because a truth of life. The myth is true and cannot but be true, because it is the charter of the tribe's life, the foundation of a world which cannot continue without that myth. On the other hand, the myth cannot continue without this world, of which it forms an organic part, as the "explanation" of its beginnings, as its original *raison d'être,* its "prologue in heaven." [10]

One might still argue by saying: I do not object to the "truth" of myth when I regard it as the child of alogical thinking, but what is true for primitive man would be a delusion for us. This reasoning has been answered satisfactorily by Karl Kerényi:

> The cult of all peoples is nothing else than a human reaction to the divine. Cultic acts are acts of the mythologems* themselves more than mythologems are "explanations" of the cultic acts. Cult and myth have reference to the same aspect of the world. For modern man this is hard to comprehend. Perhaps a comparison with poetry and music will help. No one who is at all sensitive to these arts will deny that the divine can be expressed in them. With this comparison it may become clearer what mythology is.[11]

The comparison with music is particularly fruitful. Paul Radin says that myths sometimes have far-reaching variants. Such variation used to be explained as degeneration or forgetfulness. The only way really to examine the phenomenon is to obtain the same information from different individuals, each with his own personality. With this in mind Radin obtained different versions of the same myth from three individuals.

> Two of them were brothers and had learned the myth from their father. The differences between these versions were remarkable, but the significance of the differences lay in the fact that they could be explained in terms of the temperament, literary ability, and interests of the story-teller.[12]

Radin uses this to show that the primitive community is not as compact and homogeneous as is generally supposed. There is certainly room for disposition and temperament to unfold. But his demonstration of this very important fact does not go far enough. He speaks of a "tolerant attitude" toward the form of myths—even myths that relate to the origin of the clans, to death, and to the hereafter. But what is the basis of such tolerance in the most sacred traditions of the tribes?

At this point the comparison with music is instructive. Their variability brings myth and music close. As Kerényi observes:

> Conflicting reports of the descent of the gods, their deeds and suffering, occur side by side. It is this abundance of

---

* Mythologems are the basic materials that make the subject matter of the various myths: gods, divine beings, heroic battles, descents to the netherworld, and so on.—TRANS.

inner contradiction which stands in our way when we try
to understand myth and often hampers our enjoyment. It
must be said that there is always a central theme. But it is
given in variations by the different compositions. There is
no better metaphor than that of a musical term—there are
variations on the theme, but the theme stays essentially the
same. If one approaches mythology from a musical point
of view, an obstacle is removed. After all, variations on a
theme are not "wrong" because they are novel and not
"identical" with each other. The resemblance of myth and
music is that in both the variations on a theme are not only
possible but necessary to avoid a deadening monotony.[13]

This new scholarly attitude opens a much wider vista on the
myths of ancient Hellas and Scandinavia. It is as if the whole
situation had finally ripened. Myths that were rejected as gro-
tesque fancies attract attention all over again and disclose their
secrets. No one has contributed more to the rehabilitation of the
polytheistic mythologies—already discredited by the Greek Sophists and later by the modern exegetes—than Walter F. Otto, who
restored the gods of Greece to a new life and dignity.

He says that the primeval phenomena of religion are gesture,
act and word:

> . . . in these the divine presence is manifest.
> In the word of myth the Divine assumes a particular
> shape—it is man's own shape, and this is infinitely sug-
> gestive. And that is how the Godhead appears at the center
> of every real myth. It cannot be thought of; it can only be
> experienced; it is wonderful, with all that surrounds it in
> myth—it is the greatest wonder not because it defies the
> laws of nature, but because it is something different from
> thought and all necessities of thought.[14]

The gateway to myth seems to be reopened, but not everyone
will pass through, for not everyone has the access to poetry or
music.

Part Five

EPILOGUE

Chapter Twenty-five

PAST AND FUTURE
IN THE
HISTORY OF RELIGIONS

HERE, at the end, it may be useful to look back over our shoulders. We see a long road extending over almost twenty-five centuries. It resembles a Via Appia, lined on both sides with the ruins of hypotheses. It is astonishing how self-confident man can be when he has lost his way. (At this point should we not question ourselves?)

The cause of many failures was a mistaken attitude toward the subject matter. Two eras of investigation can be clearly distinguished. The first began with the Greek natural philosophers and ended with the close of the eighteenth century; the second encompasses the post-Romantic period. The first is marked by a onesided interest in mythology, the search for significance in curious details about the gods. The adventures seemed so strange, sometimes so repulsive, that they were not understood as part of any true religion; they were called poetic imaginings or philosophy dressed in allegory. Of course, there are differences of detail in this long period. The Medieval approaches to myth are quite different from those of the Enlightenment, but whatever the approach used, the result was unsatisfactory in all respects. Consequently, we can not really speak of "history of religions" until the end of the eighteenth century. That century as a whole struggled too much with the very phenomenon of religion to allow a profound interest in questions of origin and meaning. Since men of that day were negative and critical toward their own religion, they could hardly be expected to contribute something of value.

The Romantic period was different. One might have expected it to get to the heart of the problem; yet the result of its seriously undertaken work was disappointing. Nevertheless, the Romantics made a good beginning. They found that myth—for myth is still the great issue—was more than sheer imagination. A man like Creuzer was convinced of it; this is clear in the significance he attached to religious symbolism. Yet, great progress was not made; the implements were still lacking. The newly discovered Indian texts raised high expectations; but far too little was learned of them to give a basis for research.

An even greater lack was the chance to examine myth and religion generally *in vivo corpore*—in their live significance among primitive tribes. Information about curious beliefs and customs of the primitives had been circulating since the seventeenth century, but these data were fragmentary and poorly understood. The few times when American Indian or African examples were called on for the sake of comparison, they confirmed the established opinion that it did not pay to study the Greek myths for meaning.

Ethnographical materials inundated the nineteenth century. Only then was the history of religions born as a serious discipline, comprising the study of the most primitive forms as well as the highest, exemplified in Christianity or Buddhism. The nineteenth-century scholars made abundant use of the new materials. In fact, they were perhaps even too eager and hurried. As soon as some puzzling new phenomena were found, a new theory was proposed. Animism, preanimism and totemism each took a turn as the oldest form of religion, for the oldest forms aroused the greatest interest. Obsessed by the belief that life on earth, biological and spiritual, had evolved from the simplest forms, scholars attempted to visualize the process. To be consistent, they had to begin with primeval man—a completely hypothetical creature to whom they could attribute whatever they wanted. Thus the notion of preanimism was welcomed, and finally religion was dissolved in magic.

The really elementary trouble of this period was very much like that of the first, from antiquity to the Enlightenment. There was no real access to the phenomena of religion. There were psychological and sociological explanations galore, but they were betrayed by their intellectualism. Most investigators were agnostics who considered religion *passée*, an error of pre-scientific man. What no one had ever dared to do with poetry or music—except in some circles of historical materialism—was done to the *summum bonum* of men: religion was divested of its autonomy in human life and regarded as a mental illusion or as the product of social conditions.

There was no respect for religious phenomena. Primarily, this meant there was no respect for the flexible forms the primitive peoples gave to their religious needs. The data, which came in ever increasing amounts, were dissected. Then the examiners in their conceit reported what the savages had meant to express and constructed theories that toppled one after another like a house of cards.

It is too soon to complete a history of religion, as Marett said, but the time will come when it will be possible. The last few decades have been most promising. The present generation, too, has the mark of its time; we can not know to what extent the total change of world view has imprinted itself on the study of religion or whether it will indeed be a favorable influence. We may say at least that myth and religion have come to be considered very real phenomena of the psyche of all men at all times —not only early man and not only primitives. The agnostic who does not sense what goes on beyond living and death can judge religion only as a blind man judges a rainbow. Goethe said that an eye that does not contain in itself something like the sun will never see the sun. The first necessity in our field is to treat all religious phenomena, even those which seem abhorrent, with that deep respect due all divine life.

Finally, the history of religions is history. It is not the arena for battles of mere mental constructs and hypotheses. If religion develops, let us say, changes, we can confirm that fact only with historical data. Religion is part—a vital part—of culture. A civilization reveals itself nowhere more immediately and purely than in its religious imageries. And, on the other hand, religion must be considered within the civilization. At all times a civilization announces its peculiar world view, raising its own questions and providing its own answers.

The theory of culture circles was a great advance in the context of these problems. It brought into focus the successive cultural stages. The careful investigation of every factor of culture yielded a vision of man adapting to his environment and also somehow making it serve him. The schemes that have been drawn of this so far are perhaps only sketches, and they often raise as many questions as they solve. Yet even the questions have a practical use, for they require verification and hence a closer study of primitive civilizations. Time is short, because an ever more uniform western culture spreads and threatens the life of the primitives even in the remotest parts of the world. The scholarly orientation we have arrived at may still enable us to find types of religion that have gone unnoticed. The dema-deities are religious images that all earlier investigators over-looked. Their discovery taught us many things that were totally unknown and at the same time made possible more precise formulation of questions.

Although the history of religions is also history, it is not likely to become history in the ordinary sense. The registration of successive stages or concentric patterns is not yet history of religions. The history of religions begins with the fact that there is something human that finds expression only in religion. In what ideas or forms this happens depends on time and circumstance. In any case, if one can see the seed of religious creativity that sprouts and grows in sundry ways, it would be fitting to think rather along the lines of Goethe. His morphology of plants begins with what Schiller called the idea of the "primeval plant." He had in mind an entelechy, a process of unfolding with its own immanent laws. The process is also connected to the environment—the condition of the soil, the climate, and the atmosphere. This is how it is with the forms of religion. They flourish in a geographical environs; they depend on the spiritual and intellectual make-up of a people and especially on its cultural patterns. Now we catch sight of the spiritual landscape. Growth is spontaneous in all parts of the world. There are interplays and exchanges; there are fusions that bring refinement; and there are all the phenomena of decay as cultures outlive themselves. These are the rhythms that mark every type of life.

From all this arises an image of man forever wrestling with the world and with the fact that he exists, attempting time and again a cosmic solace in an order beyond all of this, divine in nature and in origin.

NOTES

Chapter One

[1] *Politeia* 377. [2] *Fragm.* 11, 12. [3] *Odyssey* VIII, 266ff. [4] *Metaphys* I, 5, 411 a 7. [5] Scholion B on *Ilias* XX, 67. [6] *Praeparatio Evangelica* XIV, 3, 7. [7] Sextus Empiricus IX, 18. [8] *Thebais* III, 661. [9] *Apology* 28e-29a. [10] *Euthyphro* 6b-c. [11] His book is lost, but we possess excerpts by Lactantius. [12] Cf. VI, 56, 6ff.

Chapter Two

[1] Pinard de la Boullaye, S. J., *L'étude comparée des religions* (3rd ed.; Paris, 1929), I, 87. [2] See *Bibliothek der Kirchenväter*, XIV (Kempten & München: J. Kösel, 1913), 245.

Chapter Four

[1] Vossius, *De Theologia Gentili, sive de origine ac progressu Idololatriae* (Amsterdam, 1658), Lib. I, 15ff. [2] *Ibid.*, p. 138. [3] Hugo Grotius, *De veritate religionis christianae*, IV, Sec. III. For a translation of the work see the one by Symon Patrick, *The Truth of Christian Religion in Six Books* (London, 1680). [4] *Ibid.*, IV, Sec. IV. [5] *Ibid.*, Sec. V. [6] Pierre Daniel Huet, *Demonstratio evangelica*, p. 121. [7] Francis Bacon, *Sapientia veterum*, Ch. 13. [8] John Spencer, *De legibus Hebraeorum ritualibus earumque rationibus* I. III dissert. I praef.

Chapter Five

[1] David Hume, *Dialogues Concerning Natural Religion*, ed. by Norman Kemp Smith (2nd ed., London: Nelson, 1947), p. 143. [2] *Encyclopédie*, XXIX (1774), 826.

Chapter Seven

[1] Cf. Walter F. Otto, *Die Sprache*, ed. by Bayerische Akademie der schönen Künste (München, 1959), p. 123. [2] Published in 1857. [3] *Ibid.*, p. 350.

Chapter Eight

[1] E. Cassirer, *The Myth of the State* (New Haven: Yale University Press, 1946), p. 5. [2] Joseph von Görres, *Mythengeschichte der asiatischen Welt*, I (Heidelberg: Mohr und Zimmer, 1810), 18, 19. [3] Herodotus, *Historiae* II, 52. [4] *Ibid.* II, 53. [5] Pausanias, *Arcadica* Ch. 8, Sec. 2. [6] Friedrich Creuzer, *Symbolik und Mythologie der alten Völker, besonders der Griechen*, I (Leipzig und Darmstadt: Heyer und Leske, 1819-23), 6ff. [7] *Symposium* 191 D (XVI). [8] *Symbolik*, I, 36. [9] C. G. Heyne, "Sermonis mythici seu symbolici interpretatio," in *Commentationes Societatis regiae scientiarum Gottingensis*, XVI, Classis hist. et phil. (1808), 292ff.

Chapter Nine

[1] Walter F. Otto, *Theophania* (Hamburg: Rowohlt, 1956), pp. 13-14. [2] Gottfried Hermann, *Opusculae*, II, 121. [3] Carl Otfried Müller, *Prolegomena zu einer wissenschaftlichen Mythologie* (Göttingen: Vandenhoeck & Ruprecht, 1825), p. 293.

Chapter Ten

[1] Ludwig Feuerbach, *Vorlesungen über das Wesen der Religion* (2nd ed.; Stuttgart: Frommann, 1960), p. 270. [2] Herbert Spencer, *Principles of Sociology*, I (New York: Appleton, 1910), 423-24. [3] K. Kerényi, *Die antike Religion* (Düsseldorf: Diederichs, 1940), pp. 24-25.

Chapter Eleven

[1] B. Malinowski, "Myth in Primitive Psychology" (1926); reprinted in *Magic, Science and Religion* (New York: Doubleday, 1954), pp. 146-47.

Chapter Twelve

[1] Wilhelm Schwartz, *Indogermanischer Volksglaube* (Berlin: Seehagen, 1885), p. lx. [2] *Ibid.*, p. 225. [3] Wilhelm Mannhardt, *Mythologische Forschungen* (Strassburg: Trübner, 1884), p. 351. [4] *Ibid.*, p. xxv. [5] Max Müller, *Chips from a German Workshop*, II (New York: Charles Scribner's Sons, 1869), 94. [6] Malinowski, *op. cit.*, p. 97. [7] Max Müller, *Lectures on the Science of Language* (2nd series; London: Longmans, Green, 1864), pp. 484ff. [8] Müller, *Chips*, p. 56. [9] *Ibid.*, p. 76. [10] G. W. Cox, *The Mythology of Aryan Nations* (London: Longmans, Green, 1870); *An Introduction to the Science of Comparative Mythology*

and Folklore (London: Kegan Paul, 1881). [11] M. Bréal, *Mélanges de Mythologie et de Linguistique* (Paris: Hachette, 1877). [12] A. Réville, *Prolégomènes de l'Histoire des Religions* (2nd ed.; Paris: Fischbacher, 1881).

Chapter Fourteen

[1] Hugo Winckler, *Religionsgeschichtler und geschichtlicher Orient* (Leipzig: Hinrichs, 1906); *Geschichte Israels in Einzeldarstellungen* (Leipzig: Pfeiffer, 1895-1900). [2] Eduard Stucken, *Astralmythen der Hebräer, Babylonier und Aegypter* (Leipzig: Pfeiffer, 1896-97).

Chapter Fifteen

[1] E. B. Tylor, *Primitive Culture*, II (New York: Harper & Row, 1958), 194-95. [2] R. R. Marett, "Pre-animistic Religion," *Folklore*, 11 (1900), 162-82; reprinted in *The Threshold of Religion* (New York: Macmillan, 1909; 2nd ed., 1914), pp. 1-28. [3] *Ibid.*, pp. 12-13. [4] *Ibid.*, p. xi. [5] *Ibid.*, p. 119. [6] *Ibid.*, p. 120. [7] R. H. Codrington, *The Melanesians* (Oxford: Clarendon Press, 1891), p. 118. [8] *Ibid.*, p. 119. [9] *Ibid.*, p. 120. [10] F. Graebner, *Das Weltbild der Primitiven* (München: Reinhardt, 1924), p. 59. [11] Andrew Lang, *Myth, Ritual and Religion*, 2 vols. (London: Longmans, Green, 1887); *The Making of Religion* (3rd ed.; London: Longmans, Green, 1909). [12] E. B. Tylor, "Limits of Savage Religion," *Journal of the Anthropological Institute*, XXI (1892), 283-99. [13] *Folklore*, IX (1898), 290-329. [14] Arnold van Gennep, *Mythes et légendes d'Australie* (Paris: Guilmoto, 1906). [15] Marett, *op. cit.*, p. 16. [16] Andrew Lang, *The Making of Religion* (London: Longmans, Green, 1909), p. xii. [17] Andrew Lang, *Magic and Religion* (London: Longmans, Green, 1901), p. 69. [18] Wilhelm Schmidt, *Der Ursprung der Gottesidee*, I (2nd ed.; Münster: Aschendorffsche Verlagsbuchhandlung, 1926-55), 185. [19] Nathan Söderblom, *Das Werden des Gottesglaubens* (Leipzig: Hinrichs, 1916), p. 152. [20] Gerardus van der Leeuw, *Religion in Essence and Manifestation*, I. trans. by J. E. Turner (New York: Harper & Row, 1963), p. 165. [21] Schmidt, *op. cit.*, p. 596. [22] Raffaele Pettazzoni, *Dio, Formazione e sviluppo del monoteismo nella storia delle religione*, I (Roma: Soc. ed. athenaeum, 1922), xvi. [23] *Ibid.*, pp. 71ff. [24] Emile Durkheim, *The Elementary Forms of the Religious Life*, trans. by J. W. Swain (New York: Collier, 1961), p. 327. [25] Robert H. Lowie, *Primitive Religion* (Rev. ed.; New York: Grosset, 1952), p. 132. [26] *Paideuma*, III (1949), 254. [27] E. Buess, *Die Geschichte des mythischen Erkennens* (München: Kaiser, 1953), p. 101. [28] Karl Schuchhardt, *Vorgeschichte von Deutschland* (München: Oldenbourg, 1928), pp. 14-15. [29] K. J. Narr, in *Antaios*, II (Stuttgart: Klett, 1960), 132-57. [30] Arnold van Gennep, *Tabou et totémisme à Madágascar*

(Paris: Leroux, 1904), p. 305. [31] Schmidt, *op. cit.*, p. 217. [32] Van der Leeuw, *op. cit.*, p. 79. [33] F. Graebner, *Das Weltbild der Primitiven* München: E. Reinhardt, 1924), p. 55. [34] Sir James Frazer, *Totemism and Exogamy*, IV (London: Macmillan, 1910), 5. [35] Van der Leeuw, *op. cit.* [36] A. E. Jensen, *Myth and Cult among Primitive Peoples*, trans. by M. Tax Choldin and Wolfgang Weissleder (Chicago: University of Chicago Press, 1963), pp. 148-49. [37] *Transactions of the Third International Congress for the History of Religions*, II (Oxford: Clarendon Press, 1908), 118. [38] De la Boullaye, *op. cit.*, p. 407. [39] *Paideuma*, V, 44ff.

Chapter Sixteen

[1] Hermann Usener, *Götternamen, Versuch einer Lehre von der religiösen Begriffsbildung* (Bonn: F. Cohen, 1896), pp. 76-77. [2] *Ibid.*, pp. 85-108. [3] *Ibid.*, p. 280. [4] *Ibid.*, p. 316. [5] Jensen, *op. cit.*, pp. 88ff. [6] *Ibid.*, p. 114. [7] *Ibid.*, p. 179.

Chapter Seventeen

[1] Sigmund Freud, *Traumdeutung* (9th ed.; Wien: Deuticke, 1950); K. Abraham, *Traum und Mythus* (Wien: Deuticke, 1909); Rank, *Der Mythus von der Geburt des Helden* (Wien: Deuticke, 1909). [2] William James, *The Varieties of Religious Experience* (London: Longmans, Green, 1919), pp. 502-03. [3] *Ibid.*, pp. 506-07. [4] J. H. Leuba, *A Psychological Study of Religion* (New York: Macmillan, 1912), p. 53. [5] *Ibid.*, pp. 111-12.

Chapter Eighteen

[1] In the Bachofen edition by Baeumler and Schroeter, p. 198. [2] Durkheim, *op. cit.*, p. 62. [3] *Ibid.*, p. 236. [4] *Ibid.*, p. 257. [5] *Ibid.*, pp. 227-32. [6] *Ibid.*, pp. 329-33. [7] *Ibid.*, p. 328. [8] *Ibid.*, pp. 464-65.

Chapter Nineteen

[1] Lucien Lévy-Bruhl, *Primitive Mentality*, trans. by Lilian A. Clare (New York: Macmillan, 1923), p. 439. [2] Jensen, *op. cit.*, p. 23. [3] Lévy-Bruhl, *op. cit.*, p. 431. [4] Cf. J. Maritain, *Revue thomiste*, XLIV (1938), 482-83 [letter by Lévy-Bruhl to Maritain]; "Carnets de Lévy-Bruhl," in *Revue philosophique* (1947), pp. 257-81; reprinted as *Les Carnets*, préface de Maurice Leenhardt (Paris: Presses Universitaires, 1949). [5] G. van der Leeuw, *La structure de la mentalité primitive*

(Strasbourg: Imp. Alsacienne, 1928), p. 27. [6] Mircea Eliade, *The Myth of the Eternal Return,* "Bollingen Series," XLVI (New York: Pantheon, 1954), p. 48. [7] Jensen, *op. cit.,* pp. 23-24. [8] E. Cassirer, *Philosophy of Symbolic Forms,* trans. by Ralph Manheim, II (New Haven: Yale University Press, 1955), 63. [9] E. Cassirer, *Language and Myth,* trans. by S. K. Ranger (New York: Harper & Row, 1946), pp. 9-10. [10] *Anthropos,* X-XI, 325. [11] Paul Radin, "The Basic Myth of the North American Indians," *Eranos-Jahrbuch,* XVII (1949), 363. [12] Paul Radin, *Monotheism among Primitive Peoples* (1924), pp. 55-56; reprinted in 1954 by Ethnographical Museum Basel (Switzerland), pp. 24-25. [13] Paul Radin, *Die Religiöse Erfahrung der Naturvölker* (Zürich: Rhein Verlag, 1951), pp. 76-77. [14] *Ibid.,* p. 89. [15] A. E. Jensen, "Der Sittliche Gehalt primitiver Religionen," *Paideuma,* III (1949), 248. [16] Jensen, *Myth and Cult,* pp. 37-38.

Chapter Twenty

[1] Fritz Graebner, "Wanderung und Entwicklung sozialer Systeme in Australien," *Globus,* XC.

Chapter Twenty-one

[1] Georges Dumézil, *Le festin d'immortalité, étude de mythologie comparée indo-européenne* (Paris: Geuthner, 1924). [2] Georges Dumézil, *L'idéologie tripartite des Indo-Européens,* Collection Latomus XXXI (Bruxelles: Latomus, revue d'études latines, 1958).

Chapter Twenty-two

[1] *Archiv für Religionswissenschaft,* XII (1909), 545. [2] Cf. Sir James Frazer, *The Golden Bough,* I (2nd ed.; New York: Macmillan, 1900), 63ff. [3] *Folklore,* XV, 141ff. [4] H. Hubert and M. Mauss, "Esquisse d'une théorie générale de la magie," *Année Sociologique,* VII (1902-03), 1-146. [5] Irving King, *The Development of Religion* (New York: Macmillan, 1910), pp. 202-03. [6] *Globus,* 1904, 1905. [7] Karl Beth, *Religion und Magie, ein religionsgeschichtlicher Beitrag zur psychologischen Grundlegung der religiösen Prinzipienlehre* (2nd ed.; Leipzig: Teubner, 1927). [8] *Ibid.,* p. 159. [9] *Ibid.,* p. 381. [10] *Ibid.,* p. 397. [11] *Ibid.,* p. 420. [12] Van der Leeuw, *op. cit.,* II, 545.

Chapter Twenty-three

[1] Tylor, *Primitive Culture,* p. 461. [2] Herbert Spencer, *The Principles of Sociology,* I (3rd ed.; New York: Appleton, 1885), 277ff. [3] W. Rob-

ertson Smith, in *Encyclopaedia Brittanica*, XXI (9th ed.; New York: Charles Scribner's Sons, 1878-89), 132ff. ⁴ F. B. Jevons, *An Introduction to the History of Religion* (London: Methuen, 1896), pp. 96ff. ⁵ S. Reinach, *Cultes, Mythes et Religions*, I (Paris: Leroux, 1905), p. 103. ⁶ *Hastings Encyclopaedia of Religion and Ethics*, XI (New York: Charles Scribner's Sons, 1920), 3ff. ⁷ E. Westermarck, *The Origin and Development of the Moral Ideas*, I (New York: Macmillan, 1906), 469ff. ⁸ H. Hubert and M. Mauss, "Essai sur le sacrifice," *L'Année Sociologique*, II (1899). ⁹ M. Mauss, "Essai sur le don, forme archaique de l'échange," *L'Année Sociologique* NS I (1925). ¹⁰ Van der Leeuw, *op. cit.*, II, 353. ¹¹ *Ibid.*, p. 350. ¹² *Handwörterbuch des deutschen Aberglaubens*, IX (1938-41), col. 21. ¹³ Jensen, *Myth and Cult*, Ch. 8. ¹⁴ *Ibid.*, p. 173. ¹⁵ H. Lommel, *Paideuma*, III (1949), 207ff.

Chapter Twenty-four

¹ Wilhelm Wundt, *Völkerpsychologie*, 3rd ed., II, 431-32. ² K. T. Preusz, *Die geistige Kultur der Naturvölker* (2nd ed.; Leipzig: Teubner, 1923), p. 99 (1st ed. 1919). ³ Cassirer, *The Myth of the State*, p. 28. ⁴ K. T. Preusz, *Der religiöse Gehalt der Mythen*, No. 162 of the *Sammlung gemeinverständlicher Vorträge und Schriften aus dem Gebiet der Theologie und Religionsgeschichte* (Tübingen: Mohr, 1933). ⁵ B. Malinowski, *Magic, Science and Religion*, p. 108. ⁶ *Ibid.*, p. 117. ⁷ *Ibid.*, p. 145. ⁸ T. H. Gaster, "Myth and Story," *Numen*, I (1954), 186-87. ⁹ *Ibid.*, p. 198. ¹⁰ Raffaele Pettazzoni, "The Truth of Myth," *Essays on the History of Religions* (Leiden: Brill, 1954), pp. 20-21. ¹¹ K. Kerényi, "Was ist Mythologie?" in *Europäische Revue*, XVI (1939), 572. ¹² Paul Radin, *Primitive Man as Philosopher* (Rev. ed.; New York: Dover, 1956), pp. 53-54. ¹³ K. Kerényi, *Umgang mit Göttlichem* (Göttingen: Vandenhoeck & Ruprecht, 1955), p. 41. ¹⁴ Walter F. Otto, *Theophania, Der Geist der altgriechischen Religion* (Hamburg: Rowohlt, 1956), p. 25.

Index of Subjects

allegorical explanations 14, 20, 23, 34
animatism 107
animism 33, 51, 78, 101-06, 138, 140, 148
archetypes 145

burial, in crouching position 123

culture circles 175-80

deities, dema 138-42
functional, 134-38
momentary, 134-38
dynamism 107

Elementargedanken (*elementary* ideas) 146
etymologizing 16, 25, 81-82
Euhemerism 9, 10, 14, 17, 26, 32, 33, 34, 104

fear, as root of religion 8, 9, 10, 32, 34, 103, 107, 142
fetishism 32, 76, 100, 102

historicism 61, 92

language, as explanation of myth 52-53, 88-89, 136

magic 109, 126, 162, 189-97
mana 106-10, 173
matriarchy 123-24, 157

mother goddess 121-28
myth 45-46, 50-58, 91-94, 118, 169-70, 209-15
mythology, folkloristic 85, 93
nature, 11, 17, 80-91

nagualism 131
natural religion 30, 34

preanimism 106-10, 152, 165, 194
prelogic mentality 164-65
primal monotheism 113-15, 117, 120, 127
primitive thought 162-74
psychological explanations 142-56

sacrifice 198-208
shamanism 100
sociology 156-62
supreme being 110-20, 140, 142, 143, 148, 153, 160
symbol 49-50, 157, 170
symbolists 47-53

tabu 158
totemism 100, 119, 128-33, 159-61, 177-79, 199, 202-03

Urheber 116-17

Völkerpsychologie (ethnopsychology) 146-49, 156, 157

wonder, as root of religion 143

Index of Names

Anaximander 5
Aristotle 5, 8, 19
Arnobius 15
Aufrecht, Th. 67
Augustine 14

Bachhofen, J. J. 123-24, 157, 177

Bacon, F. 10, 27
Banier, Abbé 32-33
Basil 15
Bastian, A. 86, 146, 177
Bergier, N. S. 33
Beth, K. 165, 193-95, 202-03
Boccaccio 10, 22-23, 24

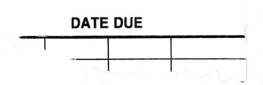

DATE DUE